EYEWITNESS TRAVEL

CYPRUS

DROITWICH

EYEWITNESS TRAVEL

CYPRUS

GRZEGORZ MICUŁA
MAGDALENA MICUŁA

LONDON, NEW YORK,
MELBOURNE, MUNICH AND DELHI
www.dk.com

Produced by Hachette Livre Polska sp. z o.o., Warsaw, Poland

SENIOR GRAPHIC DESIGNER
Paweł Pasternak

EDITORS
Agnieszka Majle,
Robert G. Pasieczny

MAIN CONTRIBUTORS
Elżbieta Makowiecka, Grzegorz Micuła, Magdalena Micuła

CARTOGRAPHERS
Magdalena Polak, Michał Zielkiewicz

PHOTOGRAPHERS
Dorota and Mariusz Jarymowicz, Krzysztof Kur

ILLUSTRATORS
Michał Burkiewicz, Paweł Marczak, Bohdan Wróblewski

TYPESETTING AND LAYOUT
Elżbieta Dudzińska, Paweł Kamiński, Grzegorz Wilk

Reproduced by Colourscan, Singapore.
Printed and bound in China by L. Rex Printing Co., Ltd.

First published in Great Britain in 2006
by Dorling Kindersley Limited
80 Strand, London WC2R 0RL

12 13 14 15 10 9 8 7 6 5 4 3 2 1

Reprinted with revisions 2008, 2010, 2012

Copyright © 2006, 2012 Dorling Kindersley Limited, London
A Penguin Company

A CIP CATALOGUE RECORD IS AVAILABLE FROM THE BRITISH LIBRARY

ISBN: 978-1-40537-059-2

Front cover main image: Sanctuary of Apollo Ylatis, Kourion

MIX
Paper from
responsible sources
FSC
www.fsc.org   FSC™ C018179

**The information in this
DK Eyewitness Travel Guide is checked regularly.**
Every effort has been made to ensure that this book is as
up-to-date as possible at the time of going to press. Some details,
however, such as telephone numbers, opening hours, prices,
gallery hanging arrangements and travel information are liable to change.
The publishers cannot accept responsibility for any consequences arising
from the use of this book, nor for any material on third party websites,
and cannot guarantee that any website address in this book will be a
suitable source of travel information. We value the views and suggestions
of our readers very highly. Please write to: Publisher, DK Eyewitness
Travel Guides, Dorling Kindersley, 80 Strand, London WC2R 0RL,
Great Britain, or email: travelguides@dk.com.

◁ Sanctuary of Apollo Ylatis, near Kourion

CONTENTS

INTRODUCING CYPRUS

**Cypriot saint, Agios Mamas, the
Byzantine Museum in Pafos**

**Beach in the bustling resort of
Agia Napa in southeast Cyprus**

Ruins of the Sanctuary of Apollo Ylatis, near Kourion

Picturesque Kyrenia harbour, one of the most beautiful in Cyprus

Baklava, a typically Cypriot dessert

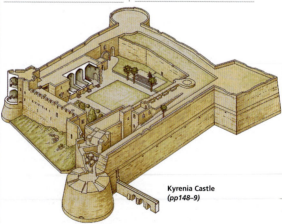

Kyrenia Castle
(pp148–9)

INTRODUCING CYPRUS

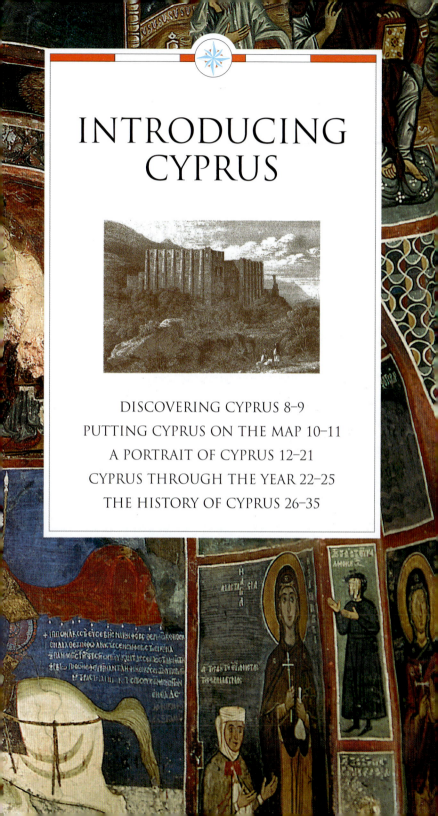

DISCOVERING CYPRUS

Cyprus has a long and illustrious history spanning more than 10,000 years. It has been influenced by periods of Hellenistic, Roman, Byzantine, Venetian, Ottoman, British and most recently Greek-Turkish rule. An island of great contrasts, each town has a vibrancy of its own. Limassol has some of the best nightlife,

A statuette of Aphrodite

Larnaka is famous for its sailing waters and Nicosia is known for its shops, universities and history. In contrast, traditional villages, many with old churches, lie in the mountainous interior, and rugged open countryside offers wildlife and sporting opportunities. Below is an overview of Cyprus' unique regions.

The crystal-clear waters along the coast of the Akamas peninsula

WEST CYPRUS

- History at Kato Pafos
- The Akamas peninsula
- Vibrant Latsi harbour

The **Kato Pafos Archaeological Park** *(see pp52–3)* includes four villas that once belonged to wealthy residents of the town: the House of Dionysos, the House of Aion, the House of Orpheus and the House of Theseus contain breathtaking mosaics with images of mythological figures, along with remains of walls, terraces and columns.

The **Akamas peninsula** *(see pp55–7)*, at the easternmost point of the island, is a delight for hikers and nature lovers. An important area for flora and fauna, the peninsula boasts around 600 different plant species and 200 different animal species. The coastline is dotted with coves where boats can anchor and the clear waters can be explored.

Just along the coast is **Latsi harbour** *(see p55)*. During the day it teems with fishermen bringing in their catch and pleasure boats vying for trade; at night the harbourside restaurants turn the fresh fish and seafood into delicious traditional dishes.

SOUTHERN CYPRUS

- Limassol's fine wine festival
- Plays at the Kourion
- Larnaka's sailing waters

A famous wine festival is held every September in **Limassol** *(see pp68–73)*. The villages around this seaside town – on the gentle south-facing slopes of the Troodos – produce some of the island's best Chardonnay, Riesling, Sauvignon Blanc, Cabernet Sauvignon and Grenache, along with Cyprus' own wine Commandaria.

It would be tough to find a better location for a play than the **Kourion** *(see pp66–7)*. This Roman theatre built in the 2nd century AD offers near-perfect acoustics and the chance to admire splendid views out to sea.

The glorious waters of **Larnaka** *(see pp78–81)* are a sailor's paradise, with little tide activity and steady winds. Drop anchor in a sheltered cove and swim in the crystal waters or dive to some of the island's shipwrecks. Larnaka marina, at the end of the town's palm tree-fringed promenade, has good amenities for sailors.

TROODOS MOUNTAINS

- Beautiful UNESCO churches
- Action-packed Platres
- The museum at Kykkos Monastery

The **Troodos mountain** region is home to some spectacular churches, ten of which *(see p109)* were awarded World Heritage status by UNESCO in recognition of their colourful Byzantine frescoes.

A cool summer climate and plentiful winter snowfalls make **Platres** *(see p93)* and the surrounding countryside perfect for all outdoor activities including hiking, mountain biking, fishing and, in winter, skiing and snowboarding.

Doorway into Kykkos church decorated with mosaics

The museum at **Kykkos Monastery** (*see pp90–91*) is reached by ascending a high flight of steps and turning into a small shop. This opens out on to an amazing collection of artifacts and paintings that is displayed alongside lavish religious robes and ceramics.

CENTRAL CYPRUS

- **Cycling in the wilderness**
- **Beautiful Machairas monastery**
- **Tamassos and Idalion**

Secluded Greek Orthodox Machairas monastery

Central Cyprus is a haven of tranquillity, with very few cars apart from the occasional tourist-hired vehicle. Cyclists will find the most challenging terrain in the **National Forest of Athalassa** (*see p106*) or the Adelfoi Forest.

Machairas (*see p110*) is one of the island's most famous monasteries. The beautiful church and cloisters date from the 20th century, and were built to house an icon of the Holy Virgin pierced by a sword, which was attributed to St Luke.

Believed to date back to 4000 BC, **Tamassos** (*see p107*) grew wealthy when copper was discovered here. Ancient remains include two well-preserved royal tombs dated to around 650–600 BC and a temple. **Idalion** (*see p108*), which dates from the Bronze Age, was an important city-state. Some of its 14 temples have been unearthed as part of ongoing excavations.

SOUTH NICOSIA

- **Charming Old City streets**
- **Must-see museums**
- **Nicosia from above**

Nicosia may be a thoroughly modern city, but examples of its long history are never far away. Head off to explore the tiny streets of the **Old Town** (*see pp116–17*) to really appreciate the city's charm. Traditional houses line the streets of Aristokyprou Street, Praxippou Street and Filokyprou Street; many of them are being turned into restaurants and little shops selling jewellery and local crafts. Another old part of the city is around the **Cathedral of St John** (*see p119*), which contains some well-preserved frescoes depicting biblical scenes.

The city has some fine museums, including the **Folk Art Museum** (*see p118*) and the **Cyprus Museum** (*see pp122–3*), which contains important artifacts, including a 2nd century AD statue of Septimius Severus, a collection of terracotta warriors and a 1st century AD Roman statuette of Aphrodite of Soloi.

See Nicosia from above, courtesy of the **Laiki Geitonia observatory** (*see p121*), which can be accessed from street level through an entrance at the side of the Debenhams store in Ledra Street. A sprawling cityscape unfolds before you in all directions, with church spires and mosque minarets peeping through the rooftops.

Pretty streets of the Old Town in South Nicosia

NORTH CYPRUS

- **Ancient Salamis**
- **Bellapais and its view**
- **Kyrenia's harbourside life**

The ruins of the ancient port of **Salamis** (*see pp134–5*) are the largest in Cyprus. They include an amphitheatre, rows of beautifully preserved columns, mosaics and a bath chamber where the underground water-heating system can still be seen.

The well-preserved ruins of **Bellapais abbey** (*see p145*) are a lovely example of Gothic architecture. The village is also worth a visit for the view down the citrus-tree-clad hillside to the sea below.

With a fort standing guard to the east and a natural horseshoe harbour, **Kyrenia** is one of the prettiest resorts on the island (*see pp146–9*). Along the harbourside are quaint buildings housing cosy seafood restaurants.

Boats moored at the picturesque harbour of Kyrenia

Putting Cyprus on the Map

Situated in the eastern Mediterranean Sea, Cyprus is its third largest island (after Sicily and Sardinia), covering an area of 9,250 sq km (3,571 sq miles) with a 720 km- (447-mile-) long coastline. Divided since 1974 into the Greek Cypriot-governed Republic of Cyprus in the south and the Turkish-sponsored Turkish Republic of North Cyprus in the north, both regions share Nicosia as a capital. The rocky Pentadaktylos mountain range runs along the north, while its central part is dominated by the mighty massif of the Troodos mountains. The wildest and least accessible areas are the Akamas and Karpasia (Karpas) peninsulas.

Satellite View of Cyprus
The entire island can be seen, with the long, narrow Karpasia (Karpas) peninsula to the right and the Troodos mountains in the centre. Turkish Anatolia is visible to the north.

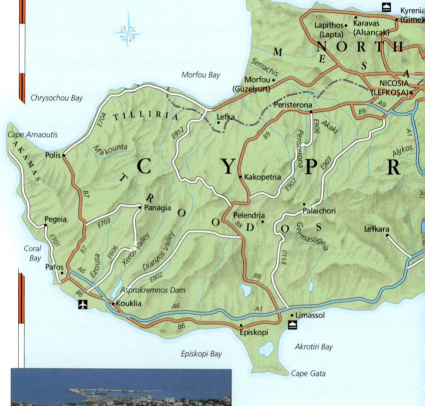

Cape Kormakiti

Kyrenia (Girne)

Lapithos (Lapta) • Karavas (Alsançak)

M E S **N O R T H** A

Serrachis

Morfou Bay

Morfou (Güzelyurt)

Peristerona

NICOSIA (LEFKOŞA)

Chrysochou Bay

A9

B9

Lefka

Peristerona

Akaki

E906

A1

T I L L I R I A

E704

E912

B9

Cape Arnaoutis

A K A M A S

Makounta

Polis

Alykos

C T R **Y P R**

Kakopetria

E903

E907

Panagia

O

Pelendria

Palaichori

Germasogeia

Lefkara

Pegeia

E703

O **D** O **S**

B8

Coral Bay

E701

B7

Ezousa

Xeros Valley

Diarizos Valley

E606

E110

Pafos

A6

E802

B8

Asprokremnos Dam

Kouklia

A6

A1

• Limassol

B6

Episkopi

Akrotiri Bay

Episkopi Bay

Cape Gata

View from St Hilarion Castle
St Hilarion Castle in North Cyprus offers a magnificent, panoramic view of the coast. The view in this particular direction shows the town and harbour of Kyrenia.

Nicosia
Located at the centre of the island, surrounded by a ring of Venetian defence walls, Nicosia is the capital and financial centre of the island. One of the old city bastions can be seen in the foreground.

Cape Apostolos Andreas

Aigialousa
(Yenirenköy)

Rizokarpaso
(Dipkarpaz)

KARPASIA

Galateia
(Mehmetcik)

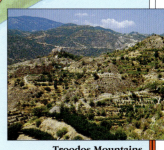

• Akanthou
(Tatlisu)

Trikomo
(İskele)

P R U S

• Kythrea
(Degirmenlik)

Pediaios

Lefkonoiko
(Gecitkale)

Famagusta Bay

R

I

Vatili (Vadili)

A

Famagusta
(Gazimağusa/
Ammochostos)

• Tymvou
(Kirklar)

Lysi •

Troodos Mountains
The volcanic massif of the Troodos mountains rises to nearly 2,000 metres (6,400 ft) above sea level. Extensive vineyards stretch over its southern slopes.

Gialias

E303

Paralimni

U

S

B3

A3

Agia Napa

Xylofagou

Cape Gkreko

A2

Aradippou

Larnaka

Larnaka Bay

KEY

✈ Airport

— Motorway

— Main road

= Secondary road

⚓ Ferry port

▰▰ Border (The "Green Line")

0 km   15

0 miles   15

Location of the Island
Cyprus lies in the eastern Mediterranean Sea, squeezed between Turkey and the coast of Syria. From here, it is 75 km (46 miles) to Turkey, 100 km (62 miles) to Syria and about 360 km (223 miles) to Egypt. The Greek island of Rhodes is 400 km (248 miles) away, and Athens about 850 km (538 miles) away.

EUROPE

THE NETHERLANDS   POLAND   BELARUS   RUSSIA

BELGIUM   GERMANY

LUXEMBOURG   CZECH REPUBLIC

SLOVAK REPUBLIC   UKRAINE

FRANCE

AUSTRIA   HUNGARY   MOLDOVA

SWITZERLAND   SLOVENIA   ROMANIA

CROATIA

SERBIA AND MONTENEGRO

BOSNIA AND HERZEGOVINA

ANDORRA   CORSICA   ITALY   KOSOVO   BULGARIA   BLACK SEA

SPAIN   SARDINIA   ALBANIA   MACEDONIA

GREECE   TURKEY

TUNISIA

MOROCCO   MEDITERRANEAN SEA   CYPRUS   SYRIA

ALGERIA   LEBANON

LIBYA   ISRAEL   JORDAN

A PORTRAIT OF CYPRUS

T*he legendary birthplace of Aphrodite, Cyprus enjoys a hot, Mediterranean climate moderated by sea breezes. Visitors bask in the sun on its many beaches, but within an hour's drive can find themselves in the mountains, enjoying the shade of cool herb- and resin-scented cedar woods, villages set amid orchards and peaceful vineyards, as though time stands still here.*

Cyprus is an idyllic destination for romantics, with so many old castles, ancient ruins and secluded mountain monasteries to explore. The exploration of these historic sights is enhanced by plentiful sunshine – over 300 days of it per year. Cyprus also has a great number of scenic beaches, and the warm waters encourage bathing and relaxation.

Mosaic of Leda with the Swan, from Kouklia

Tucked away in the shady valleys are monasteries with ancient icons of the Virgin, at least one of which was supposedly painted by St Luke. The tiny churches, listed as UNESCO World Heritage Sites, hide unique frescoes – some of the most magnificent masterpieces of Byzantine art.

In the Pafos district, valleys overgrown with pine and cedar forests provide a home to the moufflon – a shy mountain sheep. Its image can be seen on Roman mosaics in Pafos.

Cypriot meadows are at their loveliest in springtime, when covered with motley carpets of colourful flowers: anemones, cyclamens, hyacinths, irises, peonies, poppies and tulips, among others. Orchid lovers will find over 50 species of these beautiful flowers growing in the sparsely populated regions of the island – in the Akamas peninsula, in the Troodos mountains and on the Pentadaktylos mountain range.

A symbol of Cyprus – an olive tree against the backdrop of a sapphire-blue sea

◁ A chapel next to a hotel complex near Polis

View over the northern part of Nicosia, with the Turkish Cypriot flag carved into the hillside

The island lies on a route for bird migration. Thousands of birds, including flamingos, cormorants and swans, can be seen wintering on the salt lakes at Larnaka and Akrotiri.

HISTORIC DIVISIONS

The winds of history have repeatedly ravaged this beautiful island. Cyprus has been ruled in turns by Egyptians, Phoenicians, Persians, Romans, Byzantines, Crusaders, Franks, Venetians, Turks and the British. Each of these cultures has left its mark on the architecture, style, cuisine, language and the mentality of the island's inhabitants.

Above all, the island has been shaped by the conflict between the Greeks and the Turks. The Greeks first arrived over 3,000 years ago. The Turks began to settle here following the conquest of the island by Sultan Selim II in 1571.

PEOPLE AND SOCIETY

Cypriot society has been composed of two completely separate cultures since the division of the island in 1974 into the Turkish-occupied North and the Greek-speaking Republic of Cyprus in the south. Greek Cypriot society has always been highly traditional, particularly among country people. This is partly due to the power of the Orthodox Church. Life proceeds at a slow pace in the villages, where it centres around cafés where men spend hours playing backgammon and discussing politics. Village women excel in sewing and embroidery. There has been gradual change, however, with many villages becoming deserted as their residents move to towns, where life is generally easier and the

An Orthodox priest doing his shopping

standard of living higher, but this decline is gradually being reversed; old houses are frequently bought by artists, often foreigners, in search of tranquillity. In Fikardou, two abandoned houses have been turned into a museum of village life, and awarded the Europa Nostra medal for the preservation of architectural heritage. Overall, the Republic of Cyprus is highly urbanized. Women play a great role in the modern economy – running businesses, hotels and restaurants. Life in the cities of Larnaka, Nicosia and Limassol proceeds at a speedy pace.

The Cape Gkreko area – one of the most beautiful areas in Cyprus

In the Turkish North, life proceeds at a far gentler pace, partly due to the international boycott that has afflicted tourism and hampered development since 1974. The North is quite separate from southern Cyprus in both atmosphere and landscape, as well as politics. It is far less affluent and more sparsely populated, and Islam is the main religion.

A lace-maker at work

tens of thousands of its people, it seemed that the island would never recover, but the Republic of Cyprus has achieved an economic miracle. Over thirty years on, the southern part of the island is very prosperous. After the 1974 invasion, hundreds of thousands of refugees from the North found new homes and began their lives anew. Since then, national income has increased several fold. The economy is flourishing, based on tourism, maritime trade and financial services. The same cannot be said of the northern part of the island, where the standard of living is much lower, caused to a great extent by the international isolation of North Cyprus.

MODERN-DAY CYPRUS

The Republic of Cyprus lives off tourism. Its towns are bustling and – like the beaches – full of tourists. Tourist zones have been established in Limassol, Larnaka and Pafos, and around Agia Napa.

This small island provides everything for the holidaymaker, from beautiful scenery to delicious food, excellent hotels, gracious hosts and historic sights.

Following the Turkish invasion of Cyprus and the displacement of

Relaxing at an outdoor café on a summer afternoon

Landscape and Wildlife

The Cypriot landscape is surprisingly varied. Besides high mountains covered with pine and cedar forests, and the rugged crags of Kyrenia, the central part of the island is occupied by the fertile plain of Mesaoria. The crowded beaches of Limassol, Pafos and Agia Napa contrast with the less developed coastal regions of the Karpasia (Karpas) and Akamas peninsulas. In spring, the hills and meadows are covered with colourful flowers. The forests are the habitat of the moufflon – mountain sheep – while the Karpasia peninsula is home to wild donkeys.

A flock of goats grazing freely – a typical sight in the Cypriot landscape

THE COAST

Besides beautiful sandy and pebble beaches, the coastline features oddly shaped rocks jutting out of the sea and rugged cliffs, which descend steeply into the water. The northern part of Famagusta Bay and the Karpasia and Akamas peninsulas feature virtually empty sandy beaches where loggerheads and green turtles come to lay their eggs. The exposed Jurassic rocks near Coral Bay, northwest of Pafos, are being destroyed by erosion.

Lizards, *particularly the ubiquitous sand lizard, can be seen almost everywhere. The largest Cypriot lizard, Agama (Agama stelio cypriaca) can reach up to 30 cm (12 in) in length.*

Rocky coastlines *are created wherever mountain ranges reach the sea. The rocky coast near Petra tou Romiou (Rock of Aphrodite) is being worn away over time by erosion.*

Sandy coastlines *are found at Agia Napa, Famagusta Bay and the Karpasia peninsula, but the loveliest beaches are on the Akamas peninsula.*

Salt lakes – *near Larnaka and on the Akrotiri peninsula – are a haven for pink flamingos, wild ducks and the Cyprus warbler (Sylvia melanthorax).*

ROCK FORMATIONS

The Troodos mountains, in the central part of Cyprus, are formed of magma rock containing rich deposits of copper and asbestos. The Kyrenia mountains (the Pentadaktylos range), running to the Karpasia peninsula in the northeast part of the island, are made of hard, dense limestone. The lime soils in the southern part of the island, near Limassol, are ideally suited for the growing of vines.

Copper mine at Skouriotissa

MOUNTAINS

The island features two mountain ranges, separated by the fertile Mesaoria plain. The volcanic Troodos massif in central Cyprus, dominated by Mount Olympus at 1,951 m (6,258 ft) above sea level, is covered with pine and cedar forests. The constant mountain streams in the Troodos mountains even have waterfalls. Spring and autumn bring hikers to the cool forests and rugged valleys, while winter brings out skiers. The Kyrenia mountains (the Pentadaktylos or "Five-Finger" range) in North Cyprus rise a short distance inland from the coast. The highest peak is Mount Kyparissovouno, at 1,024 m (3,360 ft).

The Troodos mountains *are largely forested but vines are grown on the southern slopes and apple and cherry orchards abound in the valleys.*

In springtime *wild flowers carpet the hillsides and meadows of the island with a colourful, fragrant display.*

The Cypriot moufflon *is a spry mountain sheep, living wild in the forests of Pafos, in the western part of the island.*

Mountain streams *flow year-round, bringing cooling water to lower ground.*

OTHER REGIONS

The island's interior is occupied by the vast, fertile Mesaoria plain, given mainly to grain cultivation. The northern area around Morfou (Güzelyurt) is full of citrus groves, and to the south, in the region of Larnaka, runs a range of white semi-desert mountains stretching for kilometres. The sun-drenched region of Limassol, with its limestone soil, is a patchwork of vineyards, which yield grapes for the production of the sweet Commandaria wine.

The Akamas peninsula *is a remote region in the west of Cyprus. It features the island's most beautiful wild, sandy beaches (see pp55–7).*

Donkeys *can be seen in the Karpasia peninsula. These ageing domesticated animals have been turned loose by their owners.*

Pelicans *with wingspans up to 2.5 m (8 ft) visit the island's salt lakes. Some stop for a few days, others remain longer. These huge birds can also be seen at the harbours of Pafos, Limassol and Agia Napa, where they are a tourist attraction.*

The Karpasia peninsula *is a long, narrow strip of land jutting into the sea. Its main attractions are its wild environment and historical sights (see pp140–41).*

Cypriot Architecture

The long and rich history of Cyprus is reflected in its architecture, and some true gems can be glimpsed amid the ocean of nondescript modern development. The island has a number of Neolithic settlements as well as Bronze Age burial chambers, ruins of ancient buildings (including vast Byzantine basilicas), medieval castles, churches and monasteries. From the Ottoman era, relics include mosques and caravanserais. The British left behind colonial buildings. In villages, particularly in the mountains, people today still live in old stone houses.

The Roman II Hotel in Pafos, built to a design based on ancient Roman architecture

ANCIENT ARCHITECTURE

The Greeks, Phoenicians, Romans and Byzantines who once ruled over Cyprus left behind numerous ancient buildings. Archaeologists have uncovered the ruins of ancient Kourion, Amathous, Kition, Soloi, Salamis and Pafos with temples, theatres, basilicas, bathhouses and palaces. These ancient ruins include fragments of the old defence walls, sports stadiums, gymnasiums, and necropolises. Some Roman theatres are still in use today for shows and festivals.

The *palaestra in Salamis* (see pp134–5) *is surrounded by colonnades and statues. It was devoted to the training of athletes and to staging sporting competitions.*

Kourion, *a beautiful, prosperous city, was destroyed by an earthquake in the 4th century AD* (see pp66–7).

MEDIEVAL ARCHITECTURE

During the 300 years when Cyprus was ruled by the Crusaders and the Lusignans, many churches were built, including the opulent cathedrals in Famagusta and Nicosia. Added to these were charming village churches and chapels, Gothic monasteries and castles. The Venetians, who ruled the island for over 80 years, created the magnificent ring of defence walls around Nicosia and Famagusta, whose mighty fortifications held back the Ottoman army for almost a year.

Angeloktisi Church *in Kiti is one of a number of small stone churches on the island whose modest exteriors often hide magnificent Byzantine mosaics or splendid frescoes* (see p76).

This beautifully carved capital *crowns the surviving column of a medieval palace in South Nicosia.*

Bellapais, *with its ruins of a Gothic abbey, enchants visitors with its imposing architecture* (see p145). *Every spring international music festivals are held here* (see p22 and p25).

ISLAMIC ARCHITECTURE

Following the conquest of Cyprus by the army of Selim II, new structures appeared, including Turkish mosques (minarets were often added to Gothic cathedrals), bathhouses, caravanserais and covered bazaars. In many villages you can still see small mosques with distinctive pointed minarets.

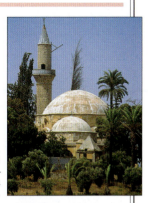

Büyük Han in North Nicosia *is a magnificent example of an Ottoman caravanserai, with a* mescit *(prayer hall) in the courtyard (see p128).*

The Hala Sultan Tekke (see p77) *is Cyprus's most sacred Muslim site. It comprises a mosque and a mausoleum with the tomb of Umm Haram, aunt of the Prophet Mohammed.*

THE COLONIAL PERIOD

British rule on the island from the 18th to 19th centuries marked the beginning of colonial-style architecture, including churches, government offices, courts of law, army barracks, civil servants' villas, bridges and other public buildings. The British administration also admired the Greek Classical style, and commissioned, designed and built a great number of Neo-Classical buildings.

The Faneromeni School in South Nicosia (see p122) *is an example of a Neo-Classical public building. When it was founded in 1852, it was seen as a connection to the students' Greek roots.*

The Pierides-Marfin Laiki Bank Museum in Larnaka *is a typical example of colonial architecture with shaded balconies resting on slender supports* (see p78). *Its flat roof and wooden shutters complement the image of a colonial residence.*

MODERN ARCHITECTURE

Following independence in 1960, the architectural style of Cypriot buildings, particularly of public buildings such as town halls, offices, banks and hotels became more modern and functional. Most of these buildings were erected in Limassol, which has since become the international business capital of Cyprus. The majority of modern buildings lack architectural merit.

Limassol's modern architecture *is largely limited to functional office buildings constructed of glass, concrete and steel, located in the eastern business district of town.*

TRADITIONAL HOMES

For centuries, Cypriot village houses, particularly in the mountains, were built of stone, offering the benefit of staying cool in summer and warm in winter. While some new homes imitate the traditional style, most are built of breeze-block and reinforced cement.

A modern stone building reminiscent of a traditional village home

Christianity and the Greek Orthodox Church

Christianity gained an early foothold in Cyprus, when saints Barnabas and Paul introduced the religion to the island in the first century AD. For 500 years the Church remained relatively unified. However, subsequent divisions led to the emergence of many parallel Christian creeds. The Great Schism of 1054 marked the split between East and West, resulting in the emergence of the Orthodox and Roman Catholic Churches. One of the groups of the Eastern Orthodox Church is the Greek Orthodox Church, and the majority of Greek Cypriots are devoutly Orthodox. Most of the churches in the south are still consecrated and can be visited; in the North, most have been converted into mosques or museums.

Byzantine frescoes, *some of the most splendid in existence, decorate the walls of small churches in the Troodos mountains. Ten of them feature on UNESCO's World Heritage List.*

Father Kallinikos *from St Barbara's Monastery (Agia Varvara) is regarded as one of the greatest icon painters of recent times. His highly sought-after icons are sold at the monastery* (see p76).

Neo-Byzantine churches *are topped by a grooved cupola with a prominent cross. They have distinctive arched windows and portals.*

Saint Nicholas

Saints' days *are celebrated by placing an icon of the saint on a small, ornamental table covered with a lace cloth.*

SAINT BARNABAS AND SAINT PAUL

Two saints are associated with Cyprus – Barnabas (a citizen of Salamis, and patron saint of the island), and Paul. Together, they spread Christianity to Cyprus in 45 AD. Paul was captured and tied to a pillar to be flogged. It is said that the saint caused his torturer to go blind. Witnessing this miracle, the Roman governor of Cyprus, Sergius Paulus, was converted to Christianity. Barnabas was stoned to death in 61 AD.

St Paul's Pillar in Kato Pafos

Royal Doors

Icons *with images of Christ or the saints, depicted in traditional Byzantine style, play a major role in the Orthodox Church. They are painted on wood, according to strictly defined rules.*

The Royal Doors *are found in the central part of an iconostasis. They symbolize the passage from the earthly to the spiritual world. The priest passes through them during the service.*

The Iconostasis is a "wall of icons" that separates the faithful from the sanctuary.

MONASTICISM

Cypriot monasteries, some of them hundreds of years old, are scattered among the mountains. These religious communities of bearded monks live in accordance with a strict regime. Built on inaccessible crags or in shadowy green valleys, they were established in the mountains to be closer to God and further from the temptations of this world. The monasteries hide an extraordinary wealth of frescoes, intricate decorations and magnificent iconostases. The best known of the Cypriot monasteries is Kykkos – the Royal Monastery *(see pp90–91)* which is a place of pilgrimage for the island's inhabitants.

DIVINE LITURGY

This is a liturgy celebrated in commemoration of the Last Supper. In the Greek Orthodox Church the service lasts longer than in the Catholic Church and there is no organ, only a choir. The service consists of two parts: the "catechumen liturgy", during which psalms and the Gospel are read; and the "liturgy of the faithful" – the main Eucharist when all worshippers (even children) receive holy communion in the form of bread and wine.

Icons on both sides of the Royal Doors depict Mary and Jesus. The second from the right usually depicts the patron saint of the church.

Two monks in the courtyard of Kykkos Monastery

CYPRUS THROUGH THE YEAR

Cypriots hold strongly to their traditions, which are manifested in the celebration of numerous religious festivals. The Orthodox Church, to which most Greek Cypriots belong, has a great influence on their lives. Besides local village fairs and public holidays, the festivities include athletic events and beauty contests. Added to this, every village has its own *panagyri* – the patron saint's day

Girl in a folk costume

celebration – the equivalent of church fairs. The villagers celebrate them with copious food, drink, dancing and song.

In North Cyprus, Muslim feasts are more common. The main ones include Şeker Bayrami, which ends the 40 days of Ramadan; Kurban Bayrami, which is held to commemorate Abraham's sacrifice (rams are slaughtered and roasted on a bonfire); and Mevlud, the birthday of Mohammed.

Olive trees flowering in the spring

SPRING

This is the most beautiful season on the island. The slopes of the hills begin to turn green and the meadows are carpeted with colourful flowers, though it is still possible to ski. The main religious festival is Easter.

MARCH

International Skiing Competition *(mid-Mar)*, Troodos. Since 1969, races have been held on the slopes of Mount Olympus *(see p92)*.
Evangelismós, Feast of the Annunciation *(25 Mar)*. Traditional folk fairs held in the villages of Kalavasos *(see p74)* and Klirou, as well as in Nicosia *(see pp112–23)*.
Easter *(varies – Mar to May)*. A week before Easter, the icon of St Lazarus is paraded through Larnaka. In all towns on Maundy Thursday, icons are covered with veils,

and on Good Friday the image of Christ adorned with flowers is carried through the streets. On Easter Saturday, icons are unveiled and in the evening an effigy of Judas is burned. Easter Day is celebrated with parties. Orthodox Easter is based on the Julian calendar, and may

Winners of the May Cyprus International Rally in Limassol

occur up to five weeks after Easter in the West.

APRIL

Wild Flower Festival *(Mar & Apr)*, Every Saturday and Sunday in many towns throughout southern Cyprus.
International Spring Concerts *(Apr & May)*, Bellapais. Performances by musical ensembles, singers and choirs are held in the Gothic abbey *(see p145)*.
Classical Music Festival *(Apr)*, Larnaka *(see pp78–81)*. Organized by the municipality, this festival features recitals and concerts by internationally known musicians and ensembles.

MAY

Anthistiria Flower Festival *(mid-May)*, Pafos, Limassol. The return of spring is celebrated with joyful processions and shows based on Greek mythology.
Orange Festival *(mid-May)*, Güzelyurt (Morfou) *(see p152)*. Held since 1977, with parades and folk concerts.
Cyprus International Rally *(May)*. Three-day car rally starting and ending in Limassol *(see pp68–71)*.
Chamber Music Festival *(May–Jun)*, Nicosia *(see pp112–23)* and Pafos *(pp48–51)*. Top international orchestras and ensembles from abroad.

AVERAGE DAILY HOURS OF SUNSHINE

Hours

Average Hours of Sunshine
In June and July, the amount of sunshine reaches nearly 13 hours per day. These months mark the peak holiday season. December, January and February have the fewest hours of sunshine, but the winter sun is pleasant and warm.

Children at the Wild Flowers Festival in Larnaka

SUMMER

Summer is rich in cultural events, especially art festivals, fairs and music concerts. Tourist resorts, hotels and attractions vie with one another to organize attractive cultural events for their guests. There are numerous folk fairs held in the mountain villages, particularly in August. This is also the hottest and sunniest time of the year.

The Limanaki Beach in Agia Napa

JUNE

Pancyprian Choirs Festival *(late Jun)*, Kato Pafos *(see pp52–3)*. During this festival, choirs perform in the ancient Roman Odeon.
St Leontios' Day *(mid-Jun)*, Pervolia village. Traditional religious fair.
Pentecost-Kataklysmos Fair (Festival of the Flood) *(7 weeks after Easter)*. Coinciding with Pentecost, this is celebrated over several days with processions and sprinkling each other with water, to symbolize cleansing.
Shakespeare at Kourion *(late Jun) (see pp66–7)*. This charity performance of a Shakespeare play takes place at the ancient amphitheatre.

JULY

International Music Festival *(Jun–Jul)*, Famagusta *(see pp136–9)*.
Moonlight Concerts *(Jul, during full moon)*, Pafos *(see pp48–51)*, Limassol *(pp68–71)*, Agia Napa *(p82)*. These concerts are organized by the Cyprus Tourism Organization.
Larnaka International Summer Festival *(Jul)*, Larnaka *(see pp78–81)*. Performances are staged by theatre, music and dance groups from Greece, the UK and other European cities.

AUGUST

Ancient Greek Drama Festival *(Aug)*, Pafos ancient Odeon *(see pp52–3)*. Theatre festival with Greek dramas.
Assumption of the Virgin Mary *(15 Aug)*. Traditional fairs in Kykko *(see pp90–91)* and Chrysorrogiastissa monasteries and in the Chrysospiliotissa church *(see p106)* in Deftera village.
Commandaria Festival *(late Aug)*. Food, wine, music and theatre at Kalo Chorio village in the Limassol district to mark the beginning of the grape harvest.
Dionysia *(late Aug)*, Stroumbi near Pafos. Cypriot and Greek dances and music. An all-night party with local wine and food.

Pomegranate from the environs of Larnaka

PUBLIC HOLIDAYS IN SOUTH CYPRUS

New Year's Day (1 Jan)
Fóta Epiphany (6 Jan)
Green Monday (varies)
Greek Independence Day (25 Mar)
Good Friday (varies)
Easter Monday (varies)
Pentecost-Kataklysmos (varies)
Greek Cypriot National Day (1 Apr)
Labour Day (1 May)
Assumption (15 Aug)
Cyprus Independence Day (1 Oct)
Ochi Day (28 Oct)
Christmas Eve (24 Dec)
Christmas Day (25 Dec)
Boxing Day (26 Dec)

AVERAGE MONTHLY RAINFALL

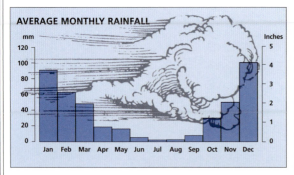

| | mm | | | | | | | | | | | | Inches |

Rainfall
The lowest rainfall occurs in July and August, the highest between November and February. Thunderstorms are rare in the summer. In the mountain regions, however, clouds may be thicker and rain more frequent than in the coastal areas.

AUTUMN

After the summer heat, autumn brings cooler weather. With the end of the peak holiday season many resorts slow down. The Cypriots celebrate successful harvests, with particular prominence given to the grape-gathering festivals. Many towns and villages hold local fairs. The Wine Festival in Limassol attracts hordes of visitors.

SEPTEMBER

Wine Festival *(early Sep)*, Limassol *(see pp68–71)*. Wine tasting and dancing in the Municipal Gardens.
Aphrodite Opera Festival *(Sep)*, Pafos *(see pp48–51)*. One of the main cultural festivals, with a cast that includes major international singers. Some years the festival starts at the end of August.
Agia Napa International Festival *(mid-Sep)*, Agia Napa *(see p82)*. This seaside resort

Troodos mountains in their autumn colours

becomes a gathering place for folk musicians and dancers, theatre groups, opera ensembles, traditional and modern singers, and magicians.
International North Cyprus Music Festival *(Sep–Oct)*, Bellapais *(see p145)*. Performances by musical virtuosos, symphony orchestras, piano recitals, vocal groups and soloists.
Elevation of the Holy Cross *(14 Sep)*. One of the oldest religious feasts in the Greek Orthodox Church calendar. In the past, men tucked basil leaves behind their ears on this day.

Participant in the Elevation of the Holy Cross

OCTOBER

Afamia Grape and Wine Festival *(early Oct)*, held in Koilani village *(see p94)* in the Limassol region.
Agios Ioannis Lampadistis *(early Oct)*, Kalopanagiotis *(see p89)*. Traditional folk festival combined with a fair.
International Dog Show *(mid-Oct)*, Pafos *(see pp48-51)* with the Kennel Club.

Agios Loukas *(mid-Oct)*. Traditional village fairs in Korakou, Koilani *(see p94)* and Aradippou.
Turkish National Day *(29 Oct)*.

NOVEMBER

Feast of Archangels Gabriel and Michael *(mid-Nov)*. Festival and fair in the St Michael monastery southwest of Nicosia *(see p106)*, in the village of Analiontas.
Cultural Winter *(Nov–Mar)*, Agia Napa *(see p82)*. A cycle of concerts, shows and exhibitions organized by the Agia Napa Municipality and Cyprus Tourism Organization.
Cultural Festival *(Nov)*, Limassol *(see pp68–71)*. Music, dancing, films, theatre and opera performances held in the Rialto theatre.
TRNC Foundation Day *(15 Nov)*. Celebrating the foundation, in 1983, of the Turkish Republic of Northern Cyprus, which is recognized only by Turkey.

Autumn harvest of grapes in the wine-growing village of Vasa

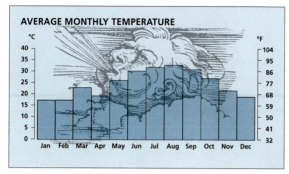

AVERAGE MONTHLY TEMPERATURE

Temperature
In the summer, temperatures may reach up to 40° C (104° F). Many people enjoy visiting the island out of the high season. Only the higher sections of the Troodos mountains, which are covered with snow in winter, record temperatures below freezing.

WINTER

The winters in Cyprus are mild, and the days are usually sunny. At times winter brings rain, but snow is limited to the upper reaches of the Troodos mountains. Many cultural events are organized by local authorities at this time. Christmas is traditionally celebrated within the family circle.

DECEMBER

Winter Solstice *(22 Dec)*. The Solstice is observed at ancient Amathous *(see p74)*, the Sanctuary of Apollo and the Sanctuary of Aphrodite, Agios Tychonas in Limassol *(see pp68–71)*.
Christmas *(25 Dec)*. Family celebrations are held after attending church.
Carols Evening *(25 Dec)*. This occurs in the central square in Agia Napa *(see p82)*. Events include carol singing, rides in Santa's sleigh and tasting traditional Cypriot dishes.

Welcoming the New Year *(31 Dec)*, in all towns. In Agia Napa *(see p82)*, free wine is served in the town's main square.

JANUARY

New Year (Agios Vassilios) *(1 Jan)*, formally celebrated with the exchange of presents.
Fóta – the Epiphany *(6 Jan)*. Greek Orthodox churches hold processions and bless water. In coastal towns and villages, young men compete with each other to retrieve a crucifix hurled into the water.
St Neofytos' Day *(late Jan)*. A traditional fair held in the Agios Neofytos monastery *(see p47)* near Pafos.
Şeker Bayrami (Sugar Festival) *(varies)*, North Cyprus. A religious feast and a family occasion marking the end of Ramadan, the annual Muslim fast.

FEBRUARY

Carnival, Limassol *(see pp68–71)*. Ten days of wild revelry preceding Lent end with

Salt excavation from the salt lake near Larnaka

Green Monday, which in Limassol features parades and fancy-dress balls.
Presentation of Jesus to the Temple *(mid-Feb)*. Traditional fair in the Chrysorrogiatissa monastery *(see p58)*, in the Pafos district.
Kite-flying Competition *(late Feb)*, Deryneia *(see p83)*.

PUBLIC HOLIDAYS IN NORTH CYPRUS

New Year's Day (1 Jan)
Children's Day (23 Apr)
Labour Day (1 May)
Youth and Sports Day (19 May)
Peace and Freedom Day (20 Jul)
Social Resistance Day (1 Aug)
Victory Day (30 Aug)
Turkish National Day (29 Oct)
Independence Day (15 Nov)
Şeker Bayrami (varies)
Kurban Bayram (varies)
Birth of the Prophet Mohammed (varies)

Winter sports on the slopes of the Troodos mountains

THE HISTORY OF CYPRUS

*L*ying at the crossroads of the eastern Mediterranean, Cyprus has long been a prize coveted by surrounding lands: Egypt and Aegia, Persia and Greece, Rome and Byzantium, and finally Venice and Turkey. Its rich copper deposits ensured the island's continuing worth to the prehistoric world. Even the name Cyprus probably derives from the late Greek word for copper – Kypros.

The location of Cyprus, at the point where the Eastern and Western civilizations met, determined its history to a large extent. Many rulers tried to conquer the island that occupied such a strategic position. Cyprus has been ruled in turn by the Egyptians, Mycenaeans, Phoenicians, Assyrians, Persians, Ptolemies, Romans, Byzantines, Crusaders, Franks, Venetians, Turks and British.

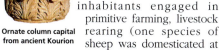

Ornate column capital from ancient Kourion

STONE AGE

Not much is known about the earliest inhabitants, who lived in coastal caves and did not leave much trace of their habitation. Recent evidence from archaeological discoveries at Aetokremmos (Eagle Cliff), however, indicates that Cyprus has been inhabited since at least 8,000 BC. The settlements of Petra tou Limnitis and Tenta existed here in the Neolithic era (late Stone Age), around 7,000-6,000 BC.

The first permanent settlements appeared in the 6th millennium BC. These early settlers are thought to have come from Asia Minor. They built round or oval huts of broken stone, covered with branches and clay. A settlement of this type was discovered in the area of Choirokotia. The inhabitants engaged in primitive farming, livestock rearing (one species of sheep was domesticated at that time) and fishing. The scarce flint stones and obsidian were used to make tools, and vessels were gouged out of limestone. Burial practices included weighing down the bodies with stones, in the belief that this would stop the dead disturbing the living.

From this period until around 4,500 BC there is a gap of information on the activities on the island. Archaeologists have discovered traces of settlements in the vicinity of Çatalköy (Agios Epikitotos), in the North, and Sotira in the South, where they found early "combed pottery" – the oldest ceramics in Cyprus. This pottery was produced by dragging a comb-like tool over the wet vessel to create straight or wavy lines.

After 4,000 BC the Chalcolithic era ushered in the first small-scale use of metal – copper, in addition to the widespread use of stone.

TIMELINE

8000 BC	5000 BC	4000 BC	3500 BC	3000 BC
c.8000 BC evidence of Neolithic era (Stone Age) human habitation				
c.6000 BC Choirokotia is Cyprus' earliest known settlement	**5250 BC** Existence of monochromatic and linear-pattern painted ceramics	**after 4000 BC** Chalcolithic settlements emerging in the western part of the island		
			3400–2300 BC The earliest copper mines are established; copper vessels and steatite (soapstone) images of female idols are produced	

Howling Man from Pierides Museum in Larnaka (5500–5000 BC)

◁ **Richard the Lionheart, who conquered Cyprus in 1191**

Neolithic settlement of Tenta

THE COPPER AND BRONZE AGES

The transitional period between the Stone and Bronze ages was known as the Chalcolithic era (after the Greek words for copper and stone: *chalkos* and *lithos*); it saw the small-scale use of copper for tools and implements. Most Chalcolithic villages were discovered in the previously unsettled western part of Cyprus. Figurines of limestone fertility goddesses from Lempa and cruciform figurines in picrolite (blue-green stone) from Yala indicate the growing cult of fertility.

The Troodos mountains contained large deposits of copper, and thanks to this the power of Cyprus began to increase in the third millennium BC. Cyprus became the largest producer and exporter of copper in the Mediterranean basin. The technology of bronze-smelting had by then spread throughout the entire Mediterranean basin. Copper, the main component of bronze, became the source of the island's wealth.

Trade with Egypt and the Middle East developed during this period. Along with vessels of fanciful, often zoomorphic shapes, human figurines and statuettes of bulls associated with the cult of fertility were produced.

By the start of the second millennium BC, there were towns trading in copper. The most important of these was the eastern harbour town of Alasia (modern-day Egkomi). At that time, cultural influences brought by settling Egyptian and Phoenician merchants intensified.

Flourishing trade necessitated the development of writing. The oldest text found in Cyprus is a Minoan incised clay tablet from the ruins of Alasia (16th century BC), a form of writing which came about through links with the Minoan civilization of Crete.

During the 16th and 15th centuries BC, the most important towns were Kition (modern-day Larnaka) and Egkomi-Alasia. Mycenaean culture left a permanent imprint on the future development of Cypriot culture.

Choirokotia, one of the earliest settlements

TIMELINE

2500 BC	2350 BC	2200 BC	2050 BC	1900 BC	1750 BC

c.2500 BC Early Bronze Age, with the earliest bronze smelting occuring in Mesaoria

2000–58 BC The island ruled by Mycenaeans, Egyptians, Phoenicians, Assyrians and Persians

Statuette of an idol, 1900 BC

c.2500 BC Red polished ceramics spread across the island; growth of the cult of fertility (its symbol a bull)

Ceramic pot from Vounous, 2500–1900 BC

1900–1650 BC Middle Bronze Age; settlements appear on the south and east of the island, as a result of overseas trade

Despite many diverse influences (from Egypt, Mesopotamia, Phoenicia and Persia), it was Greek culture that would dominate.

Around the 12th century BC, marauders known as the "sea peoples" invaded Cyprus, destroying Kition and Alasia. They settled in Maa (Paleo-kastro) in the west of the island, among other

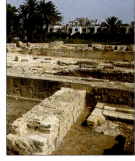

Ruins of Phoenician-populated Kition

places. But with the mass arrival of Mycenaeans in the 11th century BC, balance was restored. The Greek language, customs and culture were widely adopted, and a flourishing cult of Aphrodite also developed. The Temple of Aphrodite in Palaipafos rose in status and soon became the main shrine of the goddess in the ancient Greek world.

Female figurine from the Temple of Aphrodite

Around 1,050 BC, an earthquake devastated Cyprus, heralding the island's Dark Ages. Kition and Alasia were reduced to rubble, and their inhabitants relocated to Salamis.

IRON AGE

The first millennium BC ushered in the Iron Age throughout the entire Mediterranean area, although it in no way diminished the demand for copper from Cyprus. During this time, Cyprus was divided into kingdoms, ruled by local kings. The most important were Salamis, Marion, Lapithos, Soli, Pafos, Tamassos and Kourion. By the 9th century BC the wealth of Cyprus lured Phoenicians from nearby Tyre, who established a colony at Kition. The joint influences from the Phoenicians, Mycenaeans and the Cypriots fuelled this era of outstanding cultural achievement, with the building of new towns and the development of metallurgy.

In about the 8th century BC Amathous (east of modern-day Limassol) began to develop, and Kition (modern-day Larnaka) became a major trading hub and the centre of the cult of the Phoenician goddess, Astarte.

ARCHAIC ERA

In about 700 BC, Cyprus fell into the hands of the Assyrian kings, who did not wish to rule but merely demanded payment of tributes. This period saw the creation of Ionian-influenced limestone statues, pottery decorated with images of people and animals, and votive terracotta figurines.

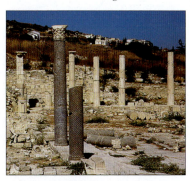

Amathous, one of the oldest Cypriot towns

1500 BC	1450 BC	1300 BC	1150 BC	1000 BC	850 BC
c.1400 BC Mycenaean merchants and craftsmen begin to settle on the island		**12th century BC** Invasion by the "sea peoples"	*Gold jewellery 1650–1150 BC* **1050–750 BC** Geometric era		
15th century BC The earliest Cypro-Minoan writing on a tablet found in the ruins of Alasia		**c.1050 BC** A violent earthquake destroys Cypriot towns, including Alasia and Kition		**c.1000 BC** Phoenicians arrive from Tyre and settle on the southern plains	

Sarcophagus from Pierides Museum in Larnaka

CLASSICAL PERIOD

In the early 6th century BC, Cyprus was ruled by Egyptians, but their influence on local art was negligible. The most distinctive architectural features of the period are the subterranean burial chambers, resembling houses, unearthed in Tamassos. In 545 BC, Egypt was conquered by the Persians, under whose control Cyprus fell. The small Cypriot kingdoms were forced to pay tributes to the Persians and to supply battle-ships in the event of war.

Although the kingdoms were not at first involved in the Persian Wars (490–480 BC), strife akin to civil war erupted. Some kingdoms declared themselves on the side of the Greeks, while others supported the Persians (especially the Phoenician inhabitants of Kition and Amathous, as well as Marion, Kourion and Salamis). In the decisive battle at Salamis, insurgents were defeated and the leader, Onesilos, was killed. The Persians went on to conquer other kingdoms. The last to fall were Palaipafos and Soloi (in 498 BC). Having quashed the revolt, the pro-Persian king of Marion built a palace to watch over Soloi.

By the start of the 5th century BC, Cyprus had ten kingdoms, the existing ones having been joined by Kyrenia, Idalion, Amathous and Kition, while Soloi submitted to the rule of the king of Marion. Cyprus became a battleground for the Greek-Persian Wars. The Athenian general, Kimon, who was sent to the island failed to conquer Cyprus, despite a few minor victories, and was killed during the siege of Kition.

Despite the difficult political situation, the influence of Greek culture on Cyprus grew considerably. This was especially noticeable in sculpture; hitherto the portrayal of gods and men had been stiff, endowed with an obligatory "archaic smile", and now it became more naturalistic.

HELLENISTIC ERA

When Alexander the Great attacked the Persian Empire in 325 BC, the Cypriot kingdoms welcomed him as a liberator, providing him with a fleet of battleships for his victorious siege of Tyre. The weakening of Phoenicia resulted in greater revenues from the copper trade for Cyprus. But the favourable situation did not last. After Alexander's death in 323 BC, Cyprus became a battleground for his successors – the victor was the Greek-Egyptian Ptolemy I Solter. Kition, Kyrenia, Lapithos and Marion were destroyed

Marble statue of Apollo from Lyra, 2nd century AD

TIMELINE

800 BC Phoenicians settle in Kition

570 BC Egyptians assume control of Cyprus

546 BC Start of Persian rule

Jug (5th century BC)

294 BC Island falls under the control of the Egyptian Ptolemys

700 BC	600 BC	500 BC	400 BC	300 BC

8th century BC Assyrians leave control of the island to Cypriot kings, demanding only an annual tribute

c.500 BC Ionian cities revolt against the Persians

381 BC Evagoras, King of Salamis, leads revolt against the Persians

333 BC Alexander the Great occupies Cyprus

Lion from a tomb stele (5th century BC)

Ruins of Kambanopetra basilica in Salamis

and Nicocreon, the King of Salamis who refused to surrender, committed suicide. Cyprus became part of the Kingdom of Egypt, and its viceroy resided in the new capital – Nea Pafos. Cultural life was influenced by Hellenism, with the Egyptian gods joining the pantheon of deities.

ROMAN RULE & CHRISTIANITY

In 58 BC, Cyprus was conquered by the legions of Rome. The island was given the status of a province ruled

by a governor, who resided in a magnificent palace in Nea Pafos. The largest town, port and main trading centre was still Salamis, which at that time numbered over 200,000 inhabitants. The imposing ruins of Salamis bear testimony to its prosperity, while the Roman floor mosaics in Pafos are among the most interesting in the Middle East. The flourishing city of Kourion was the site of the temple and oracle of Apollo – which continued to be of religious significance. Roman rule lasted in Cyprus until the end of the 4th century AD.

Mosaic from the house of Theseus in Kato Pafos

Christianity came to Cyprus with the arrival from Palestine of the apostle Paul in AD 45. He was joined by Barnabas, who was to become the first Cypriot saint. In the same year they converted the Roman governor of Cyprus, Sergius Paulus. The new religion spread slowly, until it was adopted as the state religion by Emperor Constantine. His edict of 312 granted Christianity equal status with other religions of his Empire. St Helena, the mother of Constantine the Great, stopped in Cyprus on her way back from Jerusalem, where she found fragments of the True Cross. She founded Stavrovouni monastery, which is said to house a fragment of the cross.

Saranda Kolones in Kato Pafos

Eros and Psyche
(1st century AD)

58 BC Rome annexes Cyprus

1st century BC Cyprus hit by violent earthquakes

| 00 BC | 100 BC | AD 1 | AD 100 | AD 200 | AD 300 |

313 Edict of Milan grants freedom of worship to Christians throughout the Roman Empire, including Cyprus

AD 45 The apostles Paul and Barnabas arrive as missionaries to spread Christianity to Cyprus

115–116 Jewish rebellion put down by Emperor Hadrian. Salamis destroyed

In 332 and 342, two cataclysmic earthquakes destroyed most of the Cypriot towns, including Salamis and Palaipafos, marking the end of the era.

View from St Hilarion Castle

BYZANTINE PERIOD

The official division of the Roman realm into an Eastern and Western Empire in 395 naturally left Cyprus on the eastern side of the divide, under the Byzantine sphere of influence.

The 5th and 6th centuries were flourishing times. The centres of pagan culture linked to the cults of Aphrodite and Apollo (Pafos and Kourion) lost importance, while the role of Salamis increased. Renamed Constantia, it became the island's capital. New towns also arose, such as Famagusta and Nicosia, and vast basilicas were built.

Beginning around 647, the first of a series of pillaging raids by Arabs took place. In the course of the raids, which continued over three centuries, Constantia was sacked and many magnificent buildings were destroyed.

In 965, the fleet of the Byzantine emperor Nicephorus II Phocas rid the island of Arab pirates and Cyprus again became safe. But not for long. From the 11th century, the entire Middle East became the scene of new warfare. Anatolia,

Christ Pantocrator from the church of Panagiatou tou Araka

Syria and, above all, the Holy Land were captured by the Seljuk Turks. Byzantium was incapable of resisting the onslaught, and Crusades were organized in Europe to recover the Holy Land and other lost territories.

CRUSADES & LUSIGNAN PERIOD

Successive crusades took place throughout most of the 12th and 13th centuries to recover the Holy Land from the Muslims. After considerable effort, the first succeeded in capturing Jerusalem (1099). European knights set up the Kingdom of Jerusalem, but surrounded as it was by Turkish emirates, it was unable to survive. Further crusades were launched but mainly suffered defeats. The Sultan Saladin conquered nearly the entire Kingdom of Jerusalem in 1187. The next crusade was organized in 1190. One of its leaders was Richard I (the Lionheart),

TIMELINE

Pendant from the early Byzantine period

488 Following the discovery of the tomb of St Barnabas, Emperor Zenon confirms the independence of the Cypriot Church

688 Emperor Justinian II and Caliph Abd al-Malik sign a treaty dividing control of the island

300	450	600	750

395 Partition of the Roman Empire; Cyprus becomes part of the Eastern Roman Empire

7th century Arab raids

David in the Lion's Den, *a 7th-century AD relief*

King of England, whose ships were forced onto Cyprus by a storm. The local prince, Isaac Komnenos, who had proclaimed himself King of Cyprus, plundered the ships and tried to imprison the sister and the fiancée of Richard. In reprisal, Richard smashed the Komnenos artillery on the Mesaoria plain and chased his enemy, capturing him in Kantara Castle.

As spoils of war, Cyprus passed from hand to hand. Richard turned it over to the Knights Templar, and they in turn sold the island to the knight Guy de Lusignan, who started the Cyprian Lusignan Dynasty and introduced the feudal system to Cyprus. A period of prosperity for the nobility ensued, partly due to trade with Genoa and Venice, although local Cypriots experienced terrible poverty. Magnificent cathedrals and churches were built, and small churches in the Troodos mountains were decorated with splendid frescoes. The state was weakened by a devastating raid by the increasingly powerful Genoese in 1372, who captured Famagusta. Finally, the widow of James, the last Lusignan king, ceded Cyprus to the Venetians in 1489.

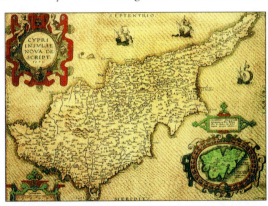

A costume from Venetian times

domains in the eastern Mediterranean from the Ottoman Empire. The most formidable fortifications around the ports and towns date from this period (including Kyrenia and Famagusta). Still, these were no match for the overwhelming power of the Ottoman Empire. When the Turkish army of Sultan Selim II landed on Cyprus in 1570, one town after another fell to the invaders. Nicosia was able to defend itself for just a few weeks; when it fell, the Turks slaughtered 20,000 people. The defence of Famagusta lasted longer – 10 months – and was one of the greatest battles of its time. The Venetian defenders did not survive to see the arrival of the relief army, and were forced to capitulate. The Turkish commander, Lala Mustafa Pasha, reneged on his promises of clemency and ordered the garrison to be slaughtered, and its leader Bragadino to be skinned alive.

VENETIAN RULE

Venetian rule over Cyprus lasted less than a century. The island was a frontier fortress, intended to defend the Venetian

A 16th-century map of Cyprus

Seal of King Henry II Lusignan

1191 Richard the Lionheart conquers Cyprus and sells the island to the Knights Templar

1372 Genoese raid, capturing of Famagusta

1489–1571 Venetian rule

1050	1200	1350	1500

965 Victory of Emperor Phokas II over the Arabs. Cyprus returns to the Byzantine Empire

1192 Knights Templar hand over Cyprus to Guy, exiled king of Jerusalem. Guy de Lusignan becomes the first king of the new Lusignan dynasty

1489 Queen Caterina Cornaro cedes the weakened island to the Venetians

THE OTTOMAN ERA

This was the start of 300 years of Turkish rule. The conquerors destroyed most of the monasteries and churches, turning others into mosques. They abolished the hated feudal system, and divided land among the peasants. The Orthodox clergy were allowed to adopt some Catholic churches and monasteries, and later the archbishop was recognized as the Greek community's representative.

The Turks brought their compatriots to settle on the island, and squashed the regular rebellions. In 1821, after the beginning of the Greek War of Independence, the Turkish governor ordered the execution of the popular Archbishop Kyprianos and many other members of the Orthodox clergy.

In the mid-19th century, Great Britain came to play an increasingly important role in the Middle East. In exchange for military aid in the war

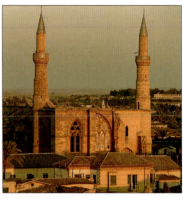
Selima Mosque in North Nicosia

with Russia, Turkey handed over occupation and administrative rights of Cyprus to Britain in perpetuity in 1878, though the island would continue to be a Turkish possession.

BRITISH RULE

Cyprus's strategic location was vital in defending the sea routes to India and in safeguarding British interests in the Middle East. During their rule, the British introduced the English justice system, reduced crime and built roads and waterworks. Following the outbreak of World War I, when Turkey declared itself on the side of Germany, Britain annexed Cyprus.

After World War II, Greek Cypriots pressed for *enosis* (unification with Greece), which was strongly opposed by the Turkish minority. Rising tensions led to the establishment of the organization EOKA (National

Hadjigeorgakis Kornesios mansion

Hoisting of the British flag in Cyprus

TIMELINE

1570 Cyprus invaded by Ottoman Turks

1754 The sultan confirms the Orthodox archbishop as a spokesman for the Greek Cypriots

The hanging of Archbishop Kyprianos

1600	1650	1700	1750	1800

1571–1878 Ottoman era

Büyük Han in North Nicosia

1660 Ottoman authorities recognize the legitimacy of the Archbishop's office with the Greeks

1779 Establishment of the dragoman (intercessor between the Turks and the Greeks)

1821 Bloody suppression of the Greek national uprising by the Turks

Organization of Cypriot Fighters) in 1954 by Archbishop Makarios and Greek General George Grivas. Its aim was to free Cyprus from British control. EOKA embarked on a terrorist campaign, first aimed at property and later, at people. In 1958, Turkish Cypriots founded the Turkish Resistance Organisation (TNT), which provided a counterbalance to EOKA.

Archbishop Makarios, first president of the Republic of Cyprus

The terror and growing costs of maintaining order led the British to grant independence to Cyprus. A constitution was drafted that, among other things, excluded *enosis* and *taksim* (partition of Cyprus between Turkey and Greece favoured by Turkish Cypriots). Britain, Greece and Turkey signed a treaty that obliged them to ensure Cyprus's independence. Archbishop Makarios, who had been interned by the British, returned to Cyprus in triumph and was elected President of the Republic of Cyprus. Independence was officially declared on 16 August 1960.

INDEPENDENT CYPRUS

In December 1963, animosity between Greek and Turkish Cypriots erupted into warfare. The Greek army intervened and the Turkish air force bombarded the environs of Polis. In 1964, United Nations troops arrived to restore peace between the warring parties within three months. The mission failed and troops remain to this day.

On 15 July 1974 a coup d'état, encouraged by Athens and staged by rebel units of the Cypriot National Guard (led by Greek army officers), ousted Makarios. The conspirators killed several hundred Greeks and Turks, which provided the Turkish government in Ankara with a pretext to send troops to Cyprus. After a short battle, the invading army controlled the north, and the resettlement of the population began. The "Green Line" buffer zone still divides the Turkish-occupied North from the South, and continues to be patrolled by UN troops.

In November 1983 the Turks declared the Turkish Republic of Northern Cyprus (TRNC), which is recognized only in Turkey. In April 2004 a referendum preceding Cyprus's entry into the European Union failed to unify the island. The leaders, President of the Republic of Cyprus Demetris Christofias and President of the TRNC Dervis Eroglu, make repeated attempts at reunification by participating in frequent rounds of talks.

Referendum on the reunification of Cyprus (2004)

1878 Great Britain takes over the administration of Cyprus	1925 Cyprus becomes a British colony	1950 Makarios is elected Archbishop	1960 (16 August) Proclamation of independence. Archbishop Makarios III becomes President of the Republic of Cyprus	

General George Grivas

1850	1900	1950	2000	2050

1914 Outbreak of World War I; Great Britain annexes Cyprus	1963–4 Fighting erupts between Greek and Turkish Cypriots; UN troops arrive	1983 TRNC is declared	2010 Festivals mark 50 years of independence

1974 Coup d'état against President Makarios. Turkish invasion of North Cyprus

2008 Southern Cyprus adopts the euro

2004 Referendum on reunification

CYPRUS REGION BY REGION

Cyprus at a Glance

Cyprus has a wide variety of historic sites. Visitors can find everything from Neolithic settlements and ancient towns to medieval cathedrals and small mountain churches decorated with exquisite frescoes, castles built by the Crusaders and Venetian fortresses, and modern buildings and museums. The island abounds in picturesque towns and villages, beautiful coastal areas, and scenic mountains, with diverse wildlife and friendly people.

Nicosia *is the world's only divided capital city. A highlight of its southern part is the Byzantine-style Archbishop Makarios Cultural Centre, housing an impressive collection of icons (see p118).*

Agios Nikolaos tis Stegis, *a UNESCO World Heritage Site, is one of the many small churches hidden in the sheltered valleys of the Troodos mountains that feature magnificent frescoes (see p98).*

SOUTH NICOSIA
Pages 112

CENTRAL CYPRUS
Pages 102–111

TROODOS MOUNTAINS
Pages 84–101

WEST CYPRUS
Pages 40–59

SOUTHERN CYPRUS
Pages 60–83

Pafos, *divided into Kato Pafos (Lower Pafos) and Ktima, is full of history. With its picturesque harbour, it is also one of the most beautiful towns in the Mediterranean (see pp48–53).*

0 km   15

0 miles   15

◁ **Herd of goats near Lara Bay in the Akamas peninsula**

Buffavento Castle *in the Kyrenia mountains was one of three castles, along with Kantara and St Hilarion, that defended Cyprus against attacks along the north coast (see p144).*

NORTH CYPRUS
Pages 124–153

Salamis *was the island's most important port and trading town for almost one thousand years, and also its capital. Now it is one of the largest archaeological sites (see pp134–5).*

In Larnaka *the remains of the 18th-century Kamares Aqueduct stand beside the Larnaka–Limassol highway. In ancient times the Kingdom of Kition, today Larnaka is a large port town with a thriving tourist zone (see pp78–81).*

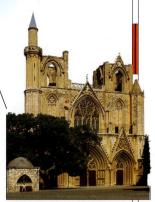

Famagusta, *a city surrounded by Venetian defence walls, contains Gothic churches that have been transformed into mosques with minarets (see pp136–7).*

WEST CYPRUS

West Cyprus is a varied region, made up of mountains, historical sights and a lovely coastline. It was once the most neglected part of the island, remote from the main cities and harbours. Now it is becoming a popular attraction due to its wild natural environment. Lovers of antiquities are sure to be enchanted by the Roman mosaics in Pafos, while mythology buffs can see the place where the goddess Aphrodite emerged from the sea at Petra tou Romiou.

Pafos's Hellenistic, Roman and Byzantine relics are among the most interesting in the island, especially the Roman mosaics.

The modern town is divided into a bustling tourist zone on the coast, with dozens of luxury hotels, taverns, pubs and restaurants, and Ktima – the old town of Pafos – which is only a short drive inland but a world away from the tourist zone.

This region has a slightly milder climate than the rest of the island, as witnessed by the banana plantations north of Pafos. And though there is practically no industry, it has the most extensive forest areas in Cyprus, including the famous Cedar Valley inhabited by wild moufflon. The Akamas peninsula, with its rugged hills overgrown with forests, is home to many species of wild animals, and the beautiful beaches provide nesting grounds for sea turtles. This is a paradise for nature lovers and is one of the best places to hike in Cyprus. Movement around the peninsula is hindered by the lack of roads, but there are trails for use by walkers.

This is the land of Aphrodite, the goddess of love, born in the south of the island by the rocks jutting out of the sea, which are named after her. In the north, on the bay of Chrysochou, is the goddess's bath, which she used after her amorous frolics with Adonis.

Pafos harbour, the most picturesque in southern Cyprus

◁ *The Bath of Achilles*, an ancient mosaic in Pafos

Exploring West Cyprus

The best place to begin exploring West Cyprus is Pafos, which has the largest concentration of hotels and the most developed tourist infrastructure. Here you will also find a wealth of historic relics that have made Pafos a UNESCO World Heritage Site. They range from Bronze Age dwellings (Maa Paleokastro at Coral Bay), royal tombs dating from the Hellenic era and Roman floor mosaics to Byzantine castles and churches. Pafos forest is home to wild moufflon. Cape Lara, to the northwest of Pafos, has beautiful beaches, and further on is the Akamas peninsula.

Lempa is a favourite place with watersports enthusiasts

GETTING THERE

The easiest way to arrive is by air to the international airport east of Pafos, where a motorway links the town with Limassol, offering easy access to the west coast. It is also possible to get here via a parallel road running along the coast and over the southern slopes of the Troodos mountains. However, the mountain roads are not of the best quality, and driving around the Akamas peninsula is best done in a four-wheel-drive vehicle.

SIGHTS AT A GLANCE

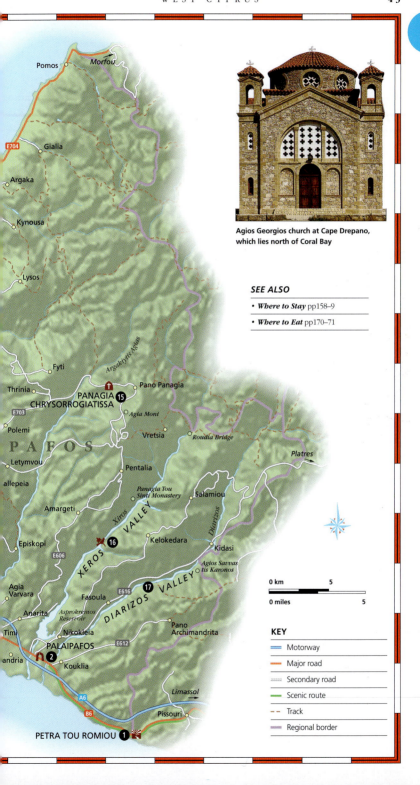

Pomos
Morfou
Gialia
E704
Argaka
Kynousa
Lysos

Fyti
Thrinia
PANAGIA
CHRYSORROGIATISSA
E703
Polemi
Letymvou
allepeia

P A F O S

Amargeti
Episkopi
E606

Agia
Varvara
Anarita
Timi
PALAIPAFOS
andria
Kouklia

Argakitis Agas

Pano Panagia
15
Agia Moni
Vretsia
Roudia Bridge

Platres

Pentalia
Panagia Tou
Simi Monastery
Salamiou

X
E
R
O
S
Xiros VALLEY

Kelokedara
16

Diarizos
Kidasi
Agios Savvas
tis Karonos

D
I
A
R
I
Z
O
S

Fasoula
E616
17
VALLEY

Asprokremos
Reservoir
Nikokleia
E612
Pano
Archimandrita

2

Limassol

A6
B6
Pissouri

PETRA TOU ROMIOU **1**

Agios Georgios church at Cape Drepano,
which lies north of Coral Bay

SEE ALSO

• *Where to Stay* pp158–9

• *Where to Eat* pp170–71

0 km   5
0 miles   5

KEY

━━━ Motorway

━━━ Major road

┅┅┅ Secondary road

━━━ Scenic route

─ ─ ─ Track

━━━ Regional border

Petra tou Romiou, the legendary birthplace of Aphrodite

Petra tou Romiou ❶

Road map B4. 25 km (16 miles) east of Pafos.

The area between Pafos and Limassol includes what is probably the most beautiful stretch of the Cyprus coast, dominated by limestone crags rising from the blue sea. At Petra tou Romiou there are three huge, white limestone rocks known collectively as the **Rock of Aphrodite**. In Greek mythology it was here that Aphrodite, goddess of love, beauty and fertility, emerged from the sea foam. She sailed to the shore on a shell towed by dolphins and rested in nearby Palaipafos, where a temple was built to her.

The location of these picturesque rocks is beautiful, with clear blue water beckoning swimmers. The large beach near the rocks is covered with fine pebbles and stones polished smooth by the action of the waves.

A word of caution, however: the road between the car park and the beach is dangerous, and you are advised to use the underground passage.

Nearby you can see trees on which infertile women tie handkerchiefs or scraps of fabric to appeal for help from Aphrodite. They are joined by others who are lonely and unlucky in love, beseeching the goddess of love to help them. A local legend says that swimming around the jutting rock at full moon will make you a year younger with each lap. Other legends lead us to believe that the amorous goddess, after a night spent in the arms of her lover, returned to this spot to regain her virginity by bathing in the sea.

On the slope of the hill above the Rock of Aphrodite, the Cyprus Tourism Organization has built a cafeteria where you can eat while taking in the beautiful view over Petra tou Romiou. Meaning "Rock of Romios",

the name Petra tou Romiou also commemorates the legendary Greek hero Digenis Akritas, also known as Romios. He lived during the Byzantine era and, during an Arab raid by Saracen corsairs on Cyprus, hurled huge boulders into the sea to destroy the Arab ships. According to legend, the rocks here are the stones thrown by Romios.

Environs
A few kilometres east of Petra tou Romiou is the small resort community of **Pissouri**, surrounded by orchards. There is a large resort here, and some smaller hotels, as well as a long, sandy beach. Nearby are two golf courses: Secret Valley and Aphrodite Hills.

Palaipafos ❷

Road map A4. In Kouklia village, 14 km (9 miles) east of Pafos, by the Pafos–Limassol road. **Tel** 264 32155. ⏰ 8am–4pm daily (to 5pm Wed). 🈲

Lying just north of the large village of Kouklia are the ruins of the famous Palaipafos (Old Pafos), which was the oldest and most powerful city-state on the island in ancient times. According to tradition, it was founded by Agaperon – a hero of the Trojan Wars and the son of the King of Tegeia in Greek Arcadia. Palaipafos was also the site of the **Temple of Aphrodite**, the most important shrine of the goddess in the ancient world, but now only of specialist interest. Archaeological evidence points to the existence of a much older town on this site, dating

---

APHRODITE

The cult of Aphrodite arrived in Cyprus from the East; she was already worshipped in Syria and Palestine as Ishtar and Astarte. She was also worshipped by the Romans as Venus. In Greek mythology Aphrodite was the goddess of love, beauty and fertility who rose from the sea foam off the shore of Cyprus. She was married to Hephaestus, but took many lovers, including Ares and Adonis. She was the mother of Eros, Hermaphrodite, Priap and Aeneas, among others. The main centres for her cult of worship were Pafos and Amathous. The myrtle plant is dedicated to her, as is the dove.

Marble statue of Aphrodite from Soloi

For hotels and restaurants in this region see pp158–9 and pp170–71

back to the Bronze Age. Legend says that Pygmalion, a local king and also a brilliant sculptor, carved many statues, including one of an extraordinarily beautiful woman with whom he fell madly in love. Aphrodite, moved by his love, turned the cold statue into a living woman. Their union produced a son, Pafos, who gave the town its name.

The most famous figure of Pafos was Kinyras, ruler of the city and great priest of Aphrodite, who introduced many religious mysteries and gave rise to the dynasty that ruled the city for centuries.

A large **centre of worship** devoted to Aphrodite was established here in the 12th century BC, at the end of the Bronze Age. All that is left now are its foundations and fragments of the walls. The sanctuary was destroyed during an earthquake and rebuilt in the 1st century, during Roman times. At this place of worship, the goddess was represented by a black stone shaped as a cone, symbolizing fertility. For centuries, crowds of pilgrims flocked to Pafos from all over the ancient world. Adorned with flowers, the pilgrims walked into the temple where they were met by the temple courtesans. Aphrodite was worshipped through ritual sexual intercourse between the pilgrims and Aphrodite's priestesses – young Cypriot women who were obliged to offer their virginity to the goddess by

The small stone church of Agios Constantinos near Kouklion

Panagia Chrysopolitissa inscription

giving themselves to a pilgrim man within the temple area. These orgiastic rites were mainly held in the spring, and elements have survived in the form of the spring flower festival – the Anthistiria.

Palaipafos was not always peaceful. It took part in the rebellion of the Ionian cities against the Persians. In 498 BC, the Persians laid siege to the city and, following a fierce battle, forced entry by scaling the ramparts, the remains of which can still be seen. In 325 BC, following a devastating earthquake that destroyed Palaipafos, its last king, Nikikles, moved the city to Nea Pafos (present day Kato Pafos), but Aphrodite's sanctuary retained its importance until the end of the 4th century, when Emperor Theodosius banned pagan cults within the empire.

The sanctuary is now a site of excavations, conducted by Swiss archaeologists.

Standing on the hill is a Gothic structure known as the **Lusignan Court**, built in the times of the Crusaders and subsequently remodelled by the Turks. It is built on a square floor plan, and leading on to a square yard is an old tower gate. The rooms in the east wing contain a museum that exhibits locally discovered ceramics, stone idols, bronze articles and the black stone worshipped by followers of Aphrodite. On the ground floor there is an impressive Gothic hall with cross vaulting.

In the nearby Roman villa, known as the **House of Leda**, archaeologists have uncovered a 2nd-century AD floor mosaic, which depicts the Spartan Queen Leda with Zeus in the guise of a swan.

Adjacent to the sanctuary is the small 12th-century church of **Panagia Chrysopolitissa**, which was built over the ruins of an Early Byzantine basilica. It is dedicated to the early Christian Madonna, whose cult derives directly from Aphrodite – the pagan goddess of love. As part of a tradition stemming from Cypriot folklore, women came here to light candles to the Virgin Mary – Giver of Mother's Milk. This church contains interesting 14th-century frescoes, and some of the colourful mosaics that covered the floor of the basilica have been preserved.

Ruins of the Sanctuary of Aphrodite

Folk Art Museum in Geroskipou

Geroskipou ❸

Road map A4. 3 km (1.8 miles) east of Pafos. 🚌 601, 606 A/B, 615, 631. 📷 Agia Paraskevi (Jul).

The name Geroskipou (*hieros kipos*) means "sacred garden" in Greek. This testifies to the fact that this former village (now a suburban district bordering Pafos) was built on the site of a forest dedicated to Aphrodite. To this day, it is notable for its many flowers and fruit trees, especially citrus and pomegranate trees – symbols of the goddess.

The main street is lined with workshops producing the local delicacy – *loukoumia* (Cyprus delight). Made from water, sugar and citrus juice, thickened through evaporation, the resulting jelly is cut into cubes and coated with icing sugar. The workshops are open to visitors, who can view the production process and, while there, also buy other sweets including sugar-coated almonds and delicious halva – made of nuts, honey and sesame seeds. The tree-shaded main square of the town is surrounded by colourful shops selling baskets, ceramics and the celebrated *loukoumia*; there are also numerous cafés serving coffee and pastries.

Standing at the southern end of the market square is **Agia Paraskevi**, one of the most interesting Byzantine churches on the island. Built in the 9th century, this stone church features five domes arranged in the shape of a cross. The sixth one surmounts the reliquary located under the 19th-century belfry. Originally, the church was a single-nave structure. Its interior is decorated with beautiful 15th-century murals depicting scenes from the New Testament, including the lives of Jesus and Mary, and the Crucifixion. The frescoes were restored in the 1970s.

The vault of the central dome has been decorated with the painting of the Praying Madonna. The three images opposite the south entrance – *The Last Supper*, *The Washing of the Feet* and *The Betrayal* – can be dated from the Lusignan period, due to the style of armour worn by the knights portrayed. Opposite are *The Birth and Presentation of the Virgin*, *The Entry into Jerusalem* and *The Raising of Lazarus*.

Another attraction, close to the market square, is the 19th-century historic house once home of the British Consul, Andreas Zamboulakis.

The stone church of Agia Paraskevi in Geroskipou

Now the building houses the **Folk Art Museum**, one of the most impressive on the island, including a collection of local folk costumes, textiles, embroidery and toys, as well as decorated gourds, furniture and domestic items.

🔒 **Agia Paraskevi Church**
Tel 26 961 859. 🕐 Apr–Oct: 8am–1pm, 2–5pm Mon–Sat; Nov–Mar: 2–4pm Mon–Sat.

🏛 **Folk Art Museum**
Leondiou. **Tel** 26 306 216.
🕐 8:30am–4pm daily. 📷

Pafos ❹

See pp48–51.

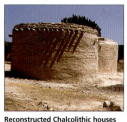

Reconstructed Chalcolithic houses in Lempa's Experimental Village

Lempa ❺

Road map A4. 4 km (2.5 miles) north of Pafos. 🚌 607 from Ktima Pafos.

Set among citrus groves between the villages of Chlorakas and Kissonerga just a short distance from the sea, Lempa is home to the **Cyprus College of Art**. The artists, craftsmen and students here have studios in restored village houses. The road to the college is lined with sculptures. The independent pottery workshops are worth visiting.

Lempa was home to the earliest islanders, who settled here more than 5,500 years ago. West of the village centre you can see the **Lempa Experimental Village** – a partially reconstructed settlement dating from the Chalcolithic (bronze) era (3500 BC). British archaeologists have rebuilt four complete houses from that era. The clay, cylindrical dwellings are covered with makeshift roofs.

Agios Neofytos monastery, founded in the 12th century

🏛 **Cyprus College of Art**
Tel 26 270 557. **www**.artcyprus.org
🗻 **Lempa Experimental Village**
⭘ *dawn–dusk daily.*

Environs
In the centre of the nearby village of Empa, some 2 km (1 mile) southeast of Lempa, is the 12th-century monastery church of **Panagia Chryse-leoussa**. Inside it are the remains of frescoes that were initially destroyed by an earthquake in the mid-1900s, and later damaged by a bad restoration job.

Agios Neofytos ❻

Road map A4. 9 km north of Pafos, 2 km NW of Tala. 🚌 *604.* ⭘ *9am–1pm, 2–6pm daily (to 4pm Nov–Mar).* 🖼 🎫 *25 Jan & 28 Sep.*

This monastery was founded in the 12th century by a monk named Neofytos, one of the main saints of the Cypriot church. He was a hermit and an ascetic, author of philosophical treatises and hymns, who spent dozens of years here. Some of his manuscripts survive, including the *Ritual Ordinance*, a handbook of monastic life, and a historic essay on the acquisition of Cyprus by the Crusaders.
The future saint dug three cells in the steep limestone rock with his bare hands. The murals covering its walls are

reputed to have been painted by Neofytos himself. This, the oldest part of the monastery, is called the *encleistra* (hermitage). In two of the caves, murals depict the final days of the life of Christ – *The Last Supper*, *Judas's Betrayal* and the *Deposition from the Cross*, featuring Joseph of Arimathea whose face is thought to be a portrait of the saint. The dome, hewn from the soft rock, features the Ascension.
The cell of the saint has bookshelves, benches and a desk at which St Neofytos used to work, all carved in the rock, as well as his sarcophagus presided over by an image of the Resurrection.
The main buildings, which are still inhabited by monks, include an inner courtyard, a small garden with an aviary, and a *katholikon* – the monastery church with a terrace dedicated to the Virgin Mary.

A woman potter

Coral Bay ❼

Road map A4. 8 km (5 miles) north of Pafos. 🚌 *610, 616, 617, 631.*

This fine sandy beach between two promontories has a tropical air. All summer long it is covered by rows of sunbeds for hire. It offers soft sand and safe swimming for families, and there is a wide choice of watersports. There are many bars, restaurants and hotels, as well as a campsite for more thrifty visitors. Live pop concerts are held here on summer evenings. This beach is popular with young Cypriots from Larnaka and Limassol, especially on summer weekends.
On the northern headland archaeologists discovered **Maa Paleokastro** – a fortified Achaian settlement dating from the Bronze Age. The site now houses the **Museum of the Mycenean Colonization of Cyprus**.

Environs
Opposite the village of Chlorakas on the road to Pafos is the **Church of St George**, which commemorates the landing of General George Grivas at this spot in 1954. The local museum has a boat that was used by EOKA guerrillas for weapons smuggling.
Several kilometres inland lies the Mavrokolympos reservoir. Above the car park are the **Adonis Baths**, whose main attraction is its 10-m- (32-ft-) high waterfall. The road running along the Mavrokolympos river leads to more waterfalls.
The region also features numerous vineyards and banana plantations.

The picturesque crescent-shaped Coral Bay

Pafos ❹

Pafos is the name given to the twin towns of Pano Pafos (Upper Pafos, known as the Old Town or Ktima by locals) and Nea Pafos or Kato Pafos (Lower Pafos) *(see pp52–3).* During the Byzantine era, when coastal towns were threatened by Arab raids, the town was moved inland to its present hilltop location. This is now the modern regional centre of trade, administration and culture, while the lower town is the site of fine Roman ruins and the majority of tourist facilities.

Exploring Pafos

Ktima is best explored on foot. Most of its major historic buildings and interesting sites, except for the Archaeological Museum, are within walking distance. The tourist area in the Old Town has been carefully restored. The main shopping street is Makarios Avenue, where you will find a wide choice of jewellery, clothing and footwear. After strolling along the streets of the Old Town it is worth stopping for a rest in the green district, to the south of town, near the acropolis and the Byzantine and Ethnographic Museums. The eastern part of town sports wide avenues lined with classical public buildings, schools and libraries. The western part is a maze of narrow streets and traditional architecture.

The façade of Agios Kendas church, which was built around 1930

🅒 Grand Mosque

(Cami Kebir) Namik Kemil.
The Grand Mosque is a relic of the past Turkish presence in this area. Standing in the former Mouttalos district, it had been the Byzantine church of Agia Sofia before being turned into a mosque.

🕍 Agora

Agoras street.
In the centre of the Old Town is an ornamental covered market hall building, dating from the early 20th century. Sweet and souvenir sellers have replaced the fruit and vegetable vendors, who now trade in the outside market.

🅘 Loutra (Turkish Baths)

Militiathou, next to the covered bazaar (agora).
Among the trees south of the Agora are the Turkish baths. Originally this dome-covered stone structure probably served as a church. After serving as the Turkish baths, some of the rooms were used to house the municipal museum, but when this moved to new premises, the building stood empty. A period of neglect followed, but the Loutra building has been restored to its former glory. It now houses a coffee shop.

🅐 Agios Kendas

Leoforos Archiepiskopou Makariou III.
Built in 1930, the exterior is not particularly exciting, but the interior is well worth a visit. Here you will find a carved wooden iconostasis, a bishop's throne and a number of 19th-century icons.

🕍 Town Hall

Plateia 28 Octovriou.
The single-storey Neo-Classical building standing on the edge of the Municipal Garden, redolent of ancient Greek architecture, houses the Town Hall and the Registry Office. This is one of the most popular wedding venues. On the opposite side, behind the slender Ionian column in the middle of the square, is the one-storey municipal library.

The Neo-Classical Town Hall and Registry Office of Pafos

🅐 Agios Theodoros (St Theodore's Cathedral)

Andrea Ioannou.
Built in 1896, Agios Theodoros is the oldest church in Ktima and is as important for the Orthodox community as St John's Cathedral (Agios Ioannis) in Nicosia.
    Close to the square stands a column commemorating the victims of the Turkish slaughter of 1821 that claimed the lives of the Bishop of Pafos, Chrysanthos, and numerous other members of the Greek clergy.

Agora covered market, Pafos

Display in the Ethnographic Museum

VISITORS' CHECKLIST

Road map A4. 🏠 *52,800.*
ℹ️ *Gladstonos 3, 26 932 841.*
🚌 *Osypa Ltd (Paphos Transport
Organization), Mesogi, 26 934
252,* **www.***pafosbuses.com.*
✈️ *15 km (9 miles).*
🎭 *Aphrodite Festival (Aug–Sep).*

🏛 Geological Exhibition

Ayios Theodoros 2. 🕐 *9am–4pm
Mon–Sat (summer).*
One of a few places on the
island where you can learn
about the geology of Cyprus,
this is a small private
collection of rocks and
minerals. On display are
sedimentary rocks with fossils;
volcanic rocks from the
Troodos Mountains and the
Akamas peninsula; and metallic
minerals, particularly copper
and asbestos that have been
mined here for millennia.

🏛 Bishop's Palace and Byzantine Museum

Andrea Ioannou 5. **Tel** *26 931 393.*
🕐 *9am–3pm Mon–Fri, 9am–1pm
Sat.* 🎫
This beautiful Byzantine-style
building is the residence of
the Bishop of Pafos and the

most important ecclesiastical
building after Agios Theodoros.
It was built in 1910 by
Iaskos, the Bishop of Pafos.
Bishop Chrysostomos subse-
quently extended the palace,

The Dormition of the Virgin Mary,
the Byzantine Museum

furnishing it with beautiful
arcades and allocating part of
it to the Byzantine Museum.
The museum houses a
collection of icons, including
the oldest on the island – the
9th-century *Agia Marina*, and
the 12th-century *Panagia
Eloussa* from the Agios Savras
monastery. There are also
religious books, including a
1472 Bible and a collection
of documents produced by
Turkish sultans.

🏛 Ethnographic Museum

Exo Vrysis 1. **Tel** *26 932 010.*
🕐 *10am–6pm Mon–Sat,
10am–1pm Sun.* 🎫
This privately run museum
houses collections of coins,
folk costumes, kitchen
utensils, baskets and ceramics
as well as axes, amphorae
and carriages. In the sunken
garden is a wood-burning
stove from an old bakery and
an authentic 3rd-century
stone sarcophagus.

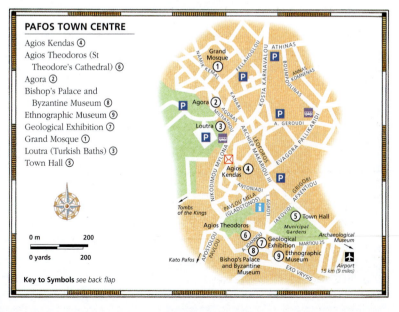

PAFOS TOWN CENTRE

0 m   200
0 yards   200

Key to Symbols *see back flap*

⌂ Tombs of the Kings

Leoforos Tafon ton Vasileon. *Tel 26 306 295.* ☐ *8am–5pm daily (to 6pm Apr, May, Sep & Oct; to 7:30pm Jun–Aug).* ⌨ ☐ *610, 615.*

The necropolis is a fascinating system of caves and rock tombs dating from the Hellenic and Roman eras (the 3rd century BC to 3rd century AD). Situated north of Kato Pafos, beyond the old city walls and close to the sea, it consists of imposing tombs carved in soft sandstone.

Eight tomb complexes have been opened for viewing; the most interesting are numbers 3, 4 and 8. Stone steps lead to underground vaults. Some tombs are surrounded by peristyles of Doric columns, beyond which you can spot burial niches. Others have been decorated with murals.

The architectural style of many tombs, particularly those in the northern section, reveals the Egyptian influence; they were inspired by the Ptolemy tombs in Alexandria. One funerary custom that has been documented is that on the anniversary of the death, relatives of the deceased would gather around the tomb for a ceremonial meal, depositing the leftovers by the actual sepulchre. Similar customs prevail to this day in some Greek Orthodox communities.

Over the following centuries the tombs were systematically

The 12th-century stone church of Agia Kyriaki

plundered. One of the more notorious looters was the American consul from Larnaka, Luigi Palma de Cesnola, who plundered many sites in Cyprus, including Kourion and the Tombs of the Kings in Pafos. These sites were built when there were no longer kings on Cyprus, and they were probably used to bury prominent citizens of Pafos, civil servants and army officers; nevertheless, in view of their opulence they became known as the Tombs of the Kings.

Inscription on one of the stones in Agia Kyriaki

During times of persecution they were used by Christians as hiding places. Later the site was used as a quarry. The place has a unique atmosphere, best experienced in the morning.

🔒 Agia Kyriaki

Odos Pafias Afroditis. ☐ *daily.*

The 12th-century stone church of Agia Kyriaki, with a later small belfry and dome, is also known as Panagia Chrysopolitissa (Our Lady of the Golden City). It was built on the ruins of an earlier seven-aisled Christian Byzantine basilica, the largest in Cyprus. A bishop's palace also stood nearby. Both buildings were destroyed by the Arabs, but the parts that have survived include 4th-century religious floor mosaics.

The road to Agia Kyriaki leads along a special platform built over the archaeological digs, from where you can see several single columns. One of them has been dubbed "St Paul's Pillar". The apostle came to Cyprus to preach Christianity, but was captured and led before the Roman governor, Sergius Paulus, who sentenced him to flogging. St Paul blinded his accuser, Elymas, thus convincing Sergius of his innocence to such an extent that the governor converted to Christianity.

Agia Kyriaki is used jointly by the Catholic and Anglican communities.

The beautiful church standing nearby, built on a rock which forms part of the Kato Pafos defence walls, is called *Panagia Theoskepasti* – "guarded by God". It is apocryphally told that during a scourging Arab attack a miraculous cloud enveloped the church, concealing it from the enemy.

⌂ Catacombs of Agia Solomoni and Fabrica Hill

Leoforos Apostolou Palou. ☐ *dawn–dusk.*

Inside a former tomb, is a subterranean church dedicated to Solomoni, a Jewess, whose seven children were tortured in her presence, and who is now regarded by the Cypriots as a saint.

In Roman times the site was probably occupied by a synagogue, and earlier on by a pagan shrine. Steep steps lead down to the sunken

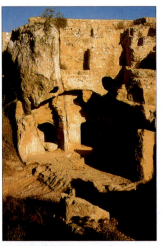

The Tombs of the Kings necropolis

sanctuary. The adjacent cave contains a tank with what is believed to be miraculous water. Similar catacombs on the opposite side of the street are called Agios Lambrianos.

Beyond Agia Solomoni, to the right, is the limestone Fabrica Hill containing carved underground chambers. They were created during Hellenic and Roman times but their purpose is unknown.

On the southern slope of the hill, Australian archaeologists have unearthed a Hellenic amphitheatre hewn out of the living rock. Nearby are two small cave churches, Agios Agapitikos and Agios Misitikos. Tradition has it that when dust collected from the floor of Agios Agapitikos is placed in someone's house, it has the power to awaken their love (*agapi* means "love"), while dust collected from Agios Misitikos will awaken hate (*misos*).

A relief from the Hellenic era, Archaeological Museum

🏛 Archaeological Museum

Leoforos Georgiou Griva Digeni 43. **Tel** 26 306 215. ⏺ 8am–3pm Tue–Fri (to 5pm Thu), 9am–3pm Sat. 🖼💻🚻

Housed in a small modern building outside the city centre, along the road leading

Fabric-festooned tree near the Catacombs of Agia Solomoni

to Geroskipou, this is one of the more interesting archaeological museums in Cyprus. The collection includes historic relics spanning thousands of years from the Neolithic era through the Bronze Age, Hellenic, Roman, Byzantine and medieval times, and up until the 18th century AD.

Particularly interesting are the Chalcolithic (copper age) figurines. There are steatite idols, a skeleton from Lempa, a 3rd-century AD mummy of a girl and an array of Hellenic ceramics, jewellery and glass. There are also ancient sarcophagi, sculptures, a coin collection, clay pots used for hot water and a set of Roman surgical instruments – evidence of the high standard of ancient medicine. There are also numerous exhibits from Kato Pafos and from Kouklia, site of the ancient city-kingdom Paliapafos and the Sanctuary of Aphrodite. The Archaeological Museum is one of the destinations featured in the Aphrodite Cultural Route, an initiative by the Cyprus Tourist

Organisation (CTO) that aims to guide visitors to key places of interest associated with the goddess. A booklet with useful information on the route is available from CTO offices.

🏖 Beaches

Pafos itself has only a few small beaches in front of hotels; these offer excellent conditions for watersports. A pleasant municipal beach is situated by Leoforos Poseidonos, at the centre of Kato Pafos, close to the Municipal Garden. Somewhat out of the way, to the north of the archaeological zone, lies the sandy-pebbly Faros Beach.

Good pebble beaches can be found north of Pafos. About 8 km (5 miles) along the coast is a small beach in the bay of Kissonerga fringed by banana plantations. The loveliest, most popular sandy beach is situated at Coral Bay, 10 km (6 miles) north of town (*see p47*). All the usual beach facilities are offered here, together with most watersports.

There are also several beaches to the east, including Alikes, Vrysoudia and Pahyammos. One of the most beautiful places to enjoy bathing is the beach near the Rock of Aphrodite, covered with smooth stones. The water here is crystal-clear and the environs truly enchanting. Facilities include a restaurant, toilets and a shower near the car park. It is worth coming to this beach either early in the morning or in the evening and staying to enjoy the beautiful sunset.

One of the alluring, popular beaches at Pafos

Kato Pafos

Column fragment

The most accessible and inspiring archaeological park on the island, the ruins at Kato (Lower) Pafos were unearthed in 1962, shedding new light on Cyprus under the Roman Empire. In ancient times, this was the capital of Cyprus. Now a UNESCO World Heritage Site, the remains found here span over 2,000 years. The lavish mosaics found on the floors of four Roman villas indicate that this was a place of ostentatious wealth.

★ House of Dionysos
Some 2,000 sq m (21,500 sq ft) of magnificent mosaics can be viewed from wooden platforms.

House of Aion
This villa, with its interesting mosaics, was destroyed by an earthquake. It takes its name from the god Aion, whose image was once to the left of the entrance.

House of Theseus
The palace of the Roman governor contains a set of interesting mosaics portraying the myth of Theseus and Ariadne. The opulent villa discovered underneath dates from the Hellenic era.

Medieval Castle
The medieval Lusignan castle remodelled by the Turks now houses a museum; its flat roof affords a lovely view over the town and the harbour.

STAR SIGHTS

★ House of Dionysos

★ Roman Odeon

The East Tower
was a defence structure, guarding the town against attacks by Arab pirates in the early Middle Ages.

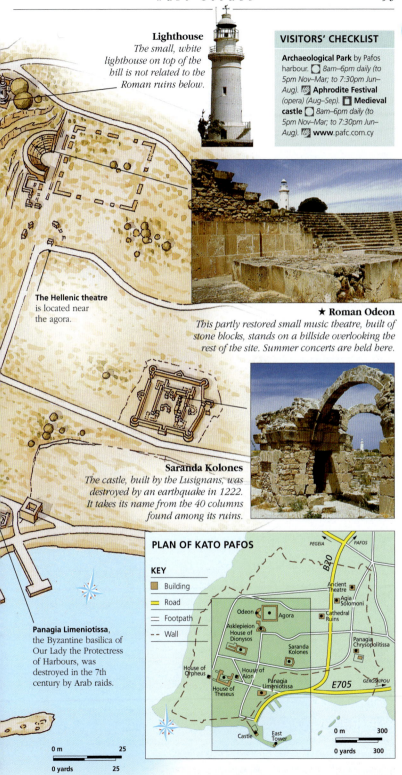

Lighthouse
The small, white lighthouse on top of the hill is not related to the Roman ruins below.

The Hellenic theatre is located near the agora.

★ Roman Odeon
This partly restored small music theatre, built of stone blocks, stands on a hillside overlooking the rest of the site. Summer concerts are held here.

Saranda Kolones
The castle, built by the Lusignans, was destroyed by an earthquake in 1222. It takes its name from the 40 columns found among its ruins.

Panagia Limeniotissa, the Byzantine basilica of Our Lady the Protectress of Harbours, was destroyed in the 7th century by Arab raids.

PLAN OF KATO PAFOS

KEY

■	Building
▬	Road
═	Footpath
--	Wall

PEGEIA · PAFOS
B70
Ancient Theatre
Agia Solomoni
Odeon · Agora
Cathedral Ruins
Asklepieion · House of Dionysos
Saranda Kolones
Panagia Chrysopolitissa
House of Orpheus
House of Aion
Panagia Limeniotissa
House of Theseus
E705
GEROSKIPOU
Castle · East Tower

0 m   300
0 yards   300

0 m   25
0 yards   25

Tree-lined avenue in the village of Pegeia

Pegeia ⓫

Road map A3. 19 km (12 miles) south of Pafos. 607, 616.

This small, picturesque hillside village, 5 km (3 miles) inland from Coral Bay, is the last sizeable settlement before entering the wilderness of Akamas. Pegeia, meaning "springs", was founded during the Byzantine era. It is famous for its abundant spring water – a great blessing in sun-parched Cyprus.

Soak up the village atmosphere in the pretty cobbled central square with its fountains, and try a bottle of the local Vasilikon wine.

Environs

On the hilltops north of Pegeia, at an altitude of some 600 m (1,970 ft), are the villages of the Laona region – **Ineia**, **Drouseia**, **Arodes** and **Kathikas**, offering sweeping views of the surrounding area. In Ineia you can visit the Basket Weaving Museum; in Drouseia the Textile Museum; the local school in Kathikas houses the Laona information centre.

Agios Georgios ⓭

Road map A3. 616.

During Roman times **Cape Drepano**, north of Coral Bay, was the site of a late Roman and early Byzantine town and harbour. The remains of a 6th-century early-Christian basilica have been unearthed here, revealing some well-preserved floor mosaics of sea creatures, a semi-circular bishop's throne and several columns.

The coastal cliffs contains several caves that served as hiding places for the local population during enemy raids. Atop one craggy section is the picturesque **Church of St George** (Agios Georgios Pegeias) built in the Byzantine style in 1928. St George, its patron saint, champions animals and those who are unlucky in love.

Close by there are several taverns and fishermen's cottages. The location affords a lovely view over the fishing harbour below, and the nearby island of Geronisos with its remains of a Neolithic settlement. There are also remains of a small temple used during Greek and Roman times.

Environs

North of Agios Georgios is the **Avakas Gorge**. This deep ravine has steep craggy banks, a dozen or so metres high, and the river Avgas runs through the base of it. The Gorge is a legally protected area; it can be visited only

The picturesque Church of St George

in organized groups led by a local guide.

Lara ⓮

Road map A3.

This sandy crescent is home to two of the most attractive beaches in southwest Cyprus. To the south lies nearly 2 km (1 mile) of uncrowded sand, while to the north there is a shallow bay with a half-moon stretch of fine white sand frequented by sea turtles.

This is one of the few remaining Mediterranean nesting grounds for the rare green and loggerhead varieties. During breeding season (June to September) staff from the Lara Turtle Conservation Project close access to the beach. They arrange occasional night-time walks along the beach, when you can see the turtles struggling ashore.

Although marine animals, sea turtles lay their eggs on dry land, crawling out onto beaches during summer nights to do this. Females lay about 100 eggs at a time, which they bury up in the sand up to half a metre (one and a half feet) deep. After laying, the eggs are carefully removed to a protected area on the beach where they are safe from dogs, foxes and other predators.

After seven weeks the eggs hatch and the hatchlings head immediately for the water. Turtles reach maturity at about the age of 20, and the females return to lay eggs on the same beach where they were born.

The sandy beach at Lara Bay – a nesting ground for rare sea turtles

Baths of Aphrodite ⓫

Road map A3. 8 km (5 miles) west of Polis, towards Akamas peninsula.
🚌 *617, 631.*

A path from the car park leads to the Baths of Aphrodite – a pool in a grotto shaded by overgrown fig trees. According to legend it was here that Aphrodite met her lover Adonis, who stopped by the spring to quench his thirst. It is said that bathing in this spot restores youth, but, sadly people are no longer allowed in the water.

Walking trails lead from the front of the Cyprus Tourism Organization (CTO) pavilion through the Akamas peninsula. The trails of Aphrodite, Adonis or Smigies will take you to the most interesting corners of the northwestern tip *(see pp56–7)*. Detailed descriptions of the trails can be found in the Nature Trails of the Akamas brochure published by the CTO.

Situated a few kilometres further west is another magnif-icent spring, the Fontana Amorosa (Fountain of Love). It was once believed that whoever took a sip of water from the spring would fall in love with the very first person they encountered afterwards.

Environs

On the way to the Baths of Aphrodite you will pass Latsi

Akamas peninsula – the westernmost point of Cyprus

(also known as Lakki and Latchi), a small town with a fishing harbour. It was once a sponge-divers' harbour, and is now also the base for pleasure boats that offer tourist cruises along the Akamas peninsula. Latsi has numerous *pensions* and hotels; the harbour features several restaurants, where you can get tasty and inexpensive fish and seafood dishes. The town has pebble and coarse sand beaches.

Akamas Peninsula ⓬

Road map A3. 18 km (11 miles) north of Agios Georgios.

Spring flowers

Stretching north of Agios Georgios and Pegeia is the wilderness of the Akamas peninsula. The hillsides and headlands form the island's last undeveloped frontier, a region of spectacular, rugged scenery, sandy coves, clear water and hillsides covered with thick woodlands of pine and juniper. Its name comes from the legendary Akamas, son of Theseus, who arrived here on his triumphant return from the Trojan War and founded the town of Akamatis. Archaeologists are still searching for this site.

The peninsula's westward plain has rocks jutting out of the arid landscape, which is overgrown with tangles

of trees and bushes. In the valleys and ravines the vegetation is lush due to more abundant water. The shoreline is characterized by steep cliffs dropping vertically into the sea, particularly around **Chrysochou Bay**.

Nowadays this area is practically deserted, inhabited only by wild animals and herds of goat, but this was not always so. In ancient times, the region had Greek towns, and later Roman and Byzantine towns, that bustled with life. On **Cape Drepano** you can see the ruins of a Roman harbour and a Byzantine basilica; in **Meleti Forest** you can visit the ruins of a Byzantine church, and tombs carved in rocks; and in the **Agios Konon region** archae-ologists have discovered an ancient settlement. The Roman settlement, which once stood on the shores of the Tyoni Bay, is now submerged in water.

The only way to travel around the wild countryside of Akamas is by a four-wheel-drive vehicle or by a cruise along the coast from Latsi.

The westernmost point of the peninsula, and of the entire island, is **Cape Arnaoutis**, where you can see an unmanned lighthouse and the wreck of a ship that ran aground. The Cape is a magnet for divers, who will find vertical crags and caves where octopuses hide; fantastic arch-shaped rocks; or even come eye-to-eye with a barracuda.

The Baths of Aphrodite

Walking in the Akamas Peninsula

This is the wildest region of Cyprus, practically uninhabited and covered with forests. Its rich flora (over 500 species, including scores of orchid varieties) and fauna, the diverse geological features, the beautiful coastline and the legends and myths associated with this fascinating country make it a paradise for ramblers and nature lovers. The shortage of surfaced roads means that many places on the peninsula can be reached only on foot.

LOCATOR MAP

Bays
A challenging section of the Aphrodite trail hugs the peninsula's wild coastline. Here you'll find the most beautiful coves and deserted beaches.

Roads
Some sections of the trails run along dirt tracks; the best way to travel here is in a four-wheel-drive vehicle.

Baths of Aphrodite

428 m

Caves
Water has carved many caves and rock niches in the lime rocks of the peninsula. These provide shelter for animals.

Rocks
Rocks, carved in fantastic shapes by wind and water, are a distinctive feature of the peninsula's landscape.

Neo Chorio
A stone church has survived here. There are plenty of places to stay in the village, as well as a few restaurants. To the south is the Petratis Gorge, famous for its bats' grotto.

Lizards
Lizards, particularly the wall lizard, are common on the island. You may be lucky enough to encounter the Agana, the largest Cypriot lizard (30 cm/12 in long).

Goats
Herds of free-ranging goats wander around the peninsula, presenting a threat to the region's natural environment.

KEY

━━	Main road
══	Other road
•••	1. Aphrodite trail (7.5 km)
•••	2. Adonis trail (7.5 km)
•••	3. Smigies trail (7.5 km)
•••	4. Pissouromouttis trail (3 km)
•••	5. Kathikas trail (2 km)
≈	River
⛺	Campsite
ℹ	Tourist information
☀	Viewpoint

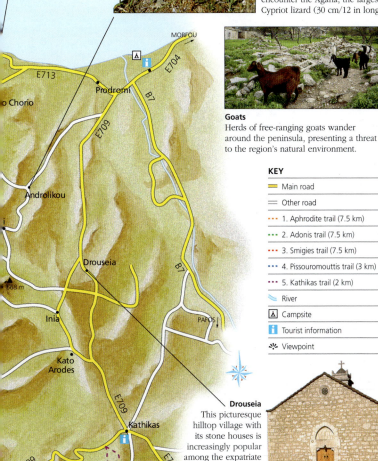

Drouseia
This picturesque hilltop village with its stone houses is increasingly popular among the expatriate community. There is a taverna and accommodation here.

The 16th-century church of Agios Andronikos in Polis

Polis ⑬

Road map A3. 35 km (22 miles) north of Pafos. 🏠 1,890. 🛈 Vasileos Stasioikou 2, 26 322 468. 🚌 626, 645. 🎭 Summer Cultural Festival (Jul, Aug).

This small town, known as Polis Chrysochou (Town of the Golden Land), stands on the site of the ancient city-state of Marion, surrounded by extensive orange groves. Polis provides an excellent base for exploring the Akamas peninsula and the wilderness of Tilliria. In the centre of Polis is the 16th-century **Agios Andronikos** church, featuring some fine frescoes. Under Ottoman rule the church was turned into a mosque. The interior of the **Agios Rafael**, a Byzantine-style church, is decorated with colourful frescoes.

Polis is one of the most attractive and fastest-growing seaside resorts of Cyprus. Popular with both backpackers and families, it offers a range of apartment complexes and a handful of small hotels, along with several campsites, including one on the beach.

Environs

Close to the town are some of the most beautiful beaches on the island, including a long sand-and-pebble beach stretching eastwards along Chrysochou Bay, a 15-minute walk from the centre of Polis. There are also picturesque villages

Carved decoration above the entrance to Agios Andronikos in Polis

and interesting churches, including the 16th-century Agia Aikaterini and the 15th-century Panagia Chorteni.

Marion ⑭

Road map A3.

Founded in the 7th century BC by Greeks, the city-state of Marion was a major trading centre during the Classical and Hellenic eras. It owed its rapid development to the nearby copper mines. In 315 BC Marion was destroyed by the Egyptian king, Ptolemy I Soter. His son, Ptolemy II, rebuilt Marion under the name Arsinoe, but the town never regained its former power.

Up to now archaeologists have managed to unearth only a small portion of the ancient town, with a burial ground dating from the Hellenic period. An interesting collection of artifacts from the site can be seen in the **Marion-Arsinoe Archaeological Museum**. Of special note are the amphorae decorated with images of people, animals and birds, as well as with geometric patterns. Growing near the museum is an olive tree, over 600 years old, which still bears fruit.

🏛 **Marion-Arsinoe Archaeological Museum**
Polis. Leoforos Makariou III. **Tel** 26 322 955. ☐ 8am–3pm Tue–Fri (to 5pm Wed), 9am–3pm Sat. 🌐

Panagia Chrysorrogiatissa ⑮

Road map A3. 40 km (25 miles) northeast of Pafos, take a right turn before the village of Stroumpi. 1.5 km (1 mile) south of Pano Panagia. **Tel** 26 722 457. ☐ summer: 9:30am–12:30pm, 1:30–6:30pm daily; winter: 10am–12:30pm, 1:30–4pm daily. **Donations** welcome. 🎭 15 Aug.

In a beautiful setting 830 m (2,723 ft) above the sea, the Chrysorrogiatissa monastery is dedicated to "Our Lady of the Golden Pomegranate". It features an unusual triangular cloister built of reddish stone.

The monastery was founded in 1152 by Ignatius, who came across an icon with the image of the Virgin Mary. The Virgin appeared and told him to build a monastery. The icon is kept in a special casket. It was supposedly painted by St Luke the Evangelist. Several other icons are also stored here; the most famous being an 18th-century image of Mary and Jesus covered

Entrance to Panagia Chrysorrogiatissa monastery

with a cloak. Other objects include old Bibles, sculptures, manuscripts and crosses.

Environs

The single-aisle **Agia Moni** church, about 2 km (1.2 miles) from the monastery, is one of the oldest in the island. Dedicated to St Nicholas, it was built in the 4th century on the site of an old pagan temple of the goddess Hera.

The nearby village of **Panagia** is the birthplace of Archbishop Makarios III, the statesman and politician, who was born the son of a shepherd here on 13 August 1913. In 1960 the Archbishop was elected president of the republic. He died on 3 August 1977 and was buried at Throni near Kykkos, overlooking his village.

🏛 **Makarios's Family Home**
Pano Panagia. ☐ *daily (key available from info centre).*
Donations *welcome.*

Tomb of Archbishop Makarios at Throni above Panagia

Xeros Valley ⑯

Road map B4.

The Xeros river flows from the western slopes of the Troodos mountains through this scenic valley. The river initially flows through Pafos Forest and Cedar Valley, which is the main home of the cedars of the local *cedrus brevifilia* species. The area, which has been declared a nature reserve, is also home to the moufflon.

A car is needed to explore the valley. Following the old road from Pafos, turn left in the village of Timi, opposite the airport, to reach **Asprokremmos** reservoir, a mecca for anglers, as it is fed by the Xeros river. The valley of

Xeros (which in Greek means "dry") was devastated by the tragic earthquake of 1953. At the heart of the valley, away from the main roads, is the abandoned stone **Panagia tou Sinti** monastery. It can be reached via local roads from the village of Pentalia or Agia Marina. Further on, the road leads through hillside villages and vineyards.

Beyond the village of Vretsia the road steadily deteriorates, but after driving for a few more kilometres you can cross the Xeros river near the historic Venetian bridge of Roudia. The deserted village of **Peravasa** marks the start of the road leading south, towards the scenic Diarizos river valley.

Diarizos Valley ⑰

Road map B3.

Greener and better irrigated than the arid Xeros valley, the Diarizos valley is studded with medieval churches, farming villages and arched Venetian bridges. The clear-flowing river trickles southwest and, like the Xeros, feeds the Asprokremmos reservoir.

The village of **Nikokleia**, near Kouklia (*see p44*), is an ancient settlement named in honour of King Nikokles, who transferred his capital to what is now Kato Pafos. The village is scenically located on the

Sheep in the Diarizos Valley

banks of the river. The old church contains fascinating icons. On the opposite side of the river, near the village of Souskiou, archaeologists unearthed a Chalcolithic settlement. In it they found pendants and figurines, as well as statues and ancient tombs. In the village of Agios Georgios are rock tombs.

Further northeast are the remains of a former monastery, **Agios Savvas tis Karonos**, built in the early 12th century and restored by the Venetians.

Above Kithasi the road climbs upwards and the views become increasingly beautiful. On the left side of the road is the restored church of **Agios Antonios**. The church in Praitori houses 16th-century icons. Above the village, the road climbs towards the resort of **Platres** and the peaks of the Troodos mountains.

The arid Xeros valley, a scenic, rugged nature reserve

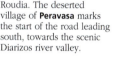

SOUTHERN CYPRUS

*T*he southern region of Cyprus features Neolithic settlements and ancient towns, medieval castles and monasteries, and the island's most beautiful beaches, around Agia Napa. Other attractions include charming hilltop villages and the ports of Limassol and Larnaka. The region is full of reminders of famous past visitors to Cyprus, including Zeno of Kition, Saint Helena, Richard the Lionheart and Leonardo da Vinci.

The coast from Pissouri to Protaras is famous for its beautiful scenery and historic sites. It has the largest ports on the island and many crowded beaches, but just a short distance inland life flows at a gentle, lazy pace.

This southern region was the site of powerful city-states, including Kition (present-day Larnaka), Kourion – of which only magnificent ruins are left, and Amathous.

Among the oldest traces of man on Cyprus are the Neolithic settlements around Choirokoitia and Kalavasos. There are reminders of subsequent settlers, too. There was a Phoenician presence at Kition; there are temples and stadia attesting to the Greek presence; and villas and theatres from the Romans.

The Byzantine legacy includes mosaics in vast basilicas, churches with beautiful murals, and monasteries – including the mountain-top Stavrovouni monastery and the cat-filled St Nicholas monastery on the Akrotiri peninsula.

The medieval castle in Limassol was used by the Crusaders; Richard the Lionheart married Berengaria of Navarre and crowned her Queen of England here; and from the Gothic castle in Kolossi knights oversaw the production of wine and sugar cane. A reminder of the Arab raids is the tomb of the Prophet's aunt at the Hala Sultan Tekke, on the shores of the salt lake near Larnaka, which attracts flamingoes, swans and pelicans.

Scenic village of Kato Lefkara

◁ **Belfry of the Agia Napa monastery**

Exploring Southern Cyprus

The best-preserved ancient town in Southern Cyprus is the Greco-Roman Kourion, with a beautifully located theatre, interesting mosaics, baths, a Byzantine stadium and the nearby Sanctuary of Apollo Ylatis. The best beaches for swimming and sunbathing are in Agia Napa and Protaras, with their enchanting clear water and lovely sandy beaches. They also offer the greatest number of attractions for young people. When exploring this part of the island be sure to visit Lefkara, a charming Cypriot village where women produce beautiful lace by hand and men make silver jewellery. Nature lovers often head for the salt lakes around Limassol and Larnaka, and are rewarded with the sight of hundreds of birds.

Stavrovouni monastery, founded by St Helena, mother of Constantine the Great

SIGHTS AT A GLANCE

0 km   10

0 miles   1

GETTING THERE

Most visitors to Cyprus arrive by air, and the biggest airport in the southern part of the island is outside Larnaka, serving a number of international flights. Motorways provide fast and safe travel links with Limassol and Agia Napa, as well as with Nicosia and Pafos. Alternatively, you can travel to Limassol by ship from Piraeus (Greece), Egypt, Lebanon and Syria. Most of the historic sites of Limassol and Larnaka are best explored on foot. Public transport in the form of buses and service taxis between major cities is good, but to reach smaller or more distant places a rental car is the best option for exploring Southern Cyprus.

SEE ALSO

- *Where to Stay* pp159–61
- *Where to Eat* pp171–3

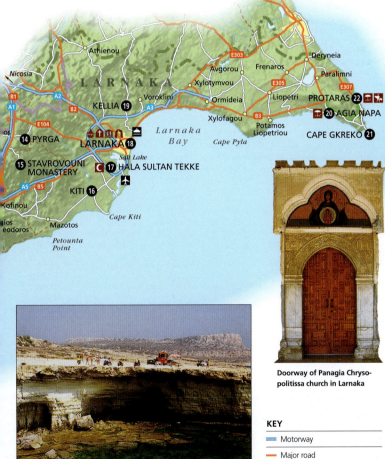

Doorway of Panagia Chrysopolitissa church in Larnaka

The craggy coastline of Cape Gkreko

KEY

▬▬▬	Motorway
▬▬▬	Major road
═══	Secondary road
▬▬▬	Scenic route
‒ ‒ ‒	Track
▬▬▬	Regional border
▬■▬	Green Line

Cape Aspro ❶

Road map B4. 4 km (2.5 miles) south of Pissouri.

Cape Aspro is the highest point along the virtually deserted coast that stretches from Kourion to Pafos. Most of the coast along this, the southernmost point of the island (excluding the Akrotiri Peninsula), is as flat as a pancake. Towering over the cape is the **Trachonas Hill**, which affords magnificent views over Episkopi Bay, the southern slopes of the Troodos mountains, the small town of Pissouri and the monastery church Moni Prophitis Ilias.

The area around **Pissouri** is famous for its orchards and vineyards; the fertile lime soil yields abundant crops of sweet grapes. The modern amphitheatre, which was built in 2000 with seating for a thousand people, affords a beautiful view over the sea and the southern coast. During the summer, plays and concerts are staged here.

The town of Pissouri has a pleasant little hotel – the Bunch of Grapes Inn – in a restored century-old home; there are also several rustic tavernas that offer typical local cuisine.

The rugged coastal cliffs rise to a height of 180 m (590 ft). They can be seen very clearly from the air, as planes usually approach Pafos airport from this direction. To the east of Cape Aspro is the pleasant and clean sandy-pebbly Pissouri beach with its clear, blue water.

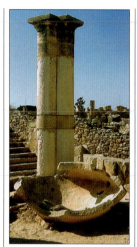

Ruins of the Sanctuary of Apollo Ylatis near Kourion

Sanctuary of Apollo Ylatis ❷

Road map B4. 3 km (2 miles) west of Kourion. **Tel** 25 991 049. ◻ 8am–5pm daily (to 6pm Apr, May, Sep & Oct; to 7:30pm Jun–Aug). 🖾

In ancient times the Sanctuary of Apollo Ylatis (also known as Hylates), was an important shrine. Stone fragments and toppled columns mark the site of this 7th-century BC shrine to the sun-god Apollo in his role as "Ylatis", or god of the woods and forests. The present ruins date from early Roman times. It was in use until the 4th century AD, when Emperor Theodosius the Great declared a battle against pagans.

The sanctuary was surrounded by a holy garden, featuring laurel trees, myrtle and palms, and was home to deer. When pilgrims arrived through the Curium and Pafian gates, they placed votive offerings by the residence of the Great Priests, which were then sent to the treasury. When the treasury became full, the priests stored the offerings (*tavissae*) in a nearby holy well. This hiding place was discovered centuries later by archaeologists, and the ancient offerings can be seen at the Kourion Archaeological Museum at Episkopi and in the Cyprus Museum in Nicosia.

Close by were baths and a *palaestra* (gymnasium), surrounded by a colonnaded portico and used as a venue for wrestling. Standing in one corner of the *palaestra* is a fragment of a large clay jug, which was used for storing water for the athletes. The remaining buildings of the complex include storehouses and pilgrims' dormitories.

The former pilgrims' inn marked the start of the holy procession route leading to the sanctuary. At the heart of the sanctuary there was a small temple with a pillared portico, devoted to Apollo. As reported by the ancient geographer Strabo, any unauthorized person who touched the altar was hurled from it to the sea, to placate Apollo. The front of the temple, with its two columns, a fragment of the wall and tympanum, has been partially reconstructed.

Earthquakes, the spread of Christianity and Arab raids all played a role in destroying the sanctuary, and now all that remains are the romantic ruins.

Some 500 m (1,640 ft) east of the sanctuary is a large, well-preserved Roman stadium that could hold 6,000 spectators. Pentathlon events – consisting of running, long jump, discus and javelin throwing, and wrestling – were staged here. The athletes appeared naked, and only men were allowed to watch. In the 4th century the stadium was closed, regarded as a symbol of paganism.

The craggy coast of Cape Aspro

Kourion ❸

See pp66–7.

Kolossi ❹

Road map B4. 14 km (9 miles) west of Limassol. **Tel** 25 934 907. 🚌 17. ⏱ 8am–5pm daily (to 6pm Apr, May, Sep & Oct; to 7:30pm Jun–Aug). 🖼

The best-preserved medieval castle in Cyprus is situated south of the village of Kolossi. In 1210 the land passed to the hands of the Knights of St John of Jerusalem, who built a castle here to be used as the Grand Master's headquarters.

At the turn of the 14th and 15th centuries the castle was sacked several times by the Genoese and Muslims.

Kolossi castle in its present shape was built in 1454 by the Grand Master, Louis de Magnac. It is a three-storey structure, laid out on a square plan, 23 m (75 ft) high with walls over 2.5 m (8 ft) thick. Entry is via a drawbridge, at the first floor level. The entrance is further guarded by a machicolation above the gate, which permitted the pouring of boiling water, oil or melted tar over attackers.

The entrance led to the dining room, whose walls were once covered with paintings. You can still see a scene of the Crucifixion with Louis de Magnac's coat of arms underneath. The adjacent room used to be the castle kitchen; stores were kept on the lower floor, and above were the living quarters; you can see stone fireplaces and windows. From here a narrow staircase leads to the flat roof surrounded by battlements, affording extensive views of the surrounding area. From here it was possible to supervise the work on plantations and in vineyards, and to spot enemy ships in the distance.

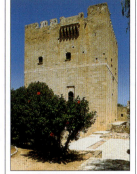

The medieval Kolossi castle, used by the Knights of Jerusalem

Standing next to the castle is a large vaulted stone building, which was once a sugar refinery. To the north are the remains of a mill, formerly used for grinding the sugar, and beyond it lies the small 13th-century church of St Eustace, which was used as castle chapel by the Knights Templar and by the Knights of St John of Jerusalem.

Agios Nikolaos ton Gaton (St Nicholas of the Cats) ❺

Road map B4. Cape Gata, 12 km (7.5 miles) from the centre of Limassol. **Tel** 25 952 621. ⏱ 8am–5pm daily.

The monastery of Agios Nikolaos ton Gaton stands on the Akrotiri peninsula, between the salt lake and the military airport. According to tradition it was founded by St Helena, mother of Constantine the Great, who visited Cyprus while returning from the Holy Land. Appalled by the plague of snakes, she sent a ship full of cats to the island to deal with them. The monks fed the cats and rallied them to fight by the ringing of the bell. Another reference to the cats is the naming of the nearby Cape Gata – the Cape of Cats.

The monastery was founded in 325, but the buildings we see now are the result of remodelling that occurred during the 14th century. At the heart of the monastery is an old church with Gothic walls and Latin coats of arms above the entrance. Candles inside the dark church illuminate the gilded iconostasis and the elongated faces on the icons, which appear to come to life.

A small section of the salt lake on the Akrotiri peninsula

Akrotiri Peninsula ❻

Road map B4.

Akrotiri is the southernmost point of Cyprus. Most of the peninsula is occupied by a sovereign British base – Akrotiri-Episkopi, which includes an air force base and a radio communications station. This base, along with a second one at Ohekelia, is a relic of the island's colonial past, when Cyprus was governed by the British.

The central part of the peninsula is occupied by a salt lake (one of the two on the island), a vantage point for watching flocks of water birds including swans, flamingoes and pelicans. Running along the east coast is the wide beach known as Lady's Mile, which was named after a mare used by an English army officer for his regular morning ride.

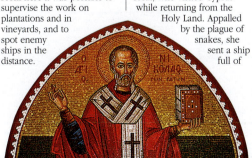

Image of St Nicholas of the Cats

Kourion ❸

Ancient Kourion (or Curium) was a major centre of cultural, political and religious life. It was home to the centuries-old site of the Sanctuary of Apollo and later the seat of a Christian bishop. Perched on a bluff, the town was founded in the 12th century BC by Mycenaean Greeks, and was a large centre in the days of the Ptolemies and the Romans. Its trump card was its defensive location, and the control it wielded over the surrounding fertile land. Kourion was destroyed by two catastrophic earthquakes in the early 4th century.

Achilles' House
This takes its name from the 4th-century mosaic discovered inside the colonnade.

The House of the Gladiators was so named after the discovery of two mosaics depicting gladiator fights.

Public baths

Baptistry & Bishop's Palace
Adjacent to the basilica and close to the bishop's palace was a large baptistry. Its remains include floor mosaics and some columns.

Basilica
The impressive triple-aisle building, erected in the 5th century AD on the site of a pagan temple, was destroyed by Arabs.

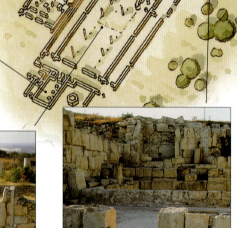

Nymphaeum
This imposing complex of stone fountains was built close to the public baths, on the spot where the aqueduct brought water to the city of Kourion.

MAP OF KOURION

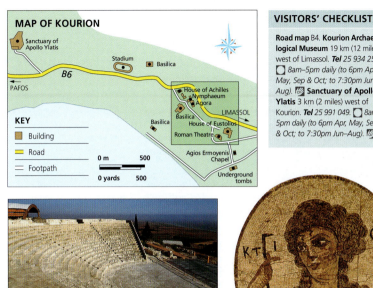

Sanctuary of Apollo Ylatis

Stadium

Basilica

B6

PAFOS

House of Achilles
Nymphaeum
Agora

Basilica

Basilica

House of Eustolios

LIMASSOL

Roman Theatre

Agios Ermoyenis Chapel

Underground tombs

KEY

☐ Building

▬ Road

═ Footpath

0 m   500
0 yards   500

VISITORS' CHECKLIST

Road map B4. **Kourion Archaeo-logical Museum** 19 km (12 miles) west of Limassol. *Tel* 25 934 250. ☐ *8am–5pm daily (to 6pm Apr, May, Sep & Oct; to 7:30pm Jun–Aug).* **Sanctuary of Apollo Ylatis** 3 km (2 miles) west of Kourion. *Tel* 25 991 049. ☐ *8am–5pm daily (to 6pm Apr, May, Sep & Oct; to 7:30pm Jun–Aug).*

★ Roman Theatre
The theatre, built in the 2nd century BC, enjoys a magnificent location overlooking the sea as well as boasting excellent acoustics.

Baths
These baths form part of the House of Eustolios, a late 4th-century AD private residence. The best mosaic depicts Ktissis as a woman holding a Roman measure, a personification of architectural art.

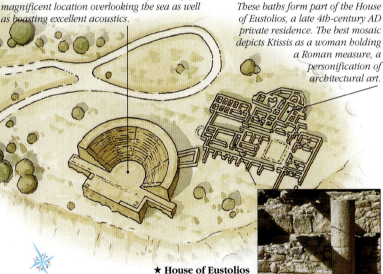

★ House of Eustolios
Built in the early Christian period, this house had some 30 rooms arranged around a colonnaded courtyard with mosaic floors. The inscription by the entrance reads "Step in and bring happiness to this house".

STAR SIGHTS

★ Roman Theatre
★ House of Eustolios

Limassol (Lemesos) ➐

8th-century silver plate

Limassol is a major centre of trade, business and tourism, and has the biggest harbour in southern Cyprus. It is probably the most fun-filled city on Cyprus in terms of the number of fairs and festivals held here. The year starts with a riotous carnival; May marks the Flower Festival; and September brings the famous Wine Festival. Hotels, restaurants and nightclubs are clustered mainly along the beach.

Strolling along the seaside promenade

Exploring Limassol

It is best to start from the medieval castle, the town's most interesting historic site. Nearby in the restored Carob Mill is the Carob Museum, where visitors can learn about this important Cypriot export. A covered bazaar and a mosque are also close by.

The area has many restaurants with Cypriot and international cuisine, a wine bar and a brewery. From here it is not far to the old harbour, now used by fishing boats and pleasure craft. You can enjoy an extended walk along the seaside promenade, passing the Orthodox Agia Napa cathedral. More material distractions can be found just inland from here, along the main shopping street, Ayiou Andhreou, which runs parallel to the coast.

🏛 Central Market

Saripolou, in the old district near the town hall. ◯ *6am–3pm Mon–Sat.*
The Central Market, housed in a graceful arcaded building dating from the British era in the early 20th century, is a great place to shop for handmade reed baskets, olive oil, *loukoumia* (Cyprus delight) and other Cypriot delicacies, as well as fruit, vegetables, cheeses and meats. The stone market hall, its roof supported by metal pillars is of particular note, featuring two arched gates with Doric columns. It has been refurbished to a design by Penelope Papadopoulou. The market is surrounded by old tavernas that make a welcome change from the modern eating-places and souvenir shops in the city's resort area. The stone-paved square in front of it is used as a venue for shows and fairs.

Colourful stalls of fruit and vegetables at the Central Market

🏛 Cyprus Handicraft Centre

Themidos 25. *Tel 25 305 118.*
◯ 7:30am–2:30pm Mon–Fri (also 3–6pm Thu except Jul–Aug).
At this centre you can buy locally made gifts and souvenirs, including jewellery, lace, ceramics, mosaics and woodcarvings produced by Cypriot craftspeople using traditional methods.

All stock is government-vetted and the fixed prices offer a good gauge of how much visitors should spend on products elsewhere.

🏛 Town Hall

Archiepiskopou Kyprianou.
www.limassolmunicipal.com.cy
The town hall is situated in the centre of Limassol, on a narrow street opposite the post office and near Agia Napa Cathedral. It was built to a design by the German architect Benjamin Gunzburg, based on the ancient Greek style of civic architecture. The columns by the entrance are redolent of the Tombs of the Kings in Pafos.

Town Hall, dating from Colonial times

🔒 Agios Andronikos Church

Agiou Andreou. 🔔 6:30pm (in summer), 4:30pm (in winter) Sat; prayers Sun (times vary).
The Church of Agios Andronikos and Athanosis (in Greek *athanosis* means immortality) was built in the 1870s in Neo-Byzantine style. For a while it served as the town's cathedral. The church is accessible only from the waterfront. It is separated from the sea by the promenade, near the Agia Napa Cathedral.

Seaside Promenade

Perfect for an evening stroll, Limassol's palm-fringed promenade stretches for nearly 3 km (2 miles) along the shoreline, starting at the old harbour and continuing eastward towards St Catherine's Church. It is lined with well-kept greenery and benches, from where you can admire the seascape and watch the ships awaiting entry to the harbour.

For hotels and restaurants in this region see pp159–61 and pp171–3

The Orthodox cathedral of Agia Napa

🔒 Agia Napa Cathedral

Genethliou Mitella.

On the fringe of Limassol's old quarter, this vast Byzantine-style structure was built in the early 20th century on the ruins of a Byzantine church. It was consecrated in 1906, and today it serves as Limassol's Orthodox cathedral.

The Greek architect Georgios Papadakis of Athens designed the cathedral, which represents Greek Orthodox religious architecture at its florid and grandiloquent best. This large stone church, sporting a twin-tower façade, is covered with a dome resting on a tambour over the intersection of the nave with the transept.

The cathedral was consecrated with the veil of St Veronica, with the imprinted image of Christ's face (the *veraikon*).

🅲 Grand Mosque

Genethliou Mitella.

⬜ vary. **Donations** welcome.

The area around the harbour and castle was once inhabited mainly by Turks, and there are some remaining Turkish inscriptions and street names. The Grand Mosque – Cami Kebir – is still used by the handful of Turkish Cypriots resident in the city, and by Muslim visitors. The city's largest mosque with a graceful minaret is squeezed between old buildings behind the Turkish Bazaar.

The Grand Mosque with its distinctive pointed minaret

⚓ Limassol Castle

See pp72–3.

🏛 Carob Museum

Vasilissis 1, by Limassol Castle.
Tel 25 342 123. ⬜ daily (times vary so call ahead).

This museum is located in a renovated former mill close to the medieval castle, in an area that is known for its art exhibitions and stylish cafés.

The Carob Museum shows how the carob is harvested, what it is used for and its relevance to the island's economy. The carob can be used in the production of honey, sweets and chocolate. Derivatives are also used for making paper, photographic filmplates and medicines. Historic machinery used to store and process the fruit is displayed alongside utensils and useful information.

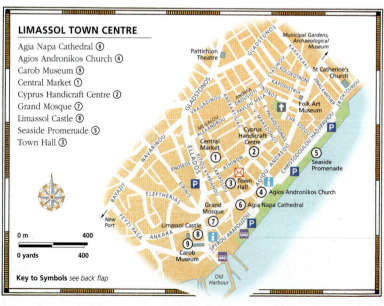

LIMASSOL TOWN CENTRE

0 m   400
0 yards   400

Key to Symbols see back flap

Artifacts in the Archaeological Museum

Further Afield

Outside the city centre are a number of sights worth visiting, including St Catherine's Catholic Church, the Municipal Gardens and mini-zoo, the District Archaeological Museum and Folk Art Museum, as well as a theatre, municipal art gallery and – among the best of the local attractions – the wineries. Stretching beyond the municipal beach to the east is the extensive tourist zone with dozens of hotels, tavernas, pubs, restaurants, souvenir shops and clubs.

🔒 St Catherine's Catholic Church

28 Oktovriou 259. *Tel* 25 362 946. ✝ 6:30pm Mon–Fri (English & Greek); 6:30pm Sat (English); 8am (Greek), 9:30am (Greek), 11am (Latin) & 6:30pm (English) Sun.
This twin-tower church stands opposite the beach, near the end of Limassol's palm-lined promenade. Consecrated in 1879, it is one of several Catholic churches in this part of the island.

🏛 District Archaeological Museum

At the junction of Kanningos and Vyronos, next to the Municipal Gardens. *Tel* 25 305 157. ⭘ 8am–3pm Tue–Fri (to 5pm Thu), 9am–3pm Sat.
At the entrance to this museum is a mosaic depicting the bath of Eros and Aphrodite. The museum's collection includes artifacts found in excavations of the ancient city-states of Kourion and Amathous, as well as Neolithic tools and jewellery.

The highlights of the collection are the statue of the Egyptian god Bes – the god of harvest depicted in the guise of a dwarf; the statue of Hathor, Egyptian goddess of heaven, music and dance; the statue of Zeus discovered at Amathous; and the head of Zeus from Fasoula, carved from limestone. Other exhibits include a collection of glass and terracotta artifacts, votive statuettes and Roman coins stamped with the images of emperors.

🍴 Municipal Gardens and Mini-Zoo

28 Oktovriou, on the seafront. *Tel* 25 588 345. ⭘ summer: 9am–7pm; winter: 9am–4pm.
The charming Municipal Gardens feature ponds and fountains. Shaded by trees, they are full of exotic greenery and flowers. The gardens include an amphitheatre and a small zoo and aviary. Zebras, cheetahs and moufflon are among the animals here. In early September the Municipal Gardens become the venue for the famous Wine Festival. As well as grape trampling and folk dances, the crowds are treated to free wine from local producers.

🏛 Folk Art Museum

Agiou Andreou 253. *Tel* 25 362 303. ⭘ 8:30am–3pm daily.
The Folk Art museum is housed in an attractive historic building dating from 1924. Arranged over six rooms is a good collection of 19th- and 20th-century Cypriot folk art.

The exhibition includes country tools, domestic utensils, wooden chests, traditional folk costumes, jewellery, tapestries and hand-crafted products such as net curtains, bedding and bedspreads, which were traditionally stored in *sentoukia* – decorative trunks used as a bride's dowry.

Costume from the Folk Art Museum

🍷 Wineries

F. Roosevelt. ☎ 25 362 756. ⭘ year-round.
Wine has been produced for over 4,000 years in Cyprus, with wine-growing a long-established tradition in the area surrounding Limassol. Along the avenue leading from the old town to the harbour are the largest wineries in Cyprus, belonging to KEO, SODAP, ETKO and LOEL. These are open to the public for both tours and tastings. You can visit the vaults themselves to see the huge barrels used to age and mellow the sweet dessert wine, Commandaria, which has been produced in Cyprus for over 800 years. At the end of the tour you will be offered a chance to taste and buy the wines. Other distilleries

The leafy, pleasantly shaded Municipal Gardens

For hotels and restaurants in this region see pp159–61 and pp171–3

produce *zivania*, a spirit distilled from grape seed left over from the production of wine and sherry. "Five Kings" brandy, commemorating a medieval banquet attended by five kings, including the King of Cyprus, is also produced here.

Pattichion Theatre

Agias Zonis. **Tel** *25 343 341.*
Musicals, drama and ballet productions are staged at the Pattichin, the oldest theatre in Limassol. The theatre was purchased by the Nicos and Despina Pattichi Foundation, then rebuilt and reopened in 1986. It is sponsored by the Limassol Municipality.

The theatre holds up to 760 people; backstage there are dressing rooms for 80 artists. The Pattichion theatre has hosted the Vienna Philharmonic Orchestra, the Athens Chamber Music Ensemble, the Vivaldi Orchestra from Moscow and Jazz Art Ballet from Paris.

Municipal Art Gallery

28 Oktovriou 103. **Tel** *25 586 212.*
7:30am–2:30pm Mon–Fri.
The gallery houses works by Cypriot painters, including early artists such as Diamantis, Kashialos, whose famous work *Chariot Drawn by Two Donkeys* is displayed, Kanthos and Frangoudis. Contemporary painters are also represented. The gallery, designed by Benjamin Gunzburg (who also designed the Town Hall), was built in the 1930s.

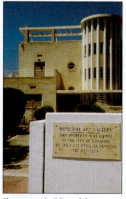

The pre-war building of the Municipal Art Gallery

Lady's Mile beach and the new harbour in Limassol

Fasouri Water Mania Waterpark

Near Trahoni village, Limassol–Pafos Road. **Tel** *25 714 235.*
May–Oct: 10am–6pm daily.
www.fasouri-watermania.com
This popular waterpark has many water attractions including swimming pools, slides and artificial waves. Great for families and kids of all ages.

New Port

4 km (2.5 miles) west of city centre. **Tel** *25 571 868.* 30.
The new port in Limassol is the largest in Cyprus. It was enlarged after 1974, when Famagusta port fell under Turkish occupation. Besides the commercial port, it includes a terminal for passenger ferries as well as cruise ships.

The old harbour, situated near Limassol castle, is now used by fishing boats and pleasure craft. The modern yachting marina at the St Raphael resort, is situated around 12 km (7.5 miles) east of the city centre, in the tourist zone, near Amathous.

Beaches

Although long and wide, the municipal beach in Limassol is not among the island's most attractive beaches; it is covered with compressed soil and pebbles, and is located near a busy street.

Better beaches can be found further afield. Beyond the new harbour, in the eastern part of the Akrotiri peninsula, is Lady's Mile – a long and relatively quiet sandy beach (*see p65*). To the west, about 17 km (10.5 miles) from the city centre, Kourion beach enjoys a lovely location at the foot of the hill where ancient Kourion once stood. You can reach it by public transport from Limassol. Avdimou beach, a further 12 km (7.5 miles) along, has nice sand and a pleasant restaurant, although no shade.

The most pleasant sandy beach is found near Pissouri, some 44 km (27 miles) from Limassol. Here you can hire a deck chair and an umbrella, and nearby are several pleasant tavernas and restaurants.

KING RICHARD THE LIONHEART

The English king, famed for his courage, was passing near Cyprus on his way to the Crusades when a storm blew one of his ships, carrying his sister and fiancée, to the shore. The ruler of Cyprus, the Byzantine Prince Isaac Komnenos, imprisoned both princesses and the crew. The outraged Richard the Lionheart landed with his army on the island, smashed the Komnenos army, imprisoned Komnenos and occupied Cyprus. In May 1191, in the chapel of Limassol castle, he married Princess Berengaria. Soon afterwards he sold the island to the Knights Templar.

English king Richard the Lionheart

Limassol Castle

Dionysos statue (4th-5th century)

This stronghold at the centre of the Old Town, near the harbour, was built by the Lusignan princes on foundations erected by the Byzantines. Later Venetian, Ottoman and British occupiers strengthened its defences. In 1191 the castle chapel was the venue for the wedding of Richard the Lionheart to Princess Berengaria of Navarre. The Turks later rebuilt the castle as a prison. During World War II it served as British Army headquarters. Nowadays it houses the Medieval Museum.

Castle Roof
The flat, stone roof of Limassol Castle was once used by its defenders. Today visitors come here to admire the panoramic view – the best in town.

The Reliefs
The section devoted to Byzantine art houses not only numerous beautiful reliefs and mosaics from the oldest Christian basilicas, but also a number of religious icons.

Grape Press
This grape press is among the stone artifacts in the castle gardens.

★ Knights' Hall
The first-floor hall, in the south wing of Limassol Castle, houses two suits of armour and a collection of antique coins.

STAR FEATURES

★ Knights' Hall

★ Main Hall

★ Main Hall
The Main Hall houses a large collection of Byzantine, Gothic and Renaissance sculptures, carvings and reliefs. Among them are carved images of the Lusignan kings from the portal of Agia Sofia Cathedral.

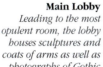

Main Lobby
Leading to the most opulent room, the lobby houses sculptures and coats of arms as well as photographs of Gothic and Renaissance architecture.

Fragment of a Portal
This fragment from Agia Sofia Cathedral forms part of the medieval stonemasonry exhibits in the museum collection.

Sarcophagi chamber
A chamber hidden in the shadowy recesses of the castle contains a collection of sarcophagi and tombstones.

Main Entrance
The castle is entered through a small bastion located on the east side of the castle.

The ruins of ancient Amathous, scenically located along the coast

Amathous ⑧

Road map C4. 12 km (7.5 miles) east of Limassol city centre. ◯ 8am–5pm daily (to 6pm Apr, May, Sep & Oct; to 7:30pm Jun–Aug). 🈺 🚻 30.

Located on a high hill east of Limassol are the stone remains of the ancient port of Amathous. Named after its legendary founder Amathus, son of Aerias and king of Pafos, this once major commercial centre was founded between the 10th and 8th centuries BC.

Amathous was the first of the island's city-states. Over the centuries it was inhabited by Greeks, Phoenicians, Egyptians and Jews.

After the arrival of Christianity on Cyprus, St Tychon founded a church here and became the first bishop of Amathous. He became the patron saint of the town.

The town existed until the 7th century AD when, together with other coastal centres, it was destroyed in Arab raids.

In later times the site was used as a quarry; huge stones were transported to Egypt for use in the construction of the Suez Canal. The American consul (and amateur archaeologist) Luigi Palma di Cesnola destroyed large areas of the city while treasure hunting.

The best-preserved part is the agora (marketplace), with a dozen remaining columns. In the north section are parts of the aqueduct system and the site of a bathhouse.

Large stone vessel from Amathous

Standing on top of the hill was the acropolis, with temples to Aphrodite and Hercules, the remains of which can still be seen. Close by, archaeologists have unearthed the ruins of an early Christian, 5th-century Byzantine basilica. Fragments of powerful defence walls can be seen on the opposite side of the road.

The coastal part of the town, together with its sea harbour, collapsed during an earthquake. Its ruins stretch a great distance into the sea.

Agios Georgios Alamanos ⑨

Road map C4.

The buildings of the Agios Georgios Alamanos monastery can be seen from the Nicosia-Limassol motorway. Although the monastery, just like the new Byzantine-style church, is not

of great architectural merit, it is interesting to watch the local monks painting icons.

In the nearby village of Pentakomo, on the opposite side of the motorway, are surviving stone houses. Close to the church is a pleasant café, where there are occasional concerts and plays.

Kalavasos ⑩

Road map C4. 40 km (25 miles) from Larnaka, 1.5 km (1 mile) from exit 15 on the motorway.

Up until the 1970s the inhabitants of this village were involved in mining copper ore from the neighbouring mountains. A symbol of this industrial past is the local steam engine, which was once used here. The Cyprus Agrotourism Company has restored some of the houses for the use of tourists.

Environs
Close by archaeologists have unearthed the Neolithic settlement of **Tenta**. Smaller than the neighbouring Choirokoitia, part of it is covered by a huge tent. The settlement, which was encircled by a defensive wall, featured a roundhouse and beehive huts built from clay and stone.

The nearby village of **Tochni** is one of the most popular agrotourism sites in Cyprus. Situated in a valley, amid olive trees and vineyards, the quiet and peaceful village is built around a small church. Picturesque narrow alleys lead to stone houses.

The Neolithic settlement of Tenta

Choirokoitia ⓫

Road map C4. 40 km (25 miles) from Limassol, 1.5 km (1 mile) from exit 14 on the motorway. **Tel** 24 322 710.
◻ Apr, May, Sep & Oct: 8am–6pm daily; Jun–Aug: 8am–7:30pm daily; Nov–Mar: 8am–5pm daily. ▨

In the village of Choirokoitia, close to the motorway that runs between Limassol and Nicosia, archaeologists discovered the ruins of a large Neolithic settlement surrounded by a stone wall. One of the oldest settlements in Cyprus, it existed as early as c.6,800 BC.

It was sited on the slope of a hill, close to the river Maroni. Its inhabitants, who numbered close to 2,000 at the peak of its development, lived in beehive huts built of stone and clay. Many of the houses unearthed by archaeologists contained under-floor graves with gifts and personal effects. The dead were laid to rest in an embryonic position, with heavy stones placed on their chests to prevent them from returning to the world of the living.

The population of Choirokoitia formed a well-organized farming community. They cultivated the fertile local soil, hunted, bred goats, spun and weaved, and produced clay figurines and other objects. The artifacts uncovered at this site include flint sickle blades, stone vases and primitive triangular fertility gods. The women wore beautiful necklaces made of shells or imported red cornelian.

The foundations of several dozens of houses have been unearthed. Some of these have been reconstructed, providing a glimpse into how the earliest Cypriots lived. Many of the items found here are now exhibited in the Cyprus Museum in Nicosia.

The settlement was abandoned suddenly, and then repopulated around 4,500 BC. These later inhabitants introduced clay pots, some of which have been unearthed. The Choirokoitia archaeological site has been declared a UNESCO World Cultural and Natural Heritage Site.

Lefkara's Lace and Silverware Museum

Agios Minas ⓬

Road map C4. Close to Lefkara. **Tel** 24 342 952. ◻ May–Sep: 8am–noon, 3–5pm daily; Oct–Apr: 8am–noon, 2–5pm daily.

Agios Minas, a small monastery located in a scenic mountain setting, was founded in the 15th century and renovated in the mid-18th century. Subsequently abandoned, it was taken by a convent in 1965. The nuns are involved in painting icons, growing flowers and fruit, and keeping bees. They sell the delicious honey.

The 15th-century convent church, which was built by the Dominicans, features wall frescoes depicting St George slaying the dragon and the martyrdom of St Minas.

Environs
The nearby village of **Vavla** has lovely stone houses, some of which are being renovated for use by tourists.

Lefkara ⓭

Road map C4. 40 km (25 miles) from Larnaka.

This village, set amid picturesque white limestone hills (*lefka ori* means white hills), is famous for the lace-making skills of its womenfolk. In the Middle Ages Lefkara was a health resort visited by Venetian ladies. While staying here they busied themselves with embroidery, which they taught the local women. One story tells of Leonardo da Vinci supposedly coming to the island in 1481 to order an altar-cloth for Milan cathedral. The lace patterns are predominantly geometric, with crosses or diamonds and occasionally flowers, birds or butterflies. While the women busy themselves with embroidery, the local men produce jewellery and other objects from silver and gold.

The village buildings, with their yellow walls and red roofs, stand in attractive contrast with the natural surroundings. At the centre of Lefkara is the 16th-century Church of the Holy Cross containing a carved and gilded wood iconostasis and a precious sacred relic – a fragment of the True Cross on which Christ was crucified. The beautiful stone Patsalos building houses the **Lace and Silverware Museum**.

🏛 **Lace and Silverware Museum**
Pano Lefkara. **Tel** 24 342 326.
◻ 8:30am–4pm Mon–Thu, 9am–4pm Fri & Sat. ▨

Reconstructed houses at Choirokoitia archaeological site

Pyrga 🔞

Road map C3. 35 km (22 miles) from Nicosia.

This village is home to the Gothic **Chapel of St Catherine**, also known as the "Chapelle Royal". Erected by the Lusignan King Janus for his wife Charlotte de Bourbon, the chapel is built of volcanic rock on a square floorplan. It has three doors and, on the altar wall, three Gothic windows. The interior features fragments of the original frescoes. These depict the *Crucifixion*, with King Janus and Queen Charlotte by the cross; the *Raising of Lazarus*; the *Last Supper*; and the Lusignan coats of arms.

Close by is the Marini river on whose banks in 1426 the Egyptian Mamelukes smashed the Cypriot army, capturing King Janus and taking him prisoner to Cairo. The king regained his freedom two years later, after a ransom was paid.

Environs
The village of **Kornos**, to the west, is famous for its oversized ceramic products, such as storage jars.

Gothic chapel of St Catherine in Pyrga

Stavrovouni Monastery 🔞

Road map D3. 40 km (25 miles) from Larnaka, 9 km (5.5 miles) from motorway. **Tel** 22 533 630. ☐ *Apr–Aug: 8am–noon, 3–6pm daily; Sep–Mar: 7–11am, 2–5pm daily.* ☒ **No women allowed.** 🎑 *14 Sep.*

Stavrovouni (Mountain of the Cross) monastery was built on a steep, 750-m

Agia Varvara (monastery of St Barbara) at the foot of Stavrovouni

(2,460-ft) mountain. In ancient times the mountain was called Olympus, and it was the site of a temple to Aphrodite.

According to tradition, the monastery was founded in 327 by St Helena, mother of Constantine the Great. On her journey back from the Holy Land, where she found the True Cross of Christ, she stopped in Cyprus and left behind fragments of the precious relic. These can be seen in a large silver reliquary in the shape of a cross.

Over the following centuries the monastery fell prey to enemy raids and earthquakes. In 1821, during the Greek independence uprising, it was burned to the ground by the Turkish governor of Cyprus. The present monastery is the result of 19th-century restoration. The small **church** contains a lovely iconostasis and a wooden cross dating from 1476,

carved with scenes from the life of Jesus. Around the church are the monks' cells and other monastic quarters. The monastery also houses a collection of monks' skulls, with the name of the deceased written on each forehead.

Today the monks produce exquisite cheeses and sultanas, and also keep honey bees.

At the foot of Stavrovouni is the **monastery of St Barbara** (Agia Varvara), known for the local monks' icon painting. Their most celebrated artist was Father Kallinikos.

Kiti 🔞

Road map D4. 7 km (4.5 miles) southwest of Larnaka. ☐ *8am–noon, 2–4pm daily (to 6pm Jun–Aug).*

The **Panagia Angeloktisti** ("Built by Angels") church, in the northwestern end of the village of Kiti, consists of three parts. The first is the 14th-century Latin chapel with the coats of arms of knights above the entrance. The second part is the 11th-century dome-covered church, built on the ruins of an early

The Stavrovouni monastery towering over the district

Byzantine basilica, whose apse has been incorporated into the present building. The 6th-century apse mosaic is the church's main attraction. It depicts Mary holding the Christ Child, flanked by the Archangels Michael and Gabriel, with peacock-feather wings.

The third part of the church is a small 12th-century chapel dedicated to Saints Cosmas and Damian (patron saints of medicine) and decorated with 15th-century murals.

Environs

The 15th-century watchtower, one kilometer (half a mile) from Kiti lighthouse, features a statue of a lion – the symbol of the Venetian Republic.

Panagia Angeloktisti church in the village of Kiti

Hala Sultan Tekke ⓱

Road map D3. 5 km (3 miles) SW of Larnaka. ◻ *8am–5pm daily (to 6pm Apr, May, Sep & Oct; to 7:30pm Jun–Aug).* 🖼

On the shores of a salt lake, surrounded by cypress, palm and olive trees, the Hala Sultan Tekke is a major Muslim sanctuary. It includes an octagonal 1816 mosque built by the Turkish governor of Cyprus, and a mausoleum with the tomb of Umm Haram.

Umm Haram, paternal aunt of the Prophet Mohammed, was killed after falling off a mule while accompanying her husband in a pillage raid on Kition in 649. The mosque has a modest interior and the mausoleum contains several sarcophagi covered with green cloth. After Mecca, Medina and Jerusalem, the Hala Sultan Tekke is among the holiest sites for Muslims.

To the west of the car park archaeological excavations

Mosque and Hala Sultan Tekke mausoleum on the shores of the Salt Lake

continue, unearthing a late-Bronze Age town. Many items found here originated from Egypt and the Middle East.

Environs

The Salt Lake, close to the mosque, is one of two such lakes on Cyprus. In winter and early spring it provides a gathering point for thousands of flamingoes, swans, pelicans and other migrating water birds. The lake lies below sea level and in winter is filled with water seeping from the sea through the lime rocks. In summer it dries out, leaving a thick deposit of salt. Until the 1980s it yielded 3 to 5 thousand tons of salt annually.

According to legend, the Salt Lake was created after Lazarus landed on this shore. Hungry and thirsty, he asked a local woman in the vineyard for a handful of fruit. She tersely refused to give him anything, so the saint, in revenge, turned her vineyard into a salt lake.

Larnaka ⓲

See pp78–81.

Kellia ⓳

Road map D3. 5 km (3 miles) north of Larnaka.

Standing to the west of Kellia, formerly a Turkish Cypriot village that derives its name from the cells of early Christian hermits who once made this their home, is the small **Church of St Anthony** (Agios Andonios) carved into the rocks.

It was first built in the 11th century, but the subsequent remodelling works have all but obliterated its original shape. The layout resembles a cross inscribed into a square, with the three aisles terminating in an apse and a 15th-century narthex.

Restoration efforts have revealed some beautiful murals. The most interesting of them is the *Crucifixion*, painted on the southeast pillar, one of the oldest paintings on the island. Other notable paintings are on the pillars and on the west wall of the church, including the *Assumption of the Virgin Mary*, *Judas' Betrayal* and *Abraham's Sacrifice*.

ZENO OF KITION (KITIUM)

Born in 334 BC, this Greek thinker founded the Stoic school of philosophy (named after Stoa Poikale – the Painted Colonnade on the Athenian agora where he taught). Zeno's philosophy embraced logic, epistemology, physics and ethics. The Stoics postulated that a life governed by reason and the harnessing of desires was of the highest virtue, leading to happiness. Stoicism left a deep mark on the philosophy and ethics of the Hellenic and Roman eras.

Bust of Zeno of Kition

Larnaka ⑱

Gargoyle

Larnaka stands on the site of ancient Kition. It takes its name from the Greek *larnax*, meaning "sarcophagus" (there were many ancient and medieval tombs in the district). The city has an international airport, a port, several interesting museums and a seaside promenade lined with numerous cafés and restaurants. The tourist zone has luxurious hotels, tavernas, nightclubs and souvenir shops.

Larnaka's seaside promenade lined with palm trees

Exploring Larnaka

The best place to begin is ancient Kition, followed by the Archaeological and Pierides-Marfin Laiki Bank Museums. From here continue with the church of St Lazarus (Agios Lazaros) and the Byzantine Museum, then proceed towards the sea, visiting the Turkish fort and mosque. The seaside promenade leads to the marina and beach.

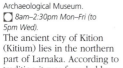

A figurine from Pierides Museum

⋔ Kition

0.5 km (0.3 mile) NE of Archaeological Museum.
◷ 8am–2:30pm Mon–Fri (to 5pm Wed).

The ancient city of Kition (Kitium) lies in the northern part of Larnaka. According to tradition it was founded by Kittim, grandson of Noah. Archaeological excavations indicate, however, that the town was founded in the 13th century BC. Soon afterwards the Mycenaeans landed on the island; they reinforced the city walls and built a temple. The Phoenicians, who conquered the city in the 9th century BC,

turned the temple into a shrine to the goddess Astarte. Kition was a major trade centre for copper, which was excavated in mines near Tamassos.

⋔ Mycenaean Site

Leoforos Archiepiskopu Kyprianou.
The main archaeological site (dubbed Area II) is near the cemetery for foreigners. There are wooden platforms from where you can view the dig. The defence walls dating from the late Bronze era were later strengthened by the Mycenaeans, who added fortifications built of stone and clay bricks.

⋔ Acropolis

Leontiou Kimonos.
Situated on top of Bamboula hill (immediately below the Archaeological Museum) was the acropolis, which had its own defence walls. In the late 1800s the hill was plundered by British soldiers, who used the rubble to cover malaria-breeding swamps. In the 1960s archaeologists stumbled upon ancient tombs filled with ceramics and jewellery, as well as alabaster sculptures and stone fragments.

🏛 Archaeological Museum

Kalograion. **Tel** 24 304 169.
◷ 8am–3pm Tue–Fri (to 5pm Thu), 9am–3pm Sat. 🖾

The Archaeological Museum displays vases, sculptures and cult statues from Larnaka and the surrounding area. It has a collection of ceramics (mostly Mycenaean), votive terracotta figurines and glass objects from Roman times. There is also an interesting exhibition of Cypriot-Minoan inscriptions, as yet undeciphered. There are also sculptures in the garden.

Interior of Larnaka's Pierides-Marfin Laiki Bank Museum

🏛 Pierides-Marfin Laiki Bank Museum

Zinonos Kitieos 4. **Tel** 24 814 555.
◷ 9am–4pm Mon–Thu, 9am–1pm Fri & Sat. 🖾 www.pierides foundation.com.cy

This museum contains the largest private collection in Cyprus. Comprising some 2,500 relics assembled by five generations of the Pierides family, the collection spans from the Neolithic era to medieval times. It was started in 1839 by Cypriot archaeologist Demetrios Pierides, who committed part of his fortune to the preservation of artifacts

Excavations of the ancient city of Kition

Natural History Museum in the municipal park

VISITORS' CHECKLIST

Road map D3. 🏛 79,000.
ℹ️ Plateia Vasileos Pavlou,
24 654 322. 🎭 Kataklysmos
Fair (50 days after Easter),
Flower Festival (early May).
🚌 by the end of the seaside
promenade, close to the
marina.

pillaged from ancient tombs by treasure hunters such as the American consul in Larnaka, Luigi Palma di Cesnola.

The most precious objects include Neolithic stone idols and 3,000-year-old ceramic vessels. There are also terracotta figurines dating from the archaic era; miniature war chariots and cavalry soldiers; amphorae and goblets in geometric and archaic styles decorated with images of fish and birds; and Hellenic statues. Of particular note is the striking astronaut-like figure jumping on springs, painted on an archaic ceramic vessel. Other exhibits include weaponry and a set of historical maps of Cyprus and of the eastern Mediterranean.

In the rooms at the back of the building is a collection of handicrafts, including jewellery, embroidery, everyday items and richly carved furniture. There are also works by the primitive artist Michael Kashialos, who was murdered by the Turks in his studio in 1974.

🏛 Natural History Museum

Leoforos Grigori Afxentiou.
Tel 24 652 569.
⏰ 9am–4pm Mon–Fri,
10am–1pm Sat.
Located in the municipal park, this small building houses a diverse collection of exhibits illustrating

the natural environment of Cyprus. Arranged across eight rooms are specimens of plants, insects and animals (from both land and sea), many of which are now rare in the wild.

There are also interesting geological exhibits. Besides the collection of copper minerals – the main source of the island's wealth since ancient times, you can see minerals belonging to the asbestos group. The large open mines from which these minerals came are located near Amiantos, on the southeastern slopes of the Troodos mountains. Other exhibits include fossils found in the island's limestone.

Fountain in front of the town hall

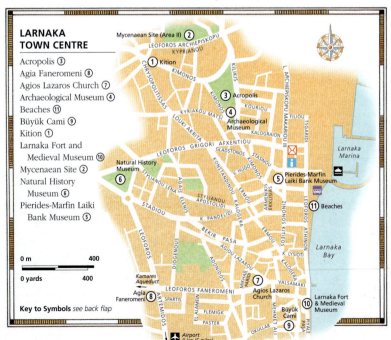

LARNAKA TOWN CENTRE

Acropolis ③
Agia Faneromeni ⑧
Agios Lazaros Church ⑦
Archaeological Museum ④
Beaches ⑪
Büyük Cami ⑨
Kition ①
Larnaka Fort and Medieval Museum ⑩
Mycenaean Site ②
Natural History Museum ⑥
Pierides-Marfin Laiki Bank Museum ⑤

0 m   400
0 yards   400

Key to Symbols see back flap

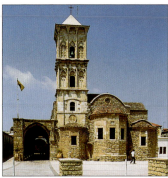

St Lazarus Church dating from the 10th century

🔒 Agios Lazaros Church

Plateia Agiou Lazarou. **Tel** 24 652 498. ⬜ 8am–12.30pm, 2–6:30pm daily (to 5:30pm Sep–Mar).

The Church of St Lazarus (Agios Lazaros) stands in the southern part of Old Larnaka. It was constructed in the early 10th century on the site of a church dating from 900 AD, which was built to house the saint's tomb.

Its architectural style reveals the influence of both eastern and western trends. Following its retrieval from the hands of the Turks in 1589, the church was used by Roman Catholic and Orthodox communities for 200 years, as evidenced by inscriptions on the portico. The interior is built around four vast pillars supporting a roof with three small domes. Its main features are the Rococo pulpit, around 300 years old, and a small icon depicting Lazarus emerging from his tomb, an image reverently paraded through

Icon from the Byzantine Museum

the church at Easter. The magnificently carved iconostasis includes a number of precious icons; the best of these dates from the 17th century and portrays Lazarus rising. On the right side of the central nave is a large gilded reliquary containing the skull of the saint. The crypt houses several stone sarcophagi. One of them supposedly housed the relics of St Lazarus. The tomb bore the Greek inscription: "Lazarus, friend of Jesus".

The graves in the courtyard are mainly of British consuls, civil servants and merchants.

Larnaka has other notable places of worship, including the metropolitan cathedral, Agios Chrysotrios, built in 1853; Agios Ioannis, featuring a beautiful iconostasis from the beginning of the 17th century; and the Roman Catholic church Terra Santa. Also of note is the 19th-century "Clown Mosque" (Zahuri Cami), with its double dome and truncated minaret.

🏛 Byzantine Museum

Plateia Agiou Lazarou. **Tel** 24 652 498. ⬜ 8:30am–12:30pm, 3–5:30pm Mon–Sat. ⬤ Wed & Sat pm. 📷

Entry to this museum is from the courtyard of Agios Lazaros church. The collection consists of icons and other objects associated with the

Orthodox religion, including chasubles and Bibles.

A previous, extensive collection vanished during the turbulent period between 1964 and 1974. It was kept in the fort, which fell into the hands of the Turks. When it was regained by the Greeks, many items had vanished.

🔒 Agia Faneromeni

At the junction of Leoforos Faneromeni and Artemidos.

This subterranean chapel is a two-chambered cave hewn into the rock. Its structure suggests a pagan tomb, probably dating from the Phoenician era. The chapel was famed for its magical properties. The sick would circle it twice, leaving behind anything from a scrap of clothing to a lock of hair in the hope that they were also leaving behind their illnesses. Girls, whose boyfriends were far away, would come here to pray for their safe return.

🎭 Amphitheatre

Leoforos Artemidos.

The open-air amphitheatre, used for staging events during the July Festival, is situated opposite the Zeno of Kition Stadium, close to the Agia Faneromeni chapel.

☪ Büyük Cami

Leoforus Athenon. ⬜ daily.

Standing beyond the fort, at the border between the Greek and Turkish districts, is the Grand Mosque (Büyük Cami). Originally the church of the Holy Cross, this building now serves Muslim visitors mostly from the Middle East. Modest attire is required, and before entering you must remove your shoes. For a

---

SAINT LAZARUS

Lazarus, brother of Martha and Mary, was resurrected by Jesus four days after his death at Bethany. He moved to Cyprus, becoming Bishop of Kition. After his final death he was buried here; his tomb was discovered in 890. Emperor Leo VI helped to build St Lazarus church, in exchange for which some of the saint's relicts were transferred to Constantinople, from where they were stolen in 1204. Today they are in Marseille Cathedral.

Painting showing the resurrection of Lazarus

small fee you can climb the narrow, steep stairs that lead to the top of the minaret. From here there is a lovely, panoramic view of Larnaka and the nearby Salt Lake. Stretching beyond the fort, right up to the fishing harbour is a large district that once belonged to the Turks. Its streets still bear Turkish names, but it is now inhabited by Greek Cypriot refugees from the area around Famagusta and the Karpasia peninsula.

The imposing mid-18th-century aqueduct

A variety of yachts moored in Larnaka marina

🛥 Larnaka Harbours

The southern part of town has a small but picturesque fishing harbour. Larnaka marina is situated several hundred metres to the north of the coastal promenade, beyond a small beach. Only boat crews are allowed entry, but you can stroll along the breakwater. Beyond the marina there are cargo and passenger terminals; the passenger terminal is the second largest in Cyprus.

♟ Larnaka Fort and Medieval Museum

On the seashore, by the south end of the coastal promenade. *Tel 24 304 576.* ⬜ *9am–5pm Mon–Fri (to 7:30pm Jun–Oct).*

The fort in Larnaka was built by the Turks in c.1625 on the site of a medieval castle which had been destroyed by Mamelukes two centuries previously. When ships sailed into the harbour (which no longer exists), they were welcomed by a gun salute fired from the castle.

During the Byzantine period, the fort was used as a police headquarters, prison and execution site. In 1833, it was partially destroyed by a lightning strike. Today the fort houses a small Medieval Museum with arms and armour dating from Turkish times, and treasure troves unearthed in Kition and at the Hala Sultan Tekke. The crenellated wall, with menacing guns and cannons, is now a viewing platform. During summer the castle yard serves as a venue for concerts, occasional plays and other cultural events.

🏖 Beaches

The sandy municipal beach by the Finikoudes promenade, in the neighbourhood of the marina, owes its popularity mainly to a double row of shade-giving palm trees. Another

A cannon at Larnaka's Fort

municipal beach is situated to the south of the fishing harbour. Although small, it is popular with locals due to its water sports facilities and the numerous restaurants and cafés in the vicinity.

The best sandy public beach in the area is located some 10 km (6 miles) east of the city and is run by the Cyprus Tourism Organization. About 10 km (6 miles) south of Larnaka, near Kiti, there is a rocky cove with patches of sand; this area is undeveloped and relatively free of people.

There are other beaches, some of them sandy, located a few kilometres north of Larnaka, within the tourist zone. However, your enjoyment of them may be hampered by the smell emanating from the nearby oil refinery.

🏛 Aqueduct (Kamares)

3 km (1.9 miles) from Larnaka.

On the outskirts of Larnaka, by the road leading to Limassol, are the remains of an aqueduct that formerly supplied the town with water taken from inlets on the River Thrimitus. The aqueduct was built in 1745 by the Turkish governor, Elhey Bekir Pasha, and functioned until 1930. Some 75 spans of this impressive structure still stand; they are illuminated at night.

Larnaka beach in high season

Octagonal fountain in the courtyard of Agia Napa monastery

Agia Napa ⑳

Road map E3. 🏛 *3,200*.
ℹ *Leoforos Kryou Nerou 12,*
23 721 796. 🎭 *Kataklysmos.*

Until the 1970s Agia Napa was a quiet fishing village with a scenic harbour. However, following the Turkish occupation of Varosha – the Greek Cypriot neighbourhood of Famagusta – Agia Napa assumed the role of Cyprus's prime bathing resort. Now a teeming holiday resort especially popular with British and Scandinavian young people, the town centre has scores of hotels, nightclubs and cafés that have given Agia Napa its reputation as the second most entertaining playground in the Mediterranean, after Ibiza.

An interesting historic relic of Agia Napa is the 16th-century Venetian **Monastery of Agia Napa**, enclosed by a high wall. According to legend, in the 16th century a hunter's dog led him to a spring in the woods where he found a sacred icon of the Virgin that had been lost 700 years earlier. (A church had been built here as early as the 8th century, hacked into the solid rock and named Agia Napa – Holy Virgin of the Forest). The spring was thus believed to have healing powers and the monastery of Agia Napa was built on the site. Soon after, Cyprus fell to the Turks and the Venetian monks fled, but villagers

Fountain detail, Agia Napa monastery

continued to use the beautiful **monastery church**.

The only church on the island with a free-standing belfry, it is built partly underground in a natural grotto. The route to its gloomy, mysterious interior leads through an entrance crowned with an arch and a rosette. Inside is a complex maze of grottoes, niches and shrines. From April until December, the church celebrates Anglican mass every Sunday at 11am and Roman Catholic mass at 5pm. At the centre of the monastery's arcaded **courtyard** is an octagonal Renaissance fountain decorated with marble reliefs and topped with a dome resting on four columns. Nearby, water supplied by a Roman aqueduct flows from the carved marble head of a wild boar.

The monastery was restored in the 1970s and now houses the **World Council of Churches Ecumenical Conference Centre**.

The **Thalassa Museum of the Sea** in Agia Napa is

designed to show the impact of the sea on the history of the island. It features a replica of the "Kyrenia Ship" dating from the times of Alexander the Great, which sank off the coast of Kyrenia some 2,300 years ago.

The majority of the museum's exhibits come from the private collection of naturalist George Tomaritis. They include a range of preserved marine fauna as well as shells and maritime exhibits.

Beautiful sandy beaches can be found in the surrounding area. One of them is **Nissi Beach**, with its small island. Neighbouring **Makronissos Beach** is linked to the town centre by bicycle routes. Nearby, on a craggy peninsula, are 19 Hellenic tombs hacked into the rock. Two kilometres (1 mile) west is a sandy beach, **Agia Thekla**, with a small chapel and an old church in a rock cave.

🏛 **Thalassa Museum of the Sea**
Leoforos Kryou Nerou.
Tel 23 816 366. ⏰ *summer:*
9am–1pm, 6–10pm Mon,
9am–5pm Tue–Sat, 9am–1pm Sun;
winter: 9am–1pm Mon, 9am–5pm
Tue–Sat, closed Sun. 🎟
www.*pieridesfoundation.com.cy*

Cape Gkreko ㉑

Road map E3.

This headland, lying at the southeastern tip of Cyprus, rises in a steep crag above the sea. The neighbouring coves with their clear water are a paradise for scuba divers and snorkellers. The entire area, with its interesting variety of

Popular sandy beach in Agia Napa

The rugged coast of Cape Gkreko with its limestone cliffs

limestone rock formations, is a **protected nature reserve**.

Archaeologists discovered the remains of two **temples**: the Hellenic temple of Aphrodite, and the Roman temple of Diana. The cape is surrounded by underwater **shipwrecks**, including a Genoese ship filled with looted treasure, which sank in the 15th century.

Walking along the shore towards Protaras you will come across a rock bridge over a small bay protruding inland, a Roman quarry, and a little further on, the **Agii Anargyri Church** above a grotto hidden in a craggy cliff underneath. The area in front of the church affords a truly magnificent view over Konnos Bay and the clifftop hotel.

Protaras ㉒

Road map E3. 🛈 *Leoforos Protaras Cape Gkreko 356, 23 832 865.*

Protaras is a conglomeration of hotels, tavernas, cafés, watersports centres and an excellent place to spend a holiday. In summer, its beautiful sandy beaches attract crowds of tourists ready to enjoy watersports, or to go for a cruise on one of the local pleasure boats.

The area is dominated by a rocky hill with the picturesque **chapel of Prophitis Elias** (the Prophet Elijah) affording a magnificent panoramic view of Protaras and nearby Varosha.

Further north are more beaches including Pernera, Minas and Agia Triada with a small church, situated in a coastal cove. Near the latter, close to the roundabout on

the road to Paralimni, is an **Aquarium**, where you can see crocodiles, penguins, fish and other marine creatures.

> **🐾 Aquarium**
> Paralimni, Protaras Ave. ⏺ 10am–6pm daily. **Tel** 23 741 111.

Environs
The area encompassing Agia Napa, Paralimni and the tourist region of Protaras is known as **Kokkinohoria** (red villages) due to its red soil, rich in iron compounds. The scenery is dominated by windmills that drive pumps, which draw water from deep underground.

After 1974, the old village of **Paralimni** became the administrative centre of the district. Situated close to the occupied, northern part of Cyprus, it received a great many refugees after the invasion and now its population numbers about 11,000.

The village skyline is dominated by three churches. The oldest of these is Panagia (Virgin Mary) dating from the 18th century and lined with porcelain tiles typical of the period. It also houses a small Byzantine museum. Paralimni is famous for delicacies such as smoked pork *(pasta)* and pork sausages *(loukanika)*.

The neighbouring farming village of **Deryneia** perches atop a hill, right by the "Green Line". From here there

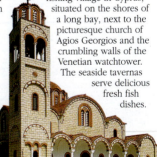
Statue of a diver in Protaras

are views of Varosha's abandoned houses, the former tourist district of Famagusta now resembling a ghost town, and the Gothic Cathedral of St Nicholas, which has been turned into a mosque.

Deryneia has three pretty churches – 15th-century Agia Marina, 17th-century Agios Georgios and the church of the Panagia.

The village of **Liopetri** is famous for the potatoes that are grown here, as well as the woven baskets used to collect them. You can still see local basket weavers at work.

The 15th-century village church of Agios Andronikos has a carved iconostasis with lovely icons and paintings in the apses.

The Akhyronas barn is Cyprus's national memorial. It was here that four EOKA fighters were killed in a battle with the British in 1958.

Potamos Liopetriou, to the south, is the most beautiful fishing village in Cyprus, situated on the shores of a long bay, next to the picturesque church of Agios Georgios and the crumbling walls of the Venetian watchtower. The seaside tavernas serve delicious fresh fish dishes.

The 18th-century church in Paralimni

TROODOS MOUNTAINS

*S*tretching some 120 km (75 miles) over southwestern Cyprus, the Troodos mountain region is truly astonishing and completely different from the rest of the sun-baked island. In winter and early spring, the peaks are often capped with snow, and the forests fill the cool air with the scent of pine and cedar. The mountain villages and monasteries hidden in the forests seem a world away from the crowded coastal areas, even during the peak holiday season.

The shady valleys and lofty peaks of the Troodos mountains have long been a refuge for people in search of calm and tranquillity, including the monks who came here looking for a place where they could be closer to God and farther from temptation.

Mount Olympus, the island's highest peak at 1,951 m (6,400 ft), rises above the other mountains in the mighty massif, crowned with the distinctive radar domes of the British army. In winter, its slopes swarm with skiers eager to enjoy a sport that is rare in this part of Europe.

The southern slopes are perfectly suited to growing the grapes used to produce the island's famous wine, the sweet Commandaria.

Almost half of the 140 species of plants unique to Cyprus grow in the Troodos region. The central section has been declared a nature reserve.

Travelling through the Troodos mountains brings visitors into contact with quiet, friendly villages, where the local people produce sweets of fruit and nuts soaked in grape juice *(soujouko)*, as well as excellent wine and flavourful goat cheese *(halloumi)*.

A trip to the region is not complete without seeing the Byzantine painted churches. The austere architecture of these Orthodox sanctuaries, hidden in remote valleys and glens, hides a wealth of amazingly rich murals (commonly referred to as frescoes) depicting scenes from the Bible.

A church hidden in the mountains – a distinctive feature of the region

◁ The forested slopes of the Troodos mountains

Exploring the Troodos Mountains

Among the highlights of a visit to the Troodos mountains are the many painted churches, some dating from the Byzantine period. Ten of these isolated churches have been listed as UNESCO World Cultural Heritage Sites. The tomb of Archbishop Makarios, the first president of Cyprus, lies near Kykkos Monastery at Throni. The Commandaria region's villages have produced the famous Cypriot dessert wine since the 12th century. The true treasures of the Troodos mountains are their waterfalls hidden among lush greenery – unusual in the eastern Mediterranean.

Theotokos Archangelos Church, one of the many small churches in the region

SIGHTS AT A GLANCE

Agios Ioannis Lampadistis ❹
Agios Nikolaos tis Stegis ⓫
Cedar Valley ❷
Kakopetria ⓴
Koilani ⓮
Kykkos pp90–91 ❸
Lofou ⓯
Monagri ⓰
Mt Olympus (Chionistra) ❼
Omodos ⓫
Panagia Forviotissa ⓶
Panagia tis Podithou ㉑

Panagia tou Araka ㉓
Panagia tou Moutoulla ❺
Pedoulas ❻
Pelendri ⓲
Platres ❿
Potamiou ⓬
Stavros tou Agiasmati ㉔
Tilliria ❶
Timios Stavros ⓱
Trooditissa ❾
Troodos ❽
Vouni ⓭

SEE ALSO

- *Where to Stay* pp162–3

- *Where to Eat* pp173–4

0 km   5

0 miles   5

For additional map symbols *see back flap*

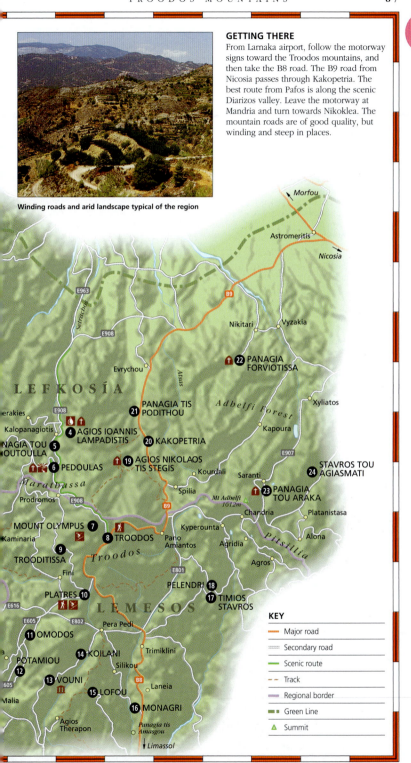

GETTING THERE
From Larnaka airport, follow the motorway signs toward the Troodos mountains, and then take the B8 road. The B9 road from Nicosia passes through Kakopetria. The best route from Pafos is along the scenic Diarizos valley. Leave the motorway at Mandria and turn towards Nikoklea. The mountain roads are of good quality, but winding and steep in places.

Winding roads and arid landscape typical of the region

Morfou
Astromeritis
Nicosia

Nikitari   Vyzakia

E963
B9

Setrachos

E908

Evrychou
Alsós

L E F K O S Í A

erakies
E908
Kalopanagiotis
4 AGIOS IOANNIS
LAMPADISTIS
5 NAGIA TOU
OUTOULLA
6 PEDOULAS

Marathrassa

Prodromos
E908

21 PANAGIA TIS
PODITHOU

22 PANAGIA
FORVIOTISSA

Adbelfi Forest

Xyliatos

Kapoura

20 KAKOPETRIA

19 AGIOS NIKOLAOS
TIS STEGIS
Kourdali
Spilia
Saranti

E907

24 STAVROS TOU
AGIASMATI

Mt Adbelfi
1612m
23 PANAGIA
TOU ARAKA
Chandria
Platanistasa

7 MOUNT OLYMPUS

Kaminaria
9
TROODITISSA
Fini

8 TROODOS
Troodos
Pano
Amiantos
Kyperounta
Agridia

Alona

Pitsillía

Agros

E801

10 PLATRES
E616

L E M E S O S

Pera Pedi
E605
E802
11 OMODOS

14 KOILANI
Trimiklini

PELENDRI 18
17 TIMIOS
STAVROS

a
POTAMIOU
12
13 VOUNI
Silikou
15 LOFOU
B8
Laneia
16 MONAGRI

605
Malia

Agios
Therapon
Panagía tis
Amasgou
↓ Limassol

KEY

———	Major road
≈≈≈	Secondary road
———	Scenic route
– – –	Track
———	Regional border
▬ ▬ ▬	Green Line
△	Summit

Tilliria ①

Road map B3.

Tilliria is a desolate region east of Polis, on the north-western slopes of the Troodos mountains. Its forested hills extend behind the former monastery, Stavros tis Psokas, in the direction of the Turkish enclave of Kokkina, Pyrgos, Kato and the sea. This region has never been inhabited, although people came here to work the long-since defunct copper ore mines. It is ideal for experienced hikers.

In ancient times, Cyprus was overgrown with dense forests, which were cut down to build ships and fire the furnaces in the copper-smelting plants.

Under British rule of the island, action was taken to restore the former character of the Cypriot forests. The extensive Pafos Forest was created in the western region of the Troodos mountains.

The wooded hills of the remote Tilliria region – a hiker's paradise

Cedar Valley ②

Road map B3.

This valley, set in the midst of the forest backwoods, contains most of the island's trees of the local *cedrus brevi-folia* variety, different from the better known Lebanese cedar. The valley is a nature reserve, and with a bit of luck visitors will see the moufflon – a wild Cypriot sheep. In the early 20th century, when the British declared these animals a protected species, only 15 of

them remained in the wild; now the forests of Cyprus are home to over 1,500 of them. The male displays powerful, curled horns. The moufflon is a symbol of Cyprus and appears on its coins.

Environs

Standing in the midst of the Pafos Forest is the abandoned 19th-century monastery of **Stavros tis Psokas**, now used by the Forestry Commission. It contains a restaurant, several guest rooms and a campsite. The locals claim it to be the coolest place on the island. Close to the campsite is an enclosure containing moufflon.

The Forestry Commission building is the starting point for hiking trails to the nearby peaks of Tripylos and Zaharou. Starting from the car park by the spring and the junction with the road leading towards the sea, you can walk or drive to Mount Tripylos – one of the highest peaks in the district at 1,362 m (4,468 ft), which offers a magnificent panorama of the Pafos and Tilliria hills.

Kykkos ③

See pp90–91.

Agios Ioannis Lampadistis ④

Road map B3. Kalopanagiotis. **Tel** 22 952 580. ⬜ 9am–12:30pm, 2–5pm daily (Nov–Apr: 9am–noon, 1–4pm). **Donations** welcome.

The monastery of St John of Lampadou (ancient Lambas) is one of the most interesting in Cyprus and has been awarded UNESCO World Heritage

Kalopanagiotis village, scenically located on a mountain slope

status. The old monastery complex includes three churches covered with one vast roof. The oldest one, dedicated to **St Irakleidios**, dates from the 11th century and is decorated with over 30 12th- and 15th-century frescoes illustrating key events in the life of Jesus. The painting on the dome depicts Christ Pantocrator. Others show the Sacrifice of Abraham, the Entry into Jerusalem and the Ascension. The 15th-century series of paintings seen on the vaults, arches and walls depicts various scenes from the New Testament.

The second church, of **Agios Ioannis (St John) Lampadistis**, dating from the 11th century, is dedicated to the saint who was born in Lampadou. He renounced marriage in favour of the monastic life, went blind, died at the age of 22, and was canonised soon afterwards. His tomb is inside the church and the niche above contains a silver reliquary with the saint's skull. The church

Monastery buildings of Agios Ioannis Lampadistis

interior is decorated with 12th-century paintings. The richly gilded iconostasis dates from the 16th century. The narthex (portico) common to both churches, which was added in the 15th century, includes a cycle of paintings depicting the miracles of Christ.

The **Latin chapel**, added in the second half of the 15th century, is decorated with 24 magnificent Byzantine wall paintings with Greek texts written in about 1500.

Environs

The mountain village of **Kalopanagiotis** is scenically located in the Setrachos Valley. It has existed since medieval times and has retained its traditional architecture, cobbled streets, and many churches and chapels. The village is now a small health resort with therapeutic sulphur springs (with beneficial properties for rheumatic conditions and gastric ailments). It is also known for its beautifully carved breadbaskets called *sanidha*. Kalopanagiotis is believed to be descended from ancient Lambas, which produced the local saints, Ioannis and Irakleidios. Nearby is an arched medieval bridge.

Panagia tou Moutoulla ❺

Road map B3. 3 km (1.8 miles) from Pedoulas. Moutoullas. ◯ *vary.* **Donations** welcome.

The village of Moutoulla, situated in a valley below Pedoulas, is renowned for its mineral water spring and its tiny church of **Our Lady of Moutoulla** (Panagia tou Moutoulla) built in 1279-80.

This is the oldest of the Troodos mountain painted churches. Its most interesting features are the pitched roof and finely carved entrance door. Beyond these doors is another set of equally beautiful doors (wood carving has been a local speciality for centuries). Above them is the image of *Christ Enthroned*, flanked by *Adam and Eve*, and *Hell and Paradise*, with a procession of

Panoramic view of Pedoulas in the Marathassa valley

saints marching into Heaven. The cycle of paintings inside the church, illustrating key events in the life of Jesus and Mary, are similar to the wall paintings in the nearby Church of the Archangel Michael. The most distinctive of these faded paintings include *Mary with the Christ Child* in a cradle, and *St Christopher and St George Fighting the Dragon* with the head of a woman in a crown. There is also a portrait of the church founder, Ioannis Moutoullas, with his wife Irene.

Remains of a wall painting in Panagia tou Moutoulla

Pedoulas ❻

Road map B3. 🚶 *190.* 🚌 *once a day from Nicosia.*

This sizeable village is located in the upper part of the Marathassa valley. The Setrakhos River that drains it flows down towards Morfou Bay. Pedoulas is famed for its surrounding orchards, gentle climate, bracing air and bottled spring water, which you can

buy in most shops in Cyprus. The most beautiful season here is spring, when the houses are completely enveloped by a sea of flowering cherry trees.

The most significant site in the village is the **Church of the Archangel Michael** (Archangelos Michail), dating from 1474. It is one of ten mountain churches listed as UNESCO World Cultural Heritage Sites, due to its magnificent interior wall paintings.

The paintings are unusually realistic. The north side of the tiny reading room is decorated with a painting of the Archangel Michael.

The renovated paintings are notable for their realistic images, including the *Sacrifice of Abraham*, the *Baptism in the Jordan River*, the *Kiss of Judas* and the *Betrayal of Christ in the Garden of Gethsemane*. The apse, usually decorated with an image of Christ Pantocrator, includes the Praying Mary (*Virgin Orans*) and the *Ascension*. Seen above the north entrance is the figure of the founder, Basil Chamados, handing a model of the church to the Archangel Michael.

Environs

The neighbouring village of Prodromos, which numbers only 150 inhabitants, is perched on top of a mountain range at an elevation of 1,400 m (4,593 ft). It is the highest village in Cyprus, and also, thanks to its decent accommodation facilities, a good base for starting to explore the Marathassa valley.

Kykkos ❸

This is the largest, most imposing and wealthiest of all the monasteries in Cyprus. Built in the middle of magnificent mountains and forests, away from human habitation, its most precious treasure is the icon of the Most Merciful Virgin, claimed to have been painted by St Luke and credited with the power to bring rain. The holy image is kept in the monastery museum.

12th-century Icon
The most beautiful icon in the museum's collection is this image of the Virgin and Child.

Collection of manuscripts, documents and books

Belfry
The new belfry, with its distinctive architectural style, stands on top of a hill near the monastery.

The rotunda has a darkened room housing the museum's most precious exhibits – the ancient, beautiful icons.

The main wing of the monastery is home to the monks' cells.

★ **Museum's Main Hall**
The monastery museum contains some important treasures: gold and silver liturgical vessels, holy books, and embroidered vestments, as well as beautiful and precious icons.

STAR FEATURES

★ Museum's
   Main Hall

★ Royal Doors
   (in the church)

General View
The hills surrounding Kykkos afford memorable views over the small monastery church and belfry, flanked by one-storey buildings with red roof tiles.

Small Courtyard
The church courtyard leads to the monastery buildings that used to house the museum.

VISITORS' CHECKLIST

Road map B3. **Monastery, church & museum** ☐ *Jun–Oct: 10am–6pm daily; Nov–May: 10am–4pm daily.* 🖼 ☐ 🚫
www.kykkos-museum.cy.net

★ **Royal Doors**
Inside the church is a richly decorated iconostasis incorporating the Royal Doors.

Church Entrance
The katholicon, or monastery church, is entered via a doorway decorated with lovely mosaics.

Main Monastery Entrance
This small, but wonderfully decorated entance is covered in beautiful mosaics.

Main Courtyard
The cloisters running along the edge of the main courtyard are decorated with mosaics depicting the history of Kykkos Monastery.

Mount Olympus (Chionistra) ❼

Road map B3. 45 km (28 miles) north of Limassol. 🚌 *bus from Nicosia in the summer.*

Chionistra, the traditional name of Olympus, means "the snowy one". The slopes of the 1,950-m (6,400-ft) mountain are covered with umbrella-shaped pine trees interspersed with cedars and junipers. The most beautiful season here is spring, when wildflowers are in bloom. In good weather the view from the top extends as far as the coast of Turkey.

In winter the mountain is covered with a layer of snow up to 3 m (nearly 10 ft) deep, making Mount Olympus popular with downhill skiers. The ski runs on the southern slopes of Sun Valley are short and easy, while the northern runs are much longer and considerably more difficult. There are also two cross-country trails. Equipment hire and lessons are available.

The nearest hotel and restaurant facilities are in Troodos and Pano Platres.

> ⏩ **Ski Station**
> ⏺ *Jan–Mar.* **www**.cyprusski.com

Umbrella pines on the slopes of Mount Olympus

Troodos ❽

Road map B3. 🎿 *15.*
ℹ️ *25 421 316.* ⏺ *8:30am–4pm Mon–Fri (second week of month: 9am–3:30pm Mon–Fri, 9am–2pm Sat).* 📷

This small resort offers a few restaurants, souvenir shops and tourist car parks. In the summer there are horse and

The iconostasis in Trooditissa church with the miraculous icon of Mary

donkey rides, while hikers have a choice of several trails. The **Troodos National Park Museum** has a collection of local natural specimens. There is also a walk along a 300-m- (984-ft-) long botanical-geological path and a short film about the natural environment of Troodos.

Hidden in the forest a few kilometres south is the former residence of the British governor of Cyprus, now used as the summer villa of the president of the Republic of Cyprus. The overseer who helped to build it in 1880 was Arthur Rimbaud, the famous French poet.

Trooditissa ❾

Road map B3. 8 km (5 miles) west of Pano Platres. ⏹ *to the public.*

This monastery is surrounded by pine forests on the southern slopes of the Troodos mountains, a few kilometres west of Platres. It was founded in 1250 on the site of an old sanctuary. During the Icono-clastic Wars of the 8th century, a monk brought here an icon of the Virgin Mary which, according to tradition, was painted by St Luke. The icon remained hidden in a cave until 990, when it was discovered, thanks to the miraculous light emanating from it.

The present **monastery church** dates from 1731.

Its carved wooden iconostasis is covered with gold leaf. The miracle-working icon – the magnificent image of the Panagia, Queen of Heaven, is to the left of the Royal Doors, covered with a curtain of silver and gold.

The monastery, whose aus-tere regime is similar to that of Stavrovouni *(see p76)*, is home to a dozen or so monks.

Environs
The nearby village of **Fini** (Foini) is renowned for its traditional handicrafts, now limited to pottery studios and a workshop producing distinctive Cypriot chairs.

The private **Pilavakion Museum**, run by Theofanis Pilavakis, displays vast ceramic jugs for storing olive oil. Adjacent to Iliovasilema bar is a small shop producing the local delicacy – *loukoumi* (Cyprus delight) said to be the best in Southern Cyprus.

Between Fini and the monastery, on a small stream running through a deep ravine where British soldiers practice climbing skills, is the picturesque **Chantara waterfall**.

Panoramic view of Fini, known for handicrafts

Platres ❿

Road map B3. 37 km (23 miles) NW of Limassol. 🚶 280. 🛈 25 421 316.

The most famous mountain resort in Cyprus, Platres lies on a steep bank above the Kyros stream. The location and surrounding forests combine to give the resort an excellent climate, making it a favourite holiday spot for Limassol and Nicosia residents.

Several colonial-style villas serve as reminders of British rule, and the few hotels and restaurants have all been designed in the same style. The town centre consists of a single street with a post office and a square next to the tourist information office, from where buses depart for Limassol *(see p203)*.

Platres is the starting point for several walking trails, including "Caledonia" that runs from the Psilodendro restaurant, past the Caledonia waterfall and ending at the former residence of the British governor; and "Pouziaris", which leads to a mountain of the same name.

Omodos ⓫

Road map B4. 8 km (5 miles) from Pano Platres. 🚶 310. 🚌 *once a day from Limassol.*

Scattered over the southern slopes of the Troodos mountains are the Krassochoria vine-growing villages, of which Omodos is the capital. Established in the 11th century, the

Courtyard of the Timiou Stavrou Monastery, in Omodos

settlement is famous for its production of wine, as well as for specialized *papilla* lace making.

Timiou Stavrou Monastery (Monastery of the Holy Cross) stands in the centre of the village. Built around 1150, it acquired its present shape in the 19th century. Timber-roofed monastic buildings surround the three-hall basilica, which contains a carved wooden iconostasis dating from 1813. According to legend, St Helena (mother of Emperor Constantine) left here a piece of the rope with which Christ was tied to the cross. The venerated relic is kept in a vast silver cross-shaped reliquary. Another holy relic St Philip's skull, kept in a silver casket.

There are no more monks in the village. The shops and stalls sell local *papilla* lace,

Famous Omodos *papilla* lace

silver jewellery, wine, honey and the ring-shaped *arkatena* bread typical of this village.

Environs
Vasa, a few kilometres west of Omodos, is a pleasant village. The Knights Hospitaller of St John, from the Kolossi commandery, were drawn to the village to escape the unbearable summer heat. The knights stayed in the monastery, which once stood here. Its 14th-century church, **Agios Georgios**, survives to this day together with its interesting frescoes. The small church museum in Vasa has religious icons and liturgical objects rescued from various abandoned churches.

Vasa has pretty white houses with red-tiled roofs and a spring flowing with pure mineral water. The village and the surrounding area offer several good restaurants, where you can get simple Cypriot dishes.

The Cypriot poet Dimitris Lipertis (1866–1937) has associations with Vasa. The house in which he lived has been made into a small museum.

The nearby archaeological site has yielded several Roman tombs, and the artifacts found in them – including amphorae and jewellery – can be viewed in Nicosia at the Cyprus Museum.

KINGDOM OF ALASHIA

For more than 100 years scientists have been searching for the mysterious Kingdom of Alashia. According to texts preserved on clay tablets in el-Amarna, its kings corresponded with the Egyptian pharaohs. Analysis of the texts has established that the copper-rich kingdom was situated at the foot of the Troodos mountains, close to present-day Alassa, where equipment for smelting and processing copper has been discovered.

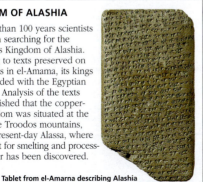
Tablet from el-Amarna describing Alashia

🛈 **Timiou Stavrou Monastery**
Omodos. ☐ *sunrise to sunset daily.*

The Donkey Sanctuary west of Vouni

Potamiou ⑫

Road map B4. 3.5 km (2 miles) south of Omodos.

This backwoods hamlet, reached via Omodos or Kissousa, is on an architectural par with the neighbouring village of Vouni. In summer its red-roofed stone houses vanish from view, swamped by creeping vines. The pride of the village is its small 16th-century church, Agia Marina, and the ruins of a Byzantine church standing near the Khapotami stream.

Vouni ⑬

Road map B4. 4 km (2.5 miles) south of Koilani.

In the mid-1990s this extra-ordinarily picturesque, partly deserted village was declared a legally protected historical site. Turned into an open-air museum, its life now centres around a handful of *kafeneia* (local cafés) and restaurants.

One of the main attractions is the **Vouni Donkey Sanctuary**, to the west of the village, which is run by the charitable foundation "Friends of the Cyprus Donkey". Mary and Patrick Skinner founded the sanctuary in 1994 with just six donkeys; today they care for about 120 elderly, sick and abandoned animals. During the grape-harvest season, strong and healthy animals are hired out to the local farmers to help them collect the grapes. Children visiting the sanctuary can enjoy donkey rides. Membership of the "Friends of the Cyprus Donkey" society is open to all.

🐴 Donkey Sanctuary
Vouni. **Tel** 25 945 488.
⏰ 10am–4pm daily. 📷
www.donkeysanctuarycyprus.org

Koilani ⑭

Road map B4.

Another tiny mountain village built on lime soil, Koilani has excellent conditions for growing grapevines and fruit trees. The scenic location, surrounded by lush vineyards, makes up for its shortage of historic sites.

A small two-room **museum** set up behind the Neo-Byzantine church of Panagia Eloussa houses a collection of icons and other religious objects gathered from old churches in the area. For a period during the 17th century, the Limassol archbishopric was based in Koilani.

Close to the village in the valley of the Kyros stream, on the site of a former monastery, is the 12th-century domed **chapel of Agia Mavra**, which was subsequently extended. Its interior, including the domed vault, is decorated with rather unsophisticated wall paintings.

Men whiling away the afternoon in the centre of Koilani

Lofou ⑮

Road map B4. 26 km (16 miles) northwest of Limassol.

This gorgeous village lies hidden amid the vineyards that cover the hillsides of the Commandaria region. The south-facing slopes and the abundance of water from the nearby Kourris and Kyros rivers produce local grapes that are large and sweet.

Lofou village spreads atop a limestone hill (*lofos* means hill). Its buildings represent the traditional stone-and-timber architecture typical of Cyprus mountain villages.

Towering above the village is the white silhouette of the

THE WINES OF CYPRUS

"The sweetness of your love is like Cyprus wine", wrote Mark Antony, offering Cyprus to Cleopatra as a wedding present. To this day vintage brands, including the sweet Commandaria, are produced on the island and continue to enjoy a good reputation. Many of the best wines are produced in monasteries, based on old recipes. The majority of white wines are of the dry variety; the most widely known are Palomino, White Lady, Aphrodite and Arsinoe. Popular red wines are Othello and Semele. The wines drunk in the north include white and red Kantara varieties.

Wine barrels in Koilani

Church of the Annunciation, with a tall, slender belfry. The present church was built in the late 19th century. Inside, among many beautiful icons, is a 16th-century image of the Mother of God.

References to Lofou appear in records dating from the Lusignan period, when it was called Loffu, but the village is probably much older, existing already in the Byzantine era.

Lofou can be reached from the north, via Pera Pedri village, or by a rough track (suitable only for four-wheel-drive vehicles) from Monagri, to the east.

Environs

The attractions of **Silikou** village, situated further north, include an olive press museum and some interesting examples of 14th-century frescoes in the Timios Stavros church.

Monagri ⑯

Road map B4. 21 km (13 miles) from Limassol.

Rising above the vine-covered hills and the Kouris valley are the walls of the **Archangelos monastery**. Built in the 10th century on the ruins of an ancient temple, the monastery was rebuilt in the mid-18th century after a tragic fire. The monastery church features a number of lovely wall paintings, some of them by Filaretos – the creator of the magnificent paintings adorning the cathedral church of John the Theologian (Agios Ioannis) in Nicosia. There are also reminders of Turkish times, when the new rulers converted the church into a mosque, including the geometric *mihrab* decorations, unique in

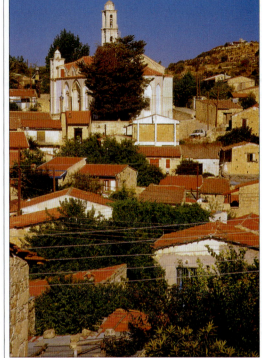

View of the hilltop Lofou village

Cyprus. The two Corinthian columns that support the portico date probably from the Roman era. The church has a carved, painted iconostasis.

Environs

A few kilometres downstream from Monagri, on the west bank of the river, is the 12th-century convent church of **Panagia tis Amasgou**, one of several Byzantine churches in the Kouris valley, near Limassol. It features beautiful but unrestored frescoes, created between the 12th and 16th centuries. These can be viewed, thanks to the generosity of the resident nuns.

The **Kouris dam**, down the river, is one of the largest structures of its kind in Cyprus; the reservoir collects rainwater used for domestic supplies and for irrigating fields and vineyards.

Situated along the main road leading from Limassol to the Troodos mountains is **Trimiklini** village. Hidden behind its church is a charming, tiny old stone chapel in a cemetery.

On the east side of the road, amid vineyards, lies another vine-growing village, **Laneia** (Lania). Its well-preserved and lovingly maintained old houses are set along narrow winding streets. Standing in the village centre is a white church with a tall belfry; next to it are two cafés. Laneia and its surrounding villages are home to local artists.

🛈 **Monastery of Archangelos**
Monagri. *Tel* 25 362 756.
⬤ by prior arrangement.

🛈 **Panagia tis Amasgou**
Tel as above. ⬤ as above.

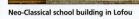

Neo-Classical school building in Lofou

Timios Stavros ⓱

Road map B3. 8 km (5 miles) west of Agros. ⬚ *vary.* **Donations** *welcome.*

The design of Timios Stavros (Holy Cross) church is different from that of other Cypriot churches. Standing on the lakeshore, at the southern end of the village, this three-aisled edifice was built on a square plan and topped with a slender dome on four columns.

Opposite the entrance are the portraits of the church's founders, as well as their coats-of-arms, and the figure of the apostle, Doubting Thomas. The painting to the right depicts the lineage of Jesus. The series of 14 superbly preserved paintings above the pulpit illustrates the life of Mary, including the *Nativity* and the *Presentation of Jesus at the Temple*, with figures dressed in Lusignan period costumes.

The iconostasis includes a silver reliquary containing fragments of the True Cross, for which the church is named.

Fragment of a painting in Timios Stavros Church

Pelendri ⓲

Road map B3. 8 km (5 miles) west of Agros, 32 km (20 miles) from Limassol.

In the Middle Ages, the village of Pelendri, on the southern slopes of the Troodos mountains, was the seat of Jean de Lusignan, son of Hugo V (the Franconian King of Cyprus).

At the centre of the village is the **Panagia Katholiki Church**, dating from the early 16th century, which has Italian-Byzantine-style paintings.

It is worth spending some time visiting the nearby **Tsiakkas Winery**, which produces local wines using traditional methods. The visit must be arranged in advance (*Tel 25 991 080*).

Agios Nikolaos tis Stegis ⓳

Road map B3. 3 km (2 miles) NW of Kakopetria. ⬚ *9am–4pm Tue–Sat, 11am–4pm Sun.* **Donations** *welcome.*

This stone church, built in the form of a cross, supports a double roof, giving it the name, St Nicholas of the Roof. The oldest section of the building dates from the 11th century; the dome and narthex were added a hundred years later, and in the 15th century the entire structure was covered with a huge ridge roof. This outer roof was designed to protect the building from snow, which falls here occasionally.

The church once served as the chapel of a monastery, no longer in existence. Inside, you can see some of the oldest wall paintings anywhere in the Troodos mountain churches. Painted over a period of about 500 years, between the 11th and the 15th centuries, they demonstrate the evolution of Orthodox religious art, making this church an excellent place to study the development of Byzantine wall painting.

Along with paintings from the early Byzantine period, known as "hieratic" or "monastic" styles influenced by the art of Syria and Cappadocia, you can also see typical Komnenos and Paleologos art styles. During the Komnenos dynasty (1081–1180), the Byzantine style, which had been rigid and highly formalized up to that point, began to move towards realism and emotional expression in the figures and in their settings.

The artists who created the wall paintings during the Paleologos dynasty continued to display similar attention to the emotional and aesthetic qualities of their art.

Paintings inside the church illustrate scenes from the New Testament. Among the earliest paintings here are the *Entry to Jerusalem*, and the warrior saints George and Theodore brandishing their panoply of arms. The ceiling of the main vault depicts the **Transfiguration of the Lord** on Mount Tabor and the **Raising of Lazarus** from the dead, conveying the startling

Interior of Timios Stavros Church

◁ **Pedoulas in the Troodos mountains**

impression the events made on the disciples of Jesus and the relatives of Lazarus.

The **Crucifixion** in the north transept shows the Sun and Moon personified weeping over the fate of the dying Jesus. Equally interesting is the painting of the **Resurrection**, in which the women coming to visit the grave are informed of the Lord's resurrection by an angel seated near the empty tomb. The painting dates from the Lusignan period.

The **Nativity** in the south transept vault shows the Virgin Mary breast-feeding the Christ Child. Painted around it is an idyllic scene with pipe-playing shepherds and gambolling animals. Adjacent is a shocking 12th-century painting of the 40 **Martyrs of Sebaste** – Roman soldiers who adopted Christianity and were killed for it – being pushed by soldiers into the freezing waters of an Anatolian lake. In the dome vault is an image of **Christ Pantocrator**.

Agios Nikolaos tis Stegis, featuring magnificent wall paintings

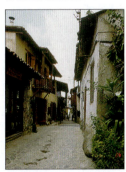

A picturesque narrow street in old Kakopetria

Kakopetria ⑳

Road map B3. 80 km (50 miles) from Nicosia.

This old village in the Solea region, in the valley of the Kargotis River, displays interesting stone architecture. At an elevation of 600 m (1,968 ft), its climate is mild enough to allow the cultivation of grapes. Besides wine, Kakopetria was once renowned for its production of silk. Now it is a weekend retreat for Nicosia residents.

The village derives its name "Accursed Rocks" from the rocks which, during an earthquake, once killed a great number of people.

The surrounding district has several intriguing churches and chapels, including the **Archangelos Church** which dates from 1514, covered with a ridge roof. It is decorated with paintings depicting the life of Jesus. The paintings in the **Agios Georgios church** are influenced by folk tradition.

Panagia tis Podithou ㉑

Road map B3. **Panagia tis Podithou** Galata. ⬜ collect key from café on the village square. **Tel** 22 922 394. **Donations** welcome.

Dating from 1502, this church is also known as Panagia Elousa (Our Lady of Mercy). Originally, it was a monastery church dedicated to St Eleanor. Later, it belonged to the Venetian family of Coro. The wall paintings that decorate the church date from the Venetian period. Created by Simeon Axenti, their style betrays both Byzantine and Italian influences. They are an example of the strong influence that Western art exerted at that time on Cypriot decorative art. The poignant **Crucifixion** is particularly interesting, painted within a triangle and revealing Italian

influences. Mary Magdalene can be seen at the foot of the Cross, her hair loose, alongside a Roman soldier and the two crucified thieves. The **Communion of the Apostles** in the apse is flanked by the figures of two Kings: Solomon and David. The painting in the narthex depicts **Our Lady the Queen of Heaven**; painted below it is the image of the church's founder – Dimitrios Coro – with his wife.

It is worth spending some time visiting the early 16th-century church, **Agios Sozomenos**, with its cycle of folk-style wall paintings created in 1513, also by Simeon Axenti. Take a closer look at the painting depicting St George fighting the dragon, whose tail is entwined around the hind legs of the knight's horse, as well as the image of St Mamas riding a lion while carrying a lamb in his arms. The nearby church of **Agia Paraskevi** features the remains of some 1514 wall paintings, probably created by a disciple of Axenti.

The charming church of Panagia tis Podithou

Fresco in Panagia Forviotissa church

Panagia Forviotissa (Panagia tis Asinou) ㉒

Road map B3. 5 km (3 miles) SW of Nikitari village. **Tel** 99 830 329. ◻ 9:30am–1pm, 2–4pm Mon–Sat, 10am–4pm Sun. **Donations** welcome.

Beyond the village of Nikitari, the road climbing towards the Troodos mountains leads through a dark forest and into a valley overgrown with pine trees. Here, on a wooded hillside, stands the small 12th-century church of Panagia Forviotissa, also known as Panagia tis Asinou. With its red tiled roof, this church dedicated to Our Lady of the Meadows is listed as a UNESCO World Cultural Heritage Site.

The church was founded in 1206 by Nikiforos Maistros, a high-ranking Byzantine official, portrayed on the paintings inside. At first glance the building, with its rough stone walls and simple ridge roof, does not resemble a church. However, this humble one-room structure hides a number of genuine treasures. There are frescoes dating from the 12th to the 16th centuries, which were restored in the 1960s and 1970s.

The wall and ceiling decorations are among the finest examples of Byzantine frescoes, starting with the *Christ Pantocrator* (Ruler of the World) on the vault of the narthex. There are also figures of the apostles, saints, prophets and martyrs. The following frescoes date from 1105: the *Baptism in the Jordan River*, the *Raising of Lazarus*, the *Last Supper*, the *Crucifixion* and the *Resurrection*. They were painted by artists from Constantinople who represented the Komnenos style.

Altogether there are over 100 frescoes here, illustrating various religious themes. It is worth taking a closer look at the extraordinarily realistic painting covering the westernmost recess of the vault – the *Forty Martyrs of Sebaste*. Next to this are the *Pentecost* and the *Raising of Lazarus*.

The cycle of paintings in the nave illustrates the life of Jesus, from the Nativity to the Crucifixion and Resurrection. Seen in the apse is the *Communion of the Apostles*; Jesus offers the Eucharist to his disciples, with Judas standing aside.

The best paintings include the *Dormition of the Virgin*, above the west entrance, and the terrifying vision of the *Last Judgment*. Above the south entrance is a portrait of the founder, Nikiforos Maistros, presenting a model of the church to Christ.

The narthex offers further surprises. The moufflon and two hunting dogs on the arch of the door herald the arrival of the Renaissance; Byzantine iconography did not employ animals. Here, too, is another image of the church founders, praying to the Virgin and Child, with Christ Pantocrator surrounded by the Apostles. Between 1965 and 1976, the frescoes underwent a process of meticulous cleaning and restoration, under supervision by experts on Byzantine art from Harvard University.

Environs
The village of **Vyzakia**, some 6 km (4 miles) down the valley from Panagia Forviotissa, is worth visiting to see the small, wooden-roofed Byzantine **Church of the Archangel Michael** with its frescoes depicting the life and the martyrdom of Jesus. Dating from the early 16th century, these wall paintings reveal a strong Venetian influence.

The little 12th-century church of Panagia Forviotissa

Panagia tou Araka ㉓

Road map C3. Lagoudera. **Tel** 99 557 369. ◻ 9am–noon, 2–5pm daily. **Donations** welcome. 🖼 *Feast of the Birth of the Virgin (6–7 Sep).*

The 12th-century church of Panagia tou Araka stands between the villages of Lagoudera and Saranti. Its interior is decorated with some of the island's most beautiful frescoes, painted in 1192 by Leon Authentou, who arrived from Constantinople and worked in the aristocratic

Panagia tou Araka Church, surrounded by mountains

Christ Pantocrator fresco in the Church of Panagia tou Araka

Komnenos style. This church contains some of the most interesting examples of pure Byzantine art in Cyprus.

The most magnificent of the paintings depicts Christ Pantocrator in a blue robe, surrounded by images of angels and prophets. In the apse are images of 12 early Christian saints, including St Barnabas, the patron saint of Cyprus. Above them is the Virgin Mary enthroned, with the Child Jesus on her knees, flanked by the Archangels Gabriel and Michael.

Relief from Panagia tou Araka

Another interesting fresco is the *Birth*, showing the Infant Jesus being bathed, watched by angels, shepherds, a flock of sheep and a white donkey.

The small, richly carved and gilded iconostasis contains only four icons. On the right is a larger-than-life painting of the Madonna of the Passion (*Panagia Arakiotissa*), to whom the church is dedicated.

Environs
The mountain hamlet of **Spilia** has a splendidly preserved oil press housed in a stone building. In the central square are monuments commemorating the EOKA combatants who fought the British, blowing themselves up in a nearby hideout used to produce bombs. Some 2 km (1.3 miles) to the north of Spilia, in the village of **Kourdali**, is a three-aisle basilica, **Koimisis tis Panagias**, which once belonged to a

former monastery. Inside, the Italian-Byzantine wall paintings depict figures dressed in Venetian clothes. The Virgin, fainting at the foot of the cross, wears a dress with exposed shoulders. Other interesting paintings here include: *Doubting Thomas*, the *Praying Virgin (Virgin Orans)* and the *Dormition of the Blessed Virgin*. The best times to visit are 14–15 August, which are local feast days.

Another site worth visiting is the diminutive **Church of Timiou Stavrou** in **Agia Eirini**, which contains more paintings depicting the life and death of Jesus. It also has a deisis – an image of the Mother of God and John the Baptist sitting on both sides of Christ, who holds in his hand the prophecy pronouncing him the Messiah and adjudicator on the Day of the Last Judgment. An attractive local walk leads along the Madhari ridge to the top of **Mount Adhelfi**, at 1,612 m (5,288 ft). From here there is a stunning panoramic view over the Troodos mountain region.

Stavros tou Agiasmati ㉔

Road map C3. 6 km (3.7 miles) north of Platanistasa. ☐ *vary, collect key from custodian in the coffee shop.* **Donations** *welcome.* ◪ *13 & 14 Sep.*

A rough road leads to this small church, in an isolated setting on the mountainside

of Madhari. Originally built as the chapel for an older monastery, its low main door was designed to prevent Arab and Turkish invaders from entering on horseback, a common way of desecrating churches.

Inside Stavros tou Agiasmati is the island's most complete cycle of paintings illustrating the Gospel. Some parts refer to the Old Testament. Another cycle of paintings illustrates the story of the Holy Cross. Together they form a fine assemblage of 15th-century frescoes.

The church's interior is divided into two horizontal zones of paintings: the lower zone displays life-size figures of the saints while the upper zone has 24 scenes from the New Testament.

Behind the iconostasis, the apse features a magnificent image of the Virgin uniting Heaven and Earth. Some of the paintings depict scenes not known anywhere else, like the fresco of the *Last Supper* in which only Christ is present; or the *Raising of Lazarus* in which a group of Jews is clearly offended by the smell of the resurrected Lazarus. The fresco of *Peter's Denial* includes a shockingly large image of a rooster. One of the niches in the north wall features a series of ten paintings that illustrate the discovery of the Holy Cross by St Helena, the mother of the Emperor Constantine. The frescoes are partly the work of Philip Goul, a Lebanese artist who is characterized by his spare yet profound style.

Standing in the north wall niche is a magnificently decorated cross, which gives Stavros tou Agiasmati (church of the Holy Cross) its name.

Stavros tou Agiasmati church, in its remote mountainside location

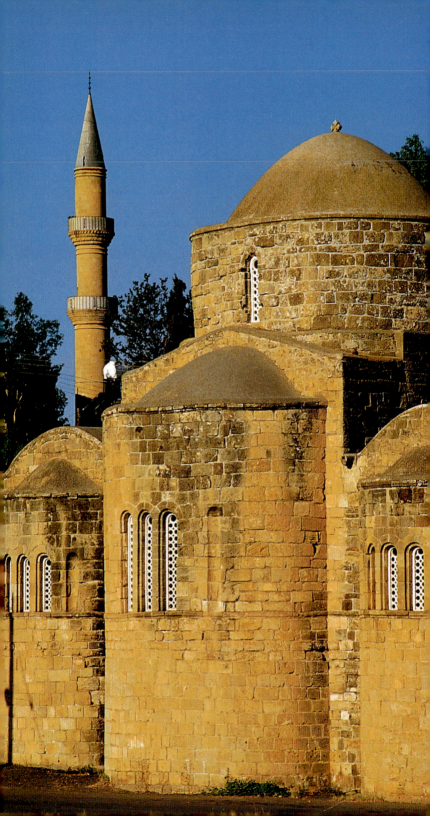

CENTRAL CYPRUS

*W*ith the exception of the divided city of Nicosia, the heartland of Cyprus remains surprisingly unexplored by visitors. The plains are covered with colourful carpets of cultivated fields, crisscrossed by roads that link the small villages. They descend radially towards Nicosia (see pp112–31), whose suburbs sprawl across the Pentadaktylos range. The eastern part of the Troodos mountains – the Pitsillia area – is incorporated in this region.

The vast plain on Mesaoria (meaning "the land between mountains") is a gently undulating area dotted with small towns and old-fashioned villages. The watchtowers and fences occasionally seen from the road are reminders of the "Green Line" – the buffer zone border. The defunct airport to the west of Nicosia once provided international service.

Central Cyprus is the island's least developed region, from a tourist's point of view. It is almost devoid of hotels and restaurants, although here and there you can find a small agrotourism farm or a *kafeneion* – a local café. Tourists usually visit this region on their way to the beautiful Troodos mountains, or to the bustling seaside resorts in the south.

The most interesting historical sites of central Cyprus are the ruins of ancient Tamassos and Idalion. Tamassos, which was established around 4,000 BC, grew rich thanks to the copper ore deposits discovered nearby. Today, items made of this metal are among the most popular souvenirs from this region.

Also of interest are the Convent of Agios Irakleidios, the unusual subterranean Church of Panagia Chrysospiliotissa and Machairas Monastery on the northeastern slopes of the Troodos mountains, in the Pitsillia area. Nearby are the mountain villages of Fikardou, Lazanias and Gourri, and further south the town of Agros, which is famous for its roses.

Roadside vineyard in central Cyprus

◁ The Byzantine Church of St Barnabas and St Hilarion at Peristerona, glowing in the light of the setting sun

Exploring Central Cyprus

Central Cyprus, stretching south of Nicosia and covering the Pitsillia area of the eastern Troodos mountains, has limited facilities for visitors. Nevertheless, when travelling to the Troodos mountains or Nicosia it is worth exploring this region, especially the ruins of ancient Tamassos, the centre of the copper-producing area since the Bronze Age. Peristerona, home to one of the most beautiful Byzantine churches in Cyprus, as well as a fine mosque, is well worth a visit. Life proceeds slowly in the picturesque villages, with their bougainvillea-clad houses.

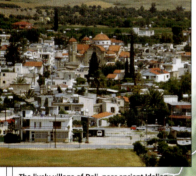

The lively village of Dali, near ancient Idalion

SEE ALSO

- *Where to Stay* p163
- *Where to Eat* p175

GETTING THERE

Central Cyprus is easily accessible. From Larnaka airport the A2 motorway runs inland towards Nicosia. From the main port in Limassol, a motorway follows the coastline and branches off as the A1 road towards Nicosia. The route from Pafos airport leads through the mountains. The road is good, and you can combine the journey with a tour of the Troodos mountains.

Kakopetria

PERISTERONA 1 C † B9 Akaki

Palaiometoc

Orounta Meniko

E906

Agia Marina

Mitsero

Xyliatos Malounta

Klir

E907

E906 E903

Fikardou

Gourri Lazanias

Troodos Platanistasa

Alona

Askas MACHAIRAS 9

AGROS 11 10 PALAICHORI

Pitsillia

Agios Ioannis Agios Theodoros

E110

L E M E S O S Melini

Kalo Chorio

Arakapas Eptagoneia

12 LOUVARAS

Lemesos Forest Kellaki

E110 Prastio

Limassol

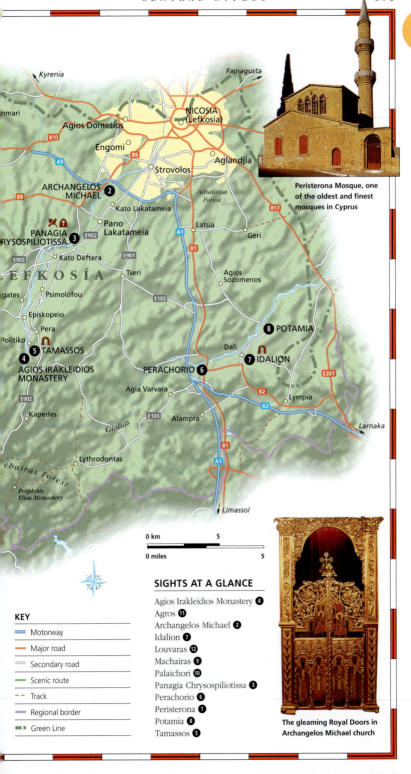

Kyrenia

Famagusta

NICOSIA
(Lefkosia)

Agios Dometios

Engomi

B10

B9

A9

Aglandjia

Strovolos

ARCHANGELOS
MICHAEL ❷

*Athalassa
Forest*

Kato Lakatameia

B17

Pano
Lakatameia

Latsia

B9

PANAGIA
RYSOSPILIOTISSA ❸

E902

A1

Geri

E903

Kato Deftera

E901

B1

EFKOSÍA

Tseri

Agios
Sozomenos

gates

Psimolofou

E102

Episkopeio

Pera

olitiko

TAMASSOS ❺

❹ AGIOS IRAKLEIDIOS
MONASTERY

❽ POTAMIA

Dali

❼ IDALION

PERACHORIO ❻

E201

E902

Agia Varvara

E103

Alampra

Kapedes

Gialias

B2

Lympia

A2

Larnaka

chairas Forest

Lythrodontas

B1

A1

*Prophitis
Elias Monastery*

Limassol

Peristerona Mosque, one
of the oldest and finest
mosques in Cyprus

0 km   5

0 miles   5

SIGHTS AT A GLANCE

KEY

▬▬	Motorway
──	Major road
═══	Secondary road
──	Scenic route
---	Track
──	Regional border
■■■	Green Line

The gleaming Royal Doors in
Archangelos Michael church

Peristerona ❶

Road map C3. 27 km (17 miles) west of Nicosia, along the road to Troodos.

Peristerona is the centre of Cyprus' watermelon-growing district. The village straddles a river that is usually dry, and features the beautiful five-domed **Church of St Barnabas and St Hilarion**, whose tall slender belfry is topped with a cross. This is a prime example of early 10th-century Byzantine architecture. The domes, resting on tall tambours with conical tips, are arranged in the shape of a cross. (A similar five-domed structure, the Agia Paraskevi Church, can be seen near Pafos, in the village of Geroskipou *see p46.*) The proprietor of the neighbouring café holds the key to the church; it is worth gaining entry.

The narthex, which houses a vast chest depicting the siege of a castle, provides a view of the nave, which is separated by arches from the side aisles. The remains of the 16th-century wall paintings illustrate the life of King David, and there is also a vast reading room. The gilded iconostasis, beautifully carved in wood, dates from 1549.

The nearby **mosque**, one of the oldest and most magnificent anywhere on the island, was built on a square floor plan. Its tall, arched tracery-laden windows indicate that this was once a Gothic church. Now the mosque stands empty, with pigeons nesting inside. The proximity of the church belfry and the mosque's minaret are reminders of a time when both

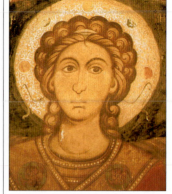

Fresco from the Archangelos Michael church

communities – Greeks and Turks – coexisted peacefully here in the village. Today, Peristerona is inhabited only by Greek Cypriots, while their Turkish Cypriot neighbours have moved north, beyond the demarcation line several kilometres away.

Environs
The Mesaoria plain lies between the Pentadaktylos mountain range to the north and the Troodos massif to the south. The village of Orounta, a few kilometres south of Peristerona, is home to the **Church of Agios Nikolaos**, part of the long deserted monastery here. Similar to other villages scattered on the north slopes of the Troodos mountains, such as Agia Marina, Xyliatos and Vyzakia, this area is home to small mountain churches, as well as numerous taverns and *kafenia* (cafés) where you can savour an original *meze* or relax over a cup of Cyprus coffee.

Archangelos Michael ❷

Road map C3. On the outskirts of south Nicosia.

The Byzantine church of the Archangel Michael on the bank of the Pediaios River was built by Archbishop Nikiforos, whose tomb can be seen in the northern section of the building. It was rebuilt in 1636 and again in 1713, when it was bought by Kykkos Monastery. The austere edifice, constructed from a yellowish stone with small windows and a simple portico, is covered with a shallow white dome resting on a tall tambour.

The church interior has a lovely wooden iconostasis and frescoes depicting, among others, the Archangel Michael. The frescoes are more lively than some of their rivals. Their colours were brightened by restoration in 1980 and include a range of Gospel and Old Testament scenes.

Environs
To the north is a complex of playing fields and a market site; next to these is the church of Panagia Make-donitissa. Nearby is a military cemetery. On the opposite side of the river, at the end of Athalassa Avenue is Athalassa forest, the largest wooded area in the vicinity of Nicosia. It features pine, cedar and eucalyptus trees. There is also a reservoir where permit holders are allowed to fish. All this makes it a pleasant place during high summer.

Panagia Chrysospiliotissa ❸

Road map C3. 12 km (8 miles) southwest of Nicosia.

This rarely visited subterranean church, situated near the village of Kato Deftera, is dedicated to Our Lady of the

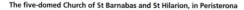

The five-domed Church of St Barnabas and St Hilarion, in Peristerona

Golden Grotto. Originally a series of ancient catacombs, these were converted into a church in the early Christian era. The interior of Panagia Chrysospiliotissa was once covered with beautiful frescoes, which are now severely damaged.

An apse, nave, narthex and a series of vestries are carved in the sandstone. This underground church is considered one of the earliest examples of a Levantine-style Christian monastery. This type of monastery, although rare in Cyprus, was common in the region that covers present-day Israel, Jordan, Lebanon and parts of Syria. On 15 August every year, a festival is held here to celebrate the monastery's name day.

Agios Irakleidios Monastery buildings

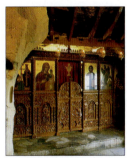
Inside the subterranean Panagia Chrysospiliotissa

Agios Irakleidios Monastery ❹

Road map C3. 20 km (12 miles) SW of Nicosia. *Tel 22 623 950.* ☐ *9am–noon, 3pm–dusk daily (groups only 9am–noon Mon, Tue & Thu).*

St Heracleidius (Agios Irakleidios) Monastery stands close to the ruins of Tamassos. In the mid-1st century, in the course of their activities as missionaries on the island of Cyprus, the apostles Barnabas and Paul appointed a local man, Heracleidius, as the first Bishop of Tamassos. Bishop Heracleidius became famous for his many miracles; he was also a well-known exorcist. At the age of 60 he was killed by pagans and buried at this spot, where a small early Christian church and monastery were built. The monastery church, built in the 5th century, was repeatedly destroyed; the present building was erected in 1759.

Inside is a fresco depicting the baptism of Heracleidius administered by the apostles Paul and Barnabas, as well as beautiful geometric Byzantine mosaics and a monogram of Jesus. Relics of St Heracleidius – including his skull and forearm – are kept in a special silver reliquary.

From the side chapel to the south, a stairway descends to the catacombs, where Heracleidius spent his final years, and where he was buried.

The present buildings date from the late 18th century. The wall paintings of the period depict scenes from the life of St Heracleidius. At that time the monastery was famous for its icons, which were painted here. Now it is inhabited by nuns, who breed canaries and make delicious rose-petal jam and sugar-coated almonds.

Tamassos ❺

Road map C3. 8 km (11 miles) SW of Nicosia. **Excavation site** *Tel 22 622 619.* ☐ *Apr–Oct: 9:30am–5pm daily; Nov–Mar: 8:30am–4pm daily.*

Near the village of Politiko, along the route leading to Machairas Monastery, archaeologists have unearthed the remains of the ancient town of Tamassos, founded by Trakofryges of Asia Minor c.4,000 BC. Around 2,500 BC, rich copper deposits were discovered here, which led to the town's growth and prosperity. Temesa (an alternative name for Tamassos) is mentioned in Homer's *Odyssey*; an excerpt describes Athena's journey to Temesa in order to trade iron for copper.

Later, in about 800 BC, the town was taken over by the Phoenicians. Their King, Atmese of Tamassos, along with other Cypriot Kings, paid tribute to the Assyrian rulers.

Alexander the Great gave the local copper mines as a present to King Protagoras of Salamis, in gratitude for his help during the siege of Tyre. In 12 AD, the Judaean King Herod the Great leased the local copper mines; many Jews arrived on the island to supervise the excavation of this valuable commodity. Archaeological works started in 1890 and continue to this day. The major discoveries are the subterranean royal tombs dating from 650–600 BC, which have long since been looted. Two of them survive in perfect condition. Other discoveries include a citadel, the site of copper processing and the Temple of Aphrodite (or Astarte). Many items discovered here are now in London's British Museum and Nicosia's Cyprus Museum.

Mosaic fragment from Tamassos

Perachorio ❻

Road map C3. 17 km (10.5 miles)
south of Nicosia.

The small village of Perachorio is the setting of the
hilltop **Church of the Holy
Apostles** (Agioi Apostoloi).
This domed, single-aisle building has several side chapels.

The church, in a scenic
setting, conceals fragments of
beautiful 12th-century frescoes,
in a style similar to those in
the Panagia tis Asinou Church
(see p100). Experts regard
these as the best examples of
the Komnenos style anywhere
on the island. The most
interesting are the images of
angels in the dome, below
the damaged painting
depicting Christ Pantocrator.
Another interesting painting
shows two shepherds
conversing casually, their
shoulder bags hanging from a
tree, while the infant Jesus is
bathed. The apse features a
picture of the Virgin, flanked
by St Peter and St Paul. Also
depicted are saints, martyrs,
emperors and demons.

Nearby is the 16th-century
church of Agios Dimitrios.

A stone church in the Potamia area

Church in Perachorio with lovely
12th-century paintings

Idalion ❼

Road map D3. 20 km (12 miles) south
of Nicosia. 🎨 Adonis Festival (spring).

The ancient Idalion, whose
remains can be seen in the
present-day village of Dali, was
one of the oldest city-states
on the island. According to
legend, it was founded by King
Chalcanor, a Trojan War hero.

The town is built on top of
two hills; only a small portion
of its ruins has so far been
unearthed, including tombs
along the road to Larnaka.

Idalion existed from the Bronze
Age up to about 1,400 BC.
The town had 14 temples,
including those dedicated to
Aphrodite, Apollo and Athena.
Archaeological excavations
are still under way. The best
artifacts can be seen in the
Cyprus Museum in Nicosia.

The remains of Idalion had
already sparked interest in the
19th century. The American
consul, Luigi Palma di
Cesnola, plundered thousands
of tombs in this area, robbing
them of all their valuable items.
Local farmers also found large
numbers of votive figurines of
Aphrodite while working in
the fields, which indicates
that this was a major site of
the cult of Aphrodite, the most
important Cypriot goddess.

Legend tells of Aphrodite's
love for Adonis, son of Zeus
and Hera. Ares, the jealous
god of war, turned himself into
a wild boar and killed Adonis
in a nearby forest. Each spring,
millions of red poppies and
anemones cover the area, said
to spring from his blood.

Ruins of the ancient city-state of
Idalion, near present-day Dali

Potamia ❽

Road map D3.

Situated close to the Green
Line, the little village of
Potamia is one of the few
places in the south with a
small Turkish community.
The village has a history of
coexistence and today elects
both a Greek- and a Turkish-
Cypriot mayor.

Not far from the village are
the ruins of the Lusignan
Kings' summer palace, and
several Gothic churches.

Environs
The surrounding area is not
of great interest, due to the
many factories and industrial
estates built in the immediate
vicinity of Nicosia. To the
southwest of the derelict
village of **Agios Sozomenos**
are the ruins of **Agios Mamas
church**, built in the Franco-
Byzantine style. This is one of
the best Gothic historic sites on
the island. Construction began
in the early 15th century, in
the Gothic style which was
prevalent on the island at that
time. However, it was never
completed. Today visitors can
see the walls of the three-
apsed aisles, separated by
intricate arcades, and the
monumental portico.

The village of Agios
Sozomenos was abandoned
early in 1964, when Greek
Cypriot police attacked the
village inhabited by Turkish
Cypriots in retaliation for the
killing of two Greeks. Both
sides suffered severe losses.
The stone wall surrounding
the village stands as a
remainder of these events.

Cypriot Church Frescoes

The shady, forested valleys of the Troodos mountains hide small Byzantine churches; ten of these have been named UNESCO World Cultural Heritage Sites. Along with a few other churches and chapels throughout the island, they conceal frescoes representing some of the most magnificent masterpieces of Byzantine art. In keeping with Orthodox canons, the interior is divided according to theological

Asinou church paintings

order. The dome symbolizes Heaven, presided over by Christ Pantocrator, the Ruler of the World, usually surrounded by archangels and prophets. Below are the main scenes from the New Testament, including the saints and fathers of the Church. The apse behind the altar features an image of the Virgin with Child. The portico usually contains the Last Judgment, painted above the exit.

Christ Pantocrator
Often painted within the dome, the Omnipotent King of the World looks down from heaven. His right hand is raised in a gesture of benediction; his left hand holds a book as a symbol of the Law.

The Life of Jesus and Mary
The life of the Holy Family has been depicted in many frescoes, as illustrations of the New Testament.

Agios Mamas
Mamas is one of the most celebrated and popular of all Cypriot saints. His name has been given to many churches throughout the island.

The Praying Virgin (Virgin Orans)
Mary raises her hand towards heaven in a pleading gesture. Her eyes are turned towards the people, urging them to trust in Christ.

The 40 Martyrs of Sebaste
In the early days of Christianity, many followers suffered death for their faith. These men, despite being subjected to freezing temperatures and then fire, held to their faith and were martyred.

The Way of the Cross
The images of the way of the cross and the Lord's Passion are among the most dramatic subjects for fresco painters.

Machairas Monastery

Road map C3. Near Deftera, 41 km (25 miles) SW of Nicosia.
◻ 8:30am–5:30pm daily (groups only 9am–noon Mon, Tue & Thu).

On the northern slopes of the Troodos mountains, in the area known as Pitsillia, stands one of Cyprus's most famous monasteries – Machairas (Panagia tou Machaira). The monastery rises like a fortress from the mountainside of Kionia, almost 800 m (2,625 ft) above sea level. Its name originates from the word *mahera*, which means 'knife' and probably derives from the knife found next to an icon hidden in a cave. The locals believe that the icon, brought here by a monk from Constantinople, was painted by the Apostle Luke. Two hermits from Palestine found the icon in a cave, and then built a church dedicated to the Virgin Mary in 1148. In 1187, Emperor Manuel Komnenos provided the funds to build a bigger church; he also exempted it from the jurisdiction of the local bishop.

The monastery buildings in their present form date from the early 20th century. The beautiful church, surrounded by cloisters, houses the icon attributed to St Luke, which depicts the Holy Virgin pierced with a sword. It also contains numerous other beautiful and well-preserved icons and cult objects. The Gospel, printed in Venice in 1588, is held in the treasury.

The monks are extremely pious; their vows are as severe as those taken by the brothers from Mount Athos in Greece.

For Cypriots, this place is associated with EOKA commander, Grigorios Afxentiou, who hid here disguised as a monk. British soldiers ambushed him in a nearby bunker. His comrades surrendered, but Afxentiou chose to fight and resisted the attacks of 60 British soldiers for several hours. Only flamethrowers could put an end to this heroic battle. On the spot where Afxentiou fell now stands a larger-than-life statue depicting the hero.

View of Palaichori village

Environs

Beyond the village of Lythrodontas, where the paved road ends, is a small monastery dedicated to the Prophet Elijah (Prophitis Elias), hidden in the Machairas Forest.

Palaichori

Road map C3.

The village of Palaichori lies in a deep valley, near the source of the Peristerona river. The village and the surrounding area feature several churches and chapels, but the most interesting of these is the **Metamorfosis tou Sotiros chapel**. Erected in the early 16th century, this small church is decorated with frescoes. On the south wall is the scene that gives the chapel its name. It shows a luminous figure of Christ, with prophets and disciples, atop Tabor Mountain at the time of the Transfiguration.

Lions are the predominant motif of the remaining paintings: in the den with Daniel, preparing to bury the body of St Mary the Beatified of Egypt and finally, St Mamas riding a particularly elongated predator.

Environs
The three picturesque villages of **Fikardou**, **Gourri** and **Lazanias** at the eastern end of the Pitsillia area form a legally protected conservation zone, due to their unique traditional architecture. The largest number of typical folk buildings have survived in Fikardou, which now looks more like an open-air museum than a village. The village has been declared a monument of national culture, being the best example of rural architecture from the past few centuries. It has narrow alleys paved with stone, and neat little timber houses, two-storeys high, with wooden balconies.

Courtyard of the Machairas Monastery

For hotels and restaurants in this region see p163 and p175

The old houses of Katsinioros and Achilleas Dimitri, which are some of the loveliest in the village, have been turned into a **Rural Museum** with a collection of tools and period furnishings. They include a loom, distillery equipment and an olive press.

🏛 **Rural Museum**
Fikardou. *Tel 22 634 731*. ☐ 9am–5pm daily (Nov–Mar: 8am–4pm). ☒

Agros ⓫

Road map C3.

Agros is a large village lying at an altitude about 1,000 m (3,280 ft) above sea level, in the picturesque Pitsillia area. The village is famous for its delicious cold meats, particularly its sausages and hams, as well as its fruit preserves and products made of rose petals. The locally cultivated Damask rose is said to have been brought here by the father of Chris Tsolakis, in 1948. Chris now owns a small factory of rose products, making rose water, liqueur, rose wine, rose-petal jam and rose-scented candles. Rose petals are harvested between late May and early June.

The charms of Agros and its environs are promoted enthusiastically by Lefkos Christodoulu who runs the largest local hotel – Rodon. His efforts have resulted in the creation of numerous walking trails. The neighbourhood is home to several Byzantine churches decorated with frescoes. Agros itself has no historic sites. The old monastery, which stood here until 1894, was pulled down by the villagers in a dispute with the local bishop. Agros boasts an excellent climate, reputedly good for a long lifespan.

Interior of the chapel of St Mamas, Louvaras, with frescoes of Jesus' life

Louvaras ⓬

Road map C4. 25 km (15.5 miles) north of Limassol.

Louvaras is a small village situated among the hills. The local attraction is the **Chapel of St Mamas**, decorated with exquisite late 15th-century frescoes depicting scenes

Detail of a colourful fresco from St Mamas Chapel

from the life of Jesus. They include the Teaching in the Temple, Meeting with the Samaritan Woman at the Well, and the Resurrection, in which the guards wear medieval suits of armour. The figures above the door, dressed in Lusignan clothes, are likely to represent the original donors.

St Mamas is one of the most popular Cypriot saints. He is portrayed on the north wall riding a lion while cradling a lamb in his arms. The scene is associated with an interesting legend. Mamas, a hermit, was ordered to pay taxes by the local governor. He refused to do so, claiming to live solely from alms. The governor lost patience and ordered Mamas to be thrown in jail. As the guards led Mamas away, a lion leapt from the bushes and attacked a lamb grazing peacefully nearby. The saint commanded the lion to stop, took the lamb into his arms and continued his journey on the back of the chastened lion. Seeing this miracle, the governor freed St Mamas, who became the patron saint of tax-evaders.

The village of Agros, scenically located among the hills

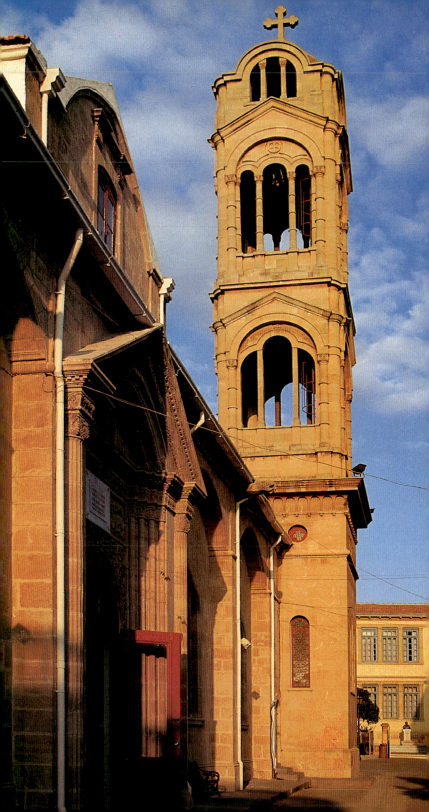

SOUTH NICOSIA

Near the centre of the island, Nicosia (Lefkosia in Greek) is Europe's only divided capital city. The numerous historic sites and traditional atmosphere of South Nicosia have been carefully preserved. The Old Town lies within an imposing defence wall erected by the Venetians in the 16th century. In the evenings, the narrow streets fill with strolling crowds of Cypriots and tourists alike who come to dine and socialize in the pedestrianized Laiki Geitonia district.

Nicosia is the business and financial centre of the Republic of Cyprus, as well as its seat of government, home to the president. It is composed of three districts: the Old Town, the modern city, and the sprawling suburbs where most families live, extending beyond the city far into the Mesaoria valley.

The charming Old Town, with its narrow, one-way streets, is surrounded by a Venetian wall stretching for 4.5 km (2.8 miles). The wall is punctuated by 11 bastions and three gates. The Porta Giuliana (Famagusta Gate) houses a Cultural Centre. Visitors heading for the border foot-crossing to Turkish-controlled North Nicosia (near the Ledra Palace Hotel) are greeted by the grim Pafos Gate, near the demarcation line. Crossing the border is much easier these days thanks to the partial lifting of restrictions.

The Laiki Geitonia district, east of Eleftheria Square (Plateia Eleftherias), has narrow, winding alleys filled with restaurants, art galleries and boutiques set between traditional houses, typical of Cypriot urban architecture. Ledra Street is a prestigious pedestrian precinct with smart boutiques and garden restaurants. One of the crossings to North Cyprus is located here. At the heart of Nicosia stands the Archbishop's Palace.

South Nicosia has a range of museums to visit, including the wonderful Cyprus Museum.

Shop-front in one of the bustling streets of Laiki Geitonia

◁ The church of Panagia Faneromeni at sunset

Exploring South Nicosia

The majority of historical sites in Nicosia are found within the mighty town walls. The main attractions, not to be missed, are the Cyprus Museum, the Archbishop's Palace and St John's Cathedral. The latter contains pristine 18th-century frescoes on Biblical themes. The Cyprus Museum holds the island's largest collection of archaeological artifacts, gathered from many sites. The restored district of Laiki Geitonia makes a pleasant place to rest with its numerous cafés, as well as providing good shopping in the local stores. The Cyprus Tourism Organization also offers free tours of the capital *(see p121)*.

5th-century BC figurine from the Cyprus Museum

KEY

▓	Street-by-Street map *See pp116–17*
🅿	Parking
ℹ	Tourist information
⊠	Post office
🚕	Taxi rank
✝	Church
☪	Mosque
🚓	Police
▬▬	City wall
▬▬	Pedestrianized street

Church along the border of South Nicosia

For additional map symbols *see back flap*

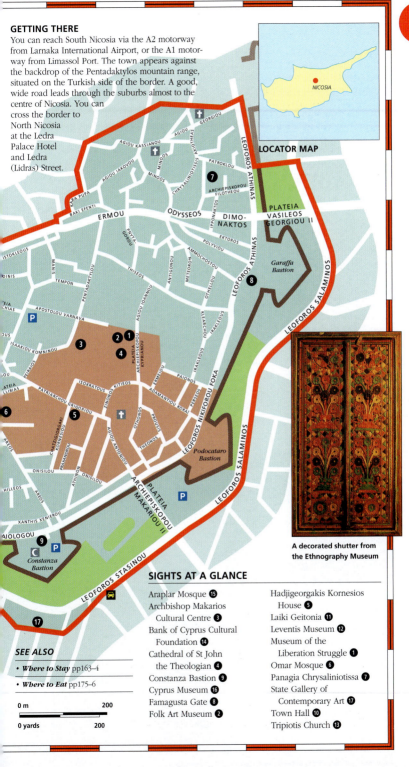

GETTING THERE

You can reach South Nicosia via the A2 motorway from Larnaka International Airport, or the A1 motorway from Limassol Port. The town appears against the backdrop of the Pentadaktylos mountain range, situated on the Turkish side of the border. A good, wide road leads through the suburbs almost to the centre of Nicosia. You can cross the border to North Nicosia at the Ledra Palace Hotel and Ledra (Lidras) Street.

LOCATOR MAP

NICOSIA

A decorated shutter from the Ethnography Museum

SIGHTS AT A GLANCE

Araplar Mosque ⑮
Archbishop Makarios
  Cultural Centre ③
Bank of Cyprus Cultural
  Foundation ⑭
Cathedral of St John
  the Theologian ④
Constanza Bastion ⑨
Cyprus Museum ⑯
Famagusta Gate ⑧
Folk Art Museum ②

Hadjigeorgakis Kornesios
  House ⑤
Laiki Geitonia ⑪
Leventis Museum ⑫
Museum of the
  Liberation Struggle ①
Omar Mosque ⑥
Panagia Chrysaliniotissa ⑦
State Gallery of
  Contemporary Art ⑰
Town Hall ⑩
Tripiotis Church ⑬

SEE ALSO

- *Where to Stay* pp163–4
- *Where to Eat* pp175–6

0 m		200

0 yards		200

Street-by-Street: South Nicosia

South Nicosia is surrounded by Venetian defence walls and bastions, and has served as the capital since the 11th century. During the Lusignan era, this was a magnificent city, home of the Royal Palace and scores of churches. Today the area within the old walls is full of museums, sacred buildings and historical buildings, which help to recreate the atmosphere of bygone centuries. It is enjoyable to stroll along the streets of old Nicosia, stopping for coffee, or taking a shopping trip to the rebuilt district of Laiki Geitonia. The only drawback is the neglected zone of no man's land dividing the city.

★ **Archbishop Makarios Cultural Centre**
The island's largest, most precious collection of magnificent icons and mosaics are housed here ❸

Richly decorated
19th-century houses are the pride of the southern part of the Old Town.

← Laiki Geitonia

The Archbishop's Palace was built in 1956–60 in Neo-Byzantine style.

Omar Mosque
A former Augustinian church was converted into a mosque in 1571, following the capture of the city by Turks. It is the largest mosque in southern Cyprus ❻

Hadjigeorgakis Kornesios House
This historic 18th-century building, a former home of the Turkish dragoman, was awarded the Europa Nostra Prize following its restoration. Now it houses a small Ethnological Museum ❺

Folk Art Museum

The highlight here is the collection of 19th- and early 20th-century Cypriot folk art. The textiles, ceramics, wooden artifacts and folk costumes are housed in a former Bishop's Palace ❷

LOCATOR MAP
See pp114–15.

Museum of the Liberation Struggle

Here are documents, photographs and weapons associated with the Greek struggle for independence from 1855 to 1959 ❶

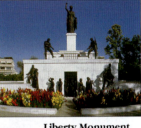

Liberty Monument

on the Podocataro Bastion symbolizes the liberation of the Cypriot nation.

Map street names:
AGIOU IOANNOU
PLATEIA ARCHIEPISKOPOU KYPRIANOU
ERMEIOU
ADAMANTOU KORAI
IRAKLEOUS
PERSEOS
PROUSIS
THEONOS
ELENIS PALEOLOGIS
LEOFOROS NIKIFOROU FOKA
OTHONOS
EOS

★ Cathedral of St John the Theologian

Erected by Archbishop Nikiforos, this small church contains beautiful 18th-century frescoes ❹

STAR SIGHTS

★ Archbishop Makarios Cultural Centre

★ Cathedral of St John the Theologian

KEY

 Suggested route

Museum of the Liberation Struggle **❶**

Plateia Archiepiskopou Kyprianou. *Tel* 22 305 878. 🕒 8am–2pm Mon–Fri (3–5:30pm Wed). 📷

Housed in a building just behind the Old Archbishop's Palace is the Museum of the Liberation Struggle. Its collection of photographs, documents, weapons and other objects chronicles the bloody struggle of the EOKA organization against the colonial British army from 1955 to 1959. The exhibits illustrate the guerrilla warfare tactics carried out by EOKA against the British and those Cypriots who objected to the armed struggle.

The collection also includes materials documenting British reprisals, including arrests, interrogations and torture. The museum is primarily intended for Cypriots and school groups.

The Folk Art Museum, housed in the old Archbishop's Palace

Folk Art Museum **❷**

Plateia Achiepiskopou Kyprianou. *Tel* 22 430 008. 🕒 8:30am–3pm Mon–Fri (to 5:30pm Wed & Sat). 📷

Behind the cathedral is the Old Archbishop's Palace, which now houses the Folk Art Museum. On display here is a diverse array of exhibits illustrating the culture of Cyprus. Outside, the main museum attractions are the wooden water wheel, olive presses and carriages. Inside are folk costumes dating from the 19th and 20th centuries,

Museum of the Liberation Struggle

household furnishings and other domestic implements, ceramics, textiles, Lefkara laces and silver jewellery.

Archbishop Makarios Cultural Centre **❸**

Plateia Achiepiskopou Kyprianou. **Byzantine Museum** *Tel* 22 430 008. 🕒 9am–4:30pm Mon–Fri, 9am–1pm Sat. 🔴 Sat pm in Aug. 📷 **www**.makariosfoundation.org.cy

This cultural centre, adjacent to the New Archbishop's Palace, houses several libraries, the School of Ecclesiastical Music and the Byzantine Museum, which was founded by Archbishop Makarios in 1982.

Also known as the Icon Museum, the Byzantine Museum contains the largest and most valuable collection of icons in Cyprus. Around 230 icons span the 8th to the 19th centuries. Through the exhibition you can follow the changing trends in the art of icon "writing", and see the idiosyncratic images of Jesus, the Virgin Mary, the saints and the apostles. The best exhibits include the 13th-century icon by the main door, portraying the Prophet Elijah being fed by a raven, and the image of the Virgin holding the dead body of Christ – the equivalent of the Roman Catholic *Pieta*.

The reconstructed apse was rescued from the church of

Crown exhibit from the Byzantine Museum

Agios Nikolaos tis Stegis in the Troodos mountains.

For several years the museum has displayed 6th-century Byzantine mosaics stolen during the 1970s from Panagia Kanakaria Church in Lythrangomi in the Turkish-occupied Karpasia peninsula. Following a lengthy court battle, the Cypriot government recovered the mosaics. They include the Virgin Mary, the archangels Michael and Gabriel, and several apostles. The figure of Jesus, depicted in one of the mosaics clutching a scroll of parchment, has the appearance of a Hellenic god. All of the figures have unnaturally large eyes, a characteristic trait of early-Christian art.

In addition to mosaics and icons, the museum's collection includes ecclesiastical garments and books.

The New Archbishop's Palace was erected in 1956–60 in the Neo-Byzantine style to a design by Greek architect George Nomikos. Usually closed to visitors, it does open occasionally, when you can visit the bedroom of Archbishop Makarios, where his heart is kept. A giant statue of Makarios, the first president of the Republic of Cyprus, stands in front of the palace. It was produced by London-based Cypriot sculptor, Nicos Kotziamanis.

Near the Makarios Cultural Centre, located in a former power plant, is the Municipal Arts Centre, a venue for major art exhibitions.

Cathedral of St John the Theologian ④

Plateia Achiepiskopou Kyprianou. **Tel** *22 432 578.* 🔲 *8am–noon, 2–4pm Mon–Fri, 8am–noon Sat.*

The small Cathedral of St John (Agios Ioannis) dates from 1662. Built of yellow stone and covered with a barrel vault, it stands on the ruins of a medieval Benedictine monastery. Its interior is decorated with magnificent paintings depicting Biblical scenes from the life of Jesus, from birth to crucifixion, including a striking Last Judgment above the entrance.

The four paintings on the right wall, next to the Archbishop's throne, show the discovery of the relics of the apostle Barnabas, founder of the Cypriot church. They also show the privileges granted by Byzantine Emperor Zeno to the Cypriot church, including *autokefalia* (independence from the Patriarch of Constantinople) and the right of the Archbishop to wear purple garments during ceremonies, to use the sceptre instead of the crosier, and to sign letters with red ink. The paintings tightly covering the walls and ceiling are by the 18th-century artist, Filaretos.

Among the furnishings are a fine carved and gilded iconostasis, and a pulpit with its double-headed eagle, a symbol of Byzantium.

To the right, by the door leading to the courtyard, stands a small marble bust of Archbishop Kyprianos, who

A fragment of the decoration in the Hadjigeorgakis Kornesios House

was hanged by the Turks in 1821 in retaliation for the outbreak of Greek national insurgence. Kyprianos founded the first secondary school in Cyprus. The Pancyprian Gymnasium, regarded as the most prestigious high school in the Greek part of the island, exists to this day. Its Neo-Greek building is on the opposite side of the street.

Hadjigeorgakis Kornesios House ⑤

Ethnological Museum Patriarchou Grigoriou 20. **Tel** *22 305 316.* 🔲 *8:30am–3:30pm Tue–Fri (to 5pm Wed), 9:30am–3:30pm Sat.* 📷

One of the town's most interesting buildings is the House of Hadjigeorgakis Kornesios, a well-preserved building from the late 18th century. Kornesios, a highly educated Greek Cypriot businessman and philanthropist, served from 1779 as a dragoman – a liaison between the Turkish government and the Greek Cypriot population. Despite serving

the Turks for a number of years, he was arrested and executed by them.

The opulent house is decorated with Anatolian-style columns and lattice-work. The bedroom and Turkish-style drawing room lined with carpets occupy the first floor. The ground floor contains servants' quarters and a *hammam* – Turkish bath. Part of the house holds a small ethnological exhibition.

Kornesios Patriarchou Grigoriou Street leads to the nearby Omar Mosque.

Omar Mosque (Ömeriye Cami) ⑥

Trikoupi and Plateia Tyllirias. 🔲 *daily, except during services.* **Donations** welcome.

This mosque takes its name from Caliph Omar, who supposedly reached Nicosia in the course of the 7th-century Arab raids on Cyprus.

The site now occupied by this mosque was once home to a 14th-century church, which served the local Augustine monastery. The Church of St Mary drew pilgrims in great numbers from Cyprus and throughout Europe to visit the tomb of the Cypriot saint John de Montfort, a member of the Knights Templar.

The church was converted into a mosque after the town was captured by the Turks, led by Lala Mustapha Pasha, in the 16th century. On the floor of the mosque are Gothic tombstones, used by the Turks as building material.

The mosque is used by resident Muslims from Arab countries. It is open to visitors; please remove your shoes before entering. It is also possible to climb to the top of the minaret, from where there are lovely views of Nicosia.

Minaret of the Omar Mosque

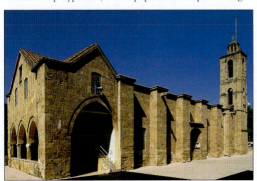

The small, yellow-stone Cathedral of St John the Theologian

Chrysaliniotissa Church, renowned for its collection of icons

Panagia Chrysaliniotissa ❼

Chrysaliniotissas.

The Chrysaliniotissa church, the capital's oldest house of worship, is dedicated to Our Lady of the Golden Flax. It stands at the centre of the district bearing the same name, right on the Green Line. It was built in c.1450 by Helen, the Greek-born wife of the Frankish King John II. The church takes its name from a miraculous icon found in a field of flax.

This L-shape building, with two domes and a slender belfry, is famous for its collection of rare Byzantine icons.

Located nearby at Dimonaktos 2 is the small **Chrysaliniotissa Crafts Centre**. Various types of Cypriot art and handicrafts can be seen and purchased in this small crafts centre. Eight workshops, a café and a souvenir shop surround the central courtyard, which is modelled on a traditional inn.

Prior to the division of Nicosia the opposite side of Ermou Street, called Tahtakale Cami after the mosque that stood here, was home to many Turkish Cypriots. Based on the Nicosia Master Plan, the old houses are being renovated and new occupants are moving in. Thanks to the founding of the Municipal Cultural Centre in Famagusta Gate, the district is becoming more attractive.

Famagusta Gate ❽

Leoforos Athinon. **Tel** 22 430 877.
⬜ 10am–1pm, 4–7pm Mon–Fri, 4–7pm Sat & Sun.

One of three city gates, Famagusta Gate is situated in the Caraffa bastion of the Venetian defence walls. Low-built and comprising a log tunnel ending at a wooden gate, it resembles the Venetian gate from Iraklion, on Crete. The side facing town is decorated with six Venetian coats-of-arms.

The structure was thoroughly renovated in the 1980s. Now it houses the **Municipal Cultural Centre**. The main room is used for exhibitions, concerts and theatrical performances. The smaller side room is devoted to art exhibitions. Thanks to the Cultural Centre, this part of town has been transformed into a pleasant artists' district.

Chrysaliniotissa church detail

Environs
The medieval Venetian defence walls are the most distinctive element of old Nicosia. They were erected during 1567–70 to a design by Italian architect Giulio Savorgnano. The present-day Famagusta Gate was originally called the Porta Giuliana, in honour of the architect.

The 5-km- (3-mile-) long Venetian walls contain 11 artillery bastions and three gates – the other two are called the Pafos and Kyrenia Gates, after the towns they face.

The defence walls fit in well with Nicosia's overall appearance. The bastions and the areas between them have been converted into car parks and market squares. The d'Avila bastion, near the Plateia Elefteria (Eleftheria Square), is the site of the town hall and the municipal library. The Podocataro bastion features the Liberty Monument, which depicts the goddess of Liberty clad in ancient robes, while two EOKA soldiers at her feet open prison bars from which a group of Cypriots emerges.

Costanza Bastion ❾

Leoforos Konstantinou Palaiologou.
🚌 Wed. Bayraktar Mosque closed to visitors.

One of the 11 bastions protruding from the Venetian walls encircling the old quarter of Nicosia, Costanza Bastion is the site of the Bayraktar mosque, which was erected to commemorate the Turkish soldier, who was killed as he scaled the defence wall during the siege of Nicosia.

Every Wednesday, the area in front of the mosque turns into a colourful fruit and vegetable market.

Famagusta Gate, housing Nicosia's Municipal Cultural Centre

Entrance to the town hall building, resting on Ionian columns

Town Hall ❿

Plateia Eleftheria (Eleftheria Square).

Built in the Classical Greek style, the single-storey town hall stands on the d'Avila bastion, next to the municipal library. An ornamental semicircular stairway leads to the portal, which rests on Ionian columns. **Plateia Eleftheria** (Eleftheria Square) opposite the town hall, is where Nicosians gather for public rallies.

Eleftheria Square is the starting point for the two main shopping streets of old Nicosia: **Onasagorou** and **Ledra**. Both are lined with dozens of shops selling shoes, clothes, textiles and souvenirs.

At the end of Ledra Street, whose name evokes the ancient town that once stood on the site of present-day Nicosia, is a barricade alongside the buffer zone, with a monument to those Greek Cypriots who disappeared during the Turkish invasion. There is also a small museum here.

Laiki Geitonia ⓫

The pedestrianized Laiki Geitonia (Popular Neighbourhood) is a restored section of Old Nicosia near the brooding Venetian defence walls, the town hall and Ledra – South Nicosia's main shopping street. Clustered within a small area of narrow, winding alleys in prettily restored houses are numerous restaurants, shady cafés, handicraft workshops and souvenir shops aimed primarily at tourists. Here you will also find tourist information offices, offering free maps and brochures.

The project to rebuild and restore the Laiki Geitonia district was honoured with the prestigious Golden Apple ("Pomme d'Or") Award, granted by the World Federation of Journalists and Travel Writers in 1988. The district has an inviting atmosphere, well suited to relaxing or a leisurely stroll.

Guided tours around South Nicosia start from outside the Cyprus Tourist Organization office located at 35 Odos Aristokyprou, in the Laiki Geitonia district. It is worth joining one of these tours, as they take visitors to many interesting sites that are normally closed to tourists.

Leventis Museum ⓬

Ippokratous 17, Laiki Geitonia. **Tel** 22 661 475. ◯ 10am–4:30pm Tue–Sun.

The fascinating Leventis Museum houses a collection devoted to the history of Nicosia, from ancient times to the 1970s.

Its creators have succeeded in putting together an intriguing exhibition showing the everyday life of Nicosia's residents. Visitors are particularly drawn to the exhibits relating to the times of the Franks and the Venetians, including medieval manuscripts and the opulent clothes of the city's rulers. Also of note are the documents and photographs dating from the colonial era.

The restored building which houses the museum was built in 1885 by a rich merchant for his daughter.

An exhibit from the Leventis Museum

Environs

The pedestrianized Ledra Street, which is full of shops, can be reached by walking along the Green Line. The military checkpoint here houses a small exhibition devoted to the island's northern territories, occupied by the Turks. Here, you can peer at the Turkish side through peepholes in the concrete barricade, and also take photographs (photography at the other checkpoints is prohibited).

Inside a souvenir shop in Laiki Geitonia

Tripiotis Church ⑬

Odos Solonos. ⏰ *9am–5pm daily.*

Dedicated to the Archangel
Gabriel, Tripiotis Church is
the loveliest of the surviving
Gothic churches in south
Nicosia. This three-aisle,
square edifice topped with a
small dome was built in 1695
by Archbishop Germanos.
Designed in the Franco-
Byzantine style, it has a rich
and interesting interior with
Gothic windows, while the
exterior has a medieval
stone relief depicting lions,
mermaids and sea monsters.
The pride of the church is its
intricately carved iconostasis,
which contains several old
icons covered with silver
revetments. The church takes
its name from the district of
Nicosia in which it stands.
This was an area that was
once inhabited by very
wealthy families.

View of the three-aisled Tripiotis Church

Bank of Cyprus Cultural Foundation ⑭

Phaneromeni 86–90. **Tel** 22 677
134. ⏰ *10am–7pm Mon–Sun.*
www.boccf.org

One of Cyprus's most
prominent private art
collections, the George
and Nefeli Giabra Pierides
collection, is housed here.
The Cultural Founda-
tion is an institution
that sponsors scientific
research and conducts
educational and cultural
activities. The magnifi-
cent exhibits represent
works from the early
Bronze Age (2,500
BC) to the end of the
Middle Ages, and are
superbly displayed
and illuminated in
modern cabinets.
The exhibits, number-
ing over 600 items,
include ancient bronze
and gold jewellery and
Mycenaean amphorae
and goblets. Also on
display are terracotta
figurines, anthropo-
morphic red-polished

Jug, Bank of
Cyprus Cultural
Foundation

vases and realistic limestone
Hellenic statues depicting,
among others, Apollo and
Hercules. Glazed ceramics
dating from the Middle Ages
can also be seen.

Close to the Bank of Cyprus
Cultural Foundation stands
the **Agia Faneromeni church**,
the largest church within the
city walls, built in 1872 on the
site of a former Greek Orthodox monastery. *Faneromeni*
in Greek means "found
through revelation". The
church was built towards the
end of Turkish rule on the
island. Inside is a beautiful
iconostas and a marble mausoleum containing the remains
of the bishops and Greek
priests who were murdered
by the Turks in 1821.

Adjacent to the church is
the imposing Neo-Classical
building of the **Faneromeni
High School**.

Araplar Mosque ⑮

Odos Lefkonos.

Standing close to
the Agia Faneromeni
church, the Araplar
Mosque was founded
in the converted
16th-century Stavros
tou Missirikou Church,
which had been
designed in the
Gothic-Byzantine style.

Although the
mosque is usually
closed, it is sometimes
possible to peek

inside and see its imposing
interior with the octagonal-
drummed dome supported
on columned arches.

Cyprus Museum ⑯

Leoforos Mouseiou 1. **Tel** 22 865
864. ⏰ *8am–4pm Tue, Wed & Fri,
8am–5pm Thu, 9am–4pm Sat,
10am–1pm Sun.* 📷

The island's largest and
best archaeological museum
occupies a late 19th-century
Neo-Classical building. The 12
or so rooms house a range of
exhibits illustrating the history
of Cyprus, from the Neolithic
Era (7,000 BC) to the end of
Roman rule (395 AD).

The museum is arranged in
chronological order. **Room 1**
displays the oldest traces of
mankind's presence on the
island. There are objects from
the mid-5th century BC, as
well as objects from Khirokitia,
stone bowls, primitive human
and animal figures carved in
andesite, limestone idols, and
jewellery made of shells and
cornelian (which would have
been imported to Cyprus).
There are also early ceramics,
both without decoration
and with simple geometric
patterns, Bronze Age amulets
and cross-shaped figurines
carved in soft, grey steatite.

Room 2 contains clay bowls
and vessels of sometimes
bizarre shapes, decorated
with figurines of animals.
Here you will find a miniature
model of a temple and a
collection of ceramic vessels
and figurines. **Room 3** houses

a collection of ceramics up to Roman times, including lovely Mycenaean vases and craters dating from the 15th century BC. Later, the ceramics became gradually more Greek in style. There is also a collection of several thousand terracotta figurines depicting smiling gods.

Room 4 holds a collection of terracotta votive figurines found in the Agis Eirini sanctuary near the Kormakitis peninsula, in the north of the island. The most interesting exhibits in the sculpture gallery, in **Room 5**, include the statue of Zeus, the God of Thunder, hurling a lightning-bolt. Also here is a stone head of Aphrodite, the famous marble statue of Aphrodite of Soloi dating from the 1st century AD (by this time under Turkish occupation), and an exquisite Sleeping Eros.

Room 6 features a larger-than-life bronze statue of the Emperor Septimius Severus (c.193-211), a masterpiece of Roman sculpture. The adjoining rooms contain a bronze statue of a Horned God from Enkomi at the eastern end of the island, as well as interesting collections of coins, jewellery, seals and other small artifacts. There are also sarcophagi, inscriptions, alabaster vases and the mosaic of Leda with the Swan found in Palea Pafos (**Room 7a**).

Further rooms contain reconstructed ancient tombs, as well as numerous items found during excavations in the Salamis area, including the marble statue of Apollo with a lyre. **Room 11** contains

a reconstructed royal tomb from Salamis with the famous bronze cauldron decorated with griffon and heads of sphinxes that was found inside. **Room 12** houses items found in the Royal Tombs, including a throne decorated with ivory and a silver-encrusted sword. Other interesting exhibits include a collection of silver and gold Byzantine vessels – part of the Lambousa Treasure.

The **Municipal Garden**, on the opposite side of the street, is a green oasis set in the town centre, providing welcome shade on hot days. It is the site of the **municipal theatre** built in 1967. With an auditorium for 1,200, it is used as a venue for drama performances, concerts, recitals and other cultural events. A short distance away, in Leoforos Nehrou, stands the **Cyprus Parliament** building.

Adjacent to the nearby Pafos Gate, right by the demarcation line that divides the city, stands the Roman Catholic **Church of the Holy Cross** and the **Apostolic Nunciature**. A short distance away, by the hotel, is a UN-controlled border crossing, linking the two parts of the town. The **Ledra Palace Hotel** is the headquarters of the UN Peacekeeping Forces in Cyprus.

State Gallery of Contemporary Art

Corner of Gonia Leoforos Stasinou and Kritis. **Tel** 22 458 228.
🕐 10am–4:45pm Mon–Fri, 10am–12:45pm Sat.

This gallery occupies a splendid building situated beyond the wall, level with the Constanza Bastion. It displays a representative collection of the best works by Cypriot artists, dating from 1930–80.

When entering Nicosia from the south you will come across the **Cyprus Handicraft Centre**, situated in Athalassa Avenue, in a building adjacent to St Barnabas Church. Here you can see the production of traditional Cypriot handicrafts, including embroidery, lace, wood-carvings, ceramics, metal-work, mosaics, the making of leather and textile goods and traditional costumes. The centre was established in order to cultivate the tradition of artistic handicrafts in Cyprus, and give employment to refugees from the occupied territories. Visitors may watch artists at work and buy their products in the local shop.

Bronze statue of Septimius Severus, the Cyprus Museum

Environs
In the suburban district of Strovolos, 2.5 km (1.5 miles) southwest of the Old Town, stands the **Presidential Palace**. It is located in an extensive park, with only its dome visible from the street. Built by the British, the palace was destroyed by fire during the riot of 1931. Rebuilt by the British Governor, Sir Ronald Storrs, it became his official residence. The first president of the independent Republic of Cyprus, Archbishop Makarios, had his office here and lived in the Archbishop's Palace in Old Nicosia.

Neo-Classical façade of the Cyprus Museum

NORTH CYPRUS

Inhabited and governed by the Turks, and isolated from the southern Greek side of the island for over 30 years, North Cyprus is probably the most beautiful region of the entire island. The sandy beaches along Famagusta Bay and the wild Karpasia (Karpas) peninsula attract thousands of tourists, although there are still far fewer here than in southern Cyprus. The heart of the region is North Nicosia, home to over one third of the population of North Cyprus.

Most hotels and facilities can be found on the northern side of the Pentadaktylos mountains, whose rugged peaks contrast with the azure of the sea. Kyrenia (Girne) has a charming yacht harbour, one of the most attractive in the Mediterranean, with a vast, old castle recalling the time the island was under Byzantine rule. Nearby, on the northern slopes of the Pentadaktylos range (Beßparmak), lies the most beautiful village in Cyprus – Bellapais, with the romantic ruins of a Gothic abbey. Nearby St Hilarion Castle is one of three fortresses in North Cyprus, alongside the castles of Buffavento and Kantara.

The western plains, in the vicinity of Morfou (Güzelyurt), are planted with citrus orchards. Wedged between the mountains and the blue sea are the archaeological excavation sites of Soli and ruins of the Persian Palace, located on top of Vouni Hill.

Numerous fascinating relics from the Lusignan, Venetian and Ottoman eras are enclosed by the Venetian walls of north Nicosia. Old Famagusta, full of Gothic remains, is equally interesting, with its Othello's Tower and several fascinating historic relics close by – including ancient Salamis (the island's first capital), as well as Enkomi, and St Barnabas monastery.

Nature lovers will be enchanted by the Karpasia peninsula, inhabited by tortoises and feral donkeys and boasting nearly 60 species of orchid.

A fruit and vegetable stall in Belediye Bazaar, in North Nicosia

◁ A view through the Gothic Bellapais Abbey

Exploring North Cyprus

Previously, this region was fairly inaccessible, but is now visited by increasing numbers of tourists. The largest choice of hotels can be found in the regions of Kyrenia and Famagusta. North Nicosia (Lefkoşa) has only two hotels recommended by the local Ministry of Tourism. The area has good main roads, and is best explored by car. Nicosia, the world's only divided capital, is full of medieval churches, caravansarais and museums. The same can be said of Famagusta, whose old town, enclosed by a ring of Venetian walls, has a unique atmosphere. Nature lovers will be drawn to the wild Karpasia peninsula, while those interested in architecture should travel to the Kyrenia mountains, with its medieval castles and Bellapais Abbey.

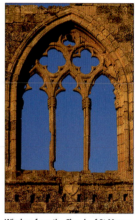

Window from the Church of St Mary of Carmel Mountain, in Famagusta

CAPE KORMAKITIS (KORUÇAM BURNU) 22
Sadrazamköy
KORMAKITIS (KORUÇAM) 21
Akdeniz
Myrtou
LAPITHOS (LAPTA) 19
LAPITHOU (KOZAN) 20
LARNAKA TIS
Morfou Bay
Syrianochori
VOUNI (VUNI SARAYI) 26
SOLOI (SOLI HARABELERI) 25
Gemikonagi
Prastio
MORFOU (GÜZELYURT) 23
Fyllia
Katokopia
LEFKA (LEFKE) 24
Petra
Kakopetria
Kontemenos
Skylloura
Gerolakkos
Kato Dikomon
Kioneli
LAMBOUSA (LAMBUSA) 18
Karman
ST HILARION CASTLE 16
BUFFAVENTO CASTLE 14
KYRENIA (GİRNE) 17
BELLAPAIS 15
Esentepe
ANTIFONI MONASTE
Kythrea
Trachoni
Marathovounc
Mia Milia
Palaikythron
NORTH NICOSIA (LEFKOŞA) 1
Tymvou
Askeia
Pyogi
Tremetousia

0 km   20
0 miles   20

Apostolos Varnavas Monastery, built near the tomb of St Barnabas

KEY

—	Major road
═	Secondary road
—	Scenic route
- -	Track
■ ■	Green Line

GETTING THERE

There are no direct flights to Ercan (Tymbou) Airport from anywhere but Turkey, and ferries sail only from Turkish ports. These include a twice-daily service from Tasucu, a three-times-a-week sailing from Mersin and a catamaran ferry from Alanya (summer only). EU passport holders may cross from the south of the island to the north via the pedestrians-only Ledra Palace crossing point or via one of three vehicle crossing points (at Agios Dometios, Pergamos and Strovilia). North Cyprus is best explored by car but you will need to take out inexpensive special insurance if using a car rented in the South.

The picturesque harbour of Kyrenia

The view from St Hilarion Castle

SEE ALSO

• *Where to Stay* pp164–5

• *Where to Eat* pp176–7

SIGHTS AT A GLANCE

North Nicosia (Lefkoşa) ❶

Atatürk

Following the invasion by Turkish troops in 1974, the northern part of Nicosia became the capital of the Turkish part of the island. It is home to over half the population of North Cyprus, as well as the seat of government. It is also the administrative, business, banking and commercial centre of North Cyprus. The majority of local historic relics are found within the old Venetian walls – Gothic churches turned into mosques, bazaars, Ottoman fountains, baths and caravansarais stand among the often ugly residential buildings.

Exploring North Nicosia

The Old Town is best explored on foot. At the bus station you can board a free bus that will take you to the centre of old Lefkoşa. Do not take photographs in the vicinity of the "Green Line" that divides the city, guarded by UN and Turkish troops.

The roof terrace of the Saray Hotel in Atatürk Square (Atatürk Meydani) provides a great view. The best place for coffee and rest is the former caravanserai, Büyük Han.

🏛 Büyük Han

Asma Alti Sokagi. ◷ 8am–7pm Mon–Fri; 8am–4pm Sat (to midnight Tue, Wed & Fri).

The Big Inn, a former caravanserai, is one of the most interesting Ottoman buildings on Cyprus. The Turks built it shortly after the capture of Nicosia in 1572, as an inn for visiting merchants. Its architectural style is redolent of other inns of that period, seen in Anatolia. Under British administration, it became Nicosia's main prison.

Following its restoration, the 68 former rooms spread

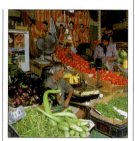

Colourful fruit and vegetable stalls in Belediy Ekpazari bazaar

around the inner courtyard now house souvenir shops, art galleries, cafés and a wine-bar. The courtyard itself features an octagonal building of a small Muslim shrine and prayer hall *(mescit)* with an ablution fountain. Büyük Han is used for theatrical performances, concerts and exhibitions.

The nearby Ottoman "Gamblers' Inn" (Kumarcilar Han), in Asma Alti Square, was built in the late 17th century. Its entrance hall features two Gothic arches, since the inn was built on the ruins of a former monastery. Now it houses the North Cyprus centre for the conservation of historic sites.

🛒 Belediye Ekpazari

◷ 7am–5pm Mon–Fri, 7am–2pm Sat.

This covered bazaar, situated between the Bedesten and the "Green Line" that bisects old Nicosia, was the main shopping area in Ottoman times. It remains a market, where you can buy fresh meat and vegetables, as well as Turkish sweets and souvenirs. Hanging by the exit from the bazaar, on the wall of one of the houses, a plaque marks the centre of the Old Town.

🏛 Bedesten

By the Selima Mosque.
🚫 for restoration.

This 12th-century Byzantine Church of St George was remodelled in the 1300s in the Gothic style by the Lusignan kings. After the 16th-century occupation of Nicosia by the Turks, it was used as a warehouse, and subsequently as a market for selling jewellery and precious metal objects. The word *bedesten* means "lockable bazaar". The north wall has an original Gothic portal, a variety of carved stonework elements and the escutcheons of the Venetian nobility.

Selima Mosque, the former Gothic Cathedral Church of St Sophia

🄲 Selima Mosque (Selimiye Cami)

At the centre of the old town, in Arasta Sokagi. ◷ 24 hours daily.

The former Cathedral Church of St Sophia (the Divine Wisdom), erected by the Lusignan kings from 1208 to 1326, is the oldest and finest example of Gothic architecture in Cyprus. It was once regarded as the most magnificent Christian sacred building in the Middle East. Its unique features include the entrance portal, stone-carved window and massive columns that support the criss-cross vaulting.

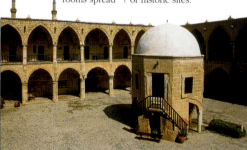

Büyük Han, a former caravanserai with a Muslim shrine in the courtyard

For hotels and restaurants in this region see pp164–5 and pp176–7

It was in this church that the Frankish rulers were crowned kings of Cyprus. This ceremony preceded a second, purely nominal, coronation as Kings of Jerusalem, performed in St Nicholas's Cathedral, in Famagusta.

The cathedral was destroyed, in turn, by the Genoese, the Mamelukes and several major earthquakes. Following the capture of Nicosia by the Turks in 1570, the cathedral was transformed into Hagia Sophia mosque, which, in 1954, was renamed Selima Mosque (Cami Selimiye).

All images of people and animals have been removed, and the Gothic stone sculptures in the main portal have been chipped away. The interior has been stripped of all ornamentation and painted white. Two 50-m (164-ft) tall minarets, entirely out of keeping with the rest of the building, have been added on the sides of the main façade.

Other adaptations made to the interior include the addition of three *mihrabs* indicating the direction of Mecca, and carpets.

🏛 Sultan Mahmut II Library

Kirilzade Sokagi. ☐ *9am–1pm, 2–4:45pm (9am–2pm in summer).* 🕮

This small domed, stone building is a classic example of

Shield above entrance to Lapidary Museum

Ottoman architecture. It was erected in 1829 by Turkish governor, Al Ruchi. It holds a collection of 1,700 books and manuscripts, richly ornamented copies of the Koran and exquisite works of Turkish and Persian calligraphers.

🏛 Lapidary Museum

Kirilzade Sokagi. ☐ *9am–1pm, 2–4:45pm (9am–2pm in summer).*

The 15th-century Venetian building at the rear of the Selima Mosque, near Sultam Mahmut II Library, houses a collection of stone sculptures removed from Gothic tombs, old houses and churches.

The garden includes a Lusignan royal sarcophagus, fragments of columns, stone rosettes and Venetian winged lions of St Mark.

🅒 Haydarpaşa Mosque

Haydarpasa Sokagi. ⬤ *to the public.*

This building was originally St Catherine's Church, erected by the Lusignans in the 14th century in flamboyant Gothic

VISITORS' CHECKLIST

Road map D3. 🏠 40,000. 🛈 *Kyrenia Gate, 0392 822 21 45.* 🚌 *Kemal Asik (next to Atatürk Cad).* ✈ *Ercan, 20 km (12 miles) southeast of North Nicosia. The border crossing to South Nicosia is by the Ledra Palace Hotel.*

style. Their coats of arms can be seen on the south portal in magnificently carved stone.

Following the occupation of Nicosia, the Turks converted the beautiful church into Camii Haydarpaşa (Haydarpaşa Mosque), adding a disproportionate minaret. Today it houses a modern art gallery.

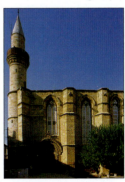

Haydarpaşa Mosque, originally the Gothic church of St Catherine

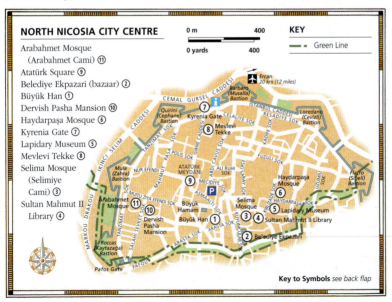

NORTH NICOSIA CITY CENTRE

Arabahmet Mosque (Arabahmet Cami) ⑪
Atatürk Square ⑨
Belediye Ekpazari (bazaar) ②
Büyük Han ①
Dervish Pasha Mansion ⑩
Haydarpaşa Mosque ⑥
Kyrenia Gate ⑦
Lapidary Museum ⑤
Mevlevi Tekke ⑧
Selima Mosque (Selimiye Cami) ③
Sultan Mahmut II Library ④

0 m   400
0 yards   400

KEY

— — Green Line

Key to Symbols *see back flap*

♛ Venetian Walls

Construction of the Venetian defence walls that encircle the Old Town of Nicosia was completed in 1567, three years before the Turkish invasion. Of the 11 bastions in the walls, five are now in the northern, Turkish sector. The **Quirini** (Cephane) bastion is now the official residence of the president of the Republic of North Cyprus. The **Barbaro** (Musalla) bastion houses the National Struggle Museum set up by the army. The **Roccas** (Kaytazağa) bastion is now a park. The other two in the Turkish sector are **Mula** (Zahra) and **Loredano** (Cevizli). A sixth bastion – **Flatro** – is split across the "Green Line" between the Greek and Turkish Cypriots.

Also on the north side is the **Kyrenia Gate**, one of the three original gates leading to the Venetian fortress.

At this point, the "no man's land" close to the Pafos Gate is at its narrowest; a mere few metres separate the Greeks strolling along the street from the Turks on the bastion.

♛ Kyrenia Gate

Girne Caddesi, by Inönü Meydani.
The Kyrenia Gate between the Quirini and Barbaro bastions was once the main entrance to north Nicosia. It was originally named Porta del Proveditore, in honour of the Venetian engineer who supervised the fortification works. The gate walls bear inscriptions dating from the Venetian and Ottoman eras. The Turks erected the square, domed building above the gate

Figures of Whirling Dervishes in Mevlevi Tekke

in 1812. The street on either side of the gate was laid out in 1931 by the British, who took down part of the Venetian wall. Today, Kyrenia Gate houses a tourist information office.

Between the gate and the Atatürk monument are two huge iron cannons; several more have been placed along the walls. Although badly corroded, some of them still display British insignia. The cannons were cast in the late 18th century and used during the Napoleonic Wars.

☪ Mevlevi Tekke

Girne Caddesi. ◯ 9am–
1pm, 2–4:45pm (9am–2pm in summer). 🖼
Less than 100 m (328 ft) south of Kyrenia Gate is the entrance to this small museum. It is housed in the former Muslim monastery (*tekke*) of the Mevlevi order (the Whirling Dervishes) that existed here until the middle of the 20th century. A kind of monastic brotherhood, it was founded in 13th century in Konya by the poet Celaleddin Rumi, later known as Mevlana and revered as one of Islam's greatest mystics. Dervishes whirl to the music of a reed flute, a Levantine lute and a drum. To them, the dance represents the spiritual search

A tombstone from Mevlevi Tekke

for Divine Love, and provides a means of inducing ecstasy that frees human beings from all suffering and fear.

The museum includes figures of Whirling Dervishes accompanied by an instrumental trio sitting in the gallery. The display cabinets contain musical instruments, traditional costumes, small metal objects (such as knives), embroidery, photographs, illuminated copies of the Koran and other Turkish mementoes. The adjacent hall features a replica of a dervish's living quarters. Next to this is a mausoleum with sarcophagi covered with green cloth, containing the bodies of 15 religious leaders, including the last leader of the order, Selim Dede, who died in 1953. In the courtyard are several tombstones from a former cemetery that occupied this site.

☪ Büyük Hamam

Irfanbey Sokagi 9. ◯ 9am–1pm,
2–4:45pm (9am–2pm in summer).
🖼 for a bath.
This 14th-century building was originally the Church of St George. After capturing the town, the Turks converted it into baths. Steep stairs lead down through a Gothic portal to the large hall, and from there to the bathing rooms.

The baths are open to the public; you can also treat yourself to a Turkish massage. Visitors are charged higher prices than the locals.

The northernmost Kyrenia Gate

🏛 Atatürk Square (Saray Square)

Atatürk Meydani, also known as Sarajönü, was the political centre of Cyprus for many centuries. On the north side of the square stood a palace inhabited, in turn, by the Frankish, Venetian and Turkish rulers, or their commissioners. In 1904, the British dismantled the 700-year-old palace complex, with its splendid throne room, opulent staterooms and cloistered courtyard.

Atatürk Square is the main square of Turkish Nicosia. The grey granite column at its centre was brought here from Salamis by the Venetians. In Venetian times, the column bore the Lion of St Mark, while its base was decorated with the coats-of-arms of the Venetian nobility. The Turks overturned the column; the British raised it again in 1915 and added a globe in place of the lion.

The northern end of the square features a stone platform with the British national emblem, erected here in 1953 to commemorate the coronation of Queen Elizabeth II.

Nearby are the courts of law, police headquarters, numerous banks and a post office, which was built by the British.

Atatürk Meydani, the main square in the Turkish zone of Nicosia

The Dervish Pasha Mansion

🏛 Dervish Pasha Mansion

Belig Paşa Sokagi. ⏰ 9am–1pm, 2–4:45pm (9am–7pm in summer). 📷

This two-storey building, typical of early 19th-century Turkish architecture, was owned by Dervish Pasha, the publisher of Cyprus's first Turkish newspaper, *Zaman* (meaning "Time"). Archival copies of the paper, published since 1891, can be seen among the other exhibits here.

Following its restoration, the building has been turned into an ethnographic museum, where you can see a panelled and carpet-lined drawing room, dining room, bedroom, and even a bridal room. The exhibits include embroidery, jewellery, hookahs, lamps, ceramics and copperware.

The ground floor, intended as servants' quarters, is built of stone, while the upper floor, which was occupied by the owner, is built of brick.

🏛 Arabahmet District

Stretching southwest of Kyrenia Gate (Girne Caddesi), the Arabahmet district is full of imposing Ottoman houses, restored partly with funding from the European Union. At the junction of Zahra and Tanzimat, close to the Mula bastion, is an octagonal Ottoman fountain, somewhat neglected today.

Until 1963, this district was home to residents from a variety of countries, including Greece and Armenia. There was even an Armenian church dedicated to the Virgin Mary, which was originally a Benedictine monastery. Nowadays the church stands in the closed military zone.

The **Holy Cross Church**, straddling the border, has an entrance from the Greek side. Its tower, topped with a cross, dominates the entire Arabahmet district.

The **Roccas bastion** (Kaytazaga), which overlooks the "Green Line", was turned into a municipal garden in the 1990s. This is the only place in Nicosia where the buffer zone vanishes and the inhabitants of both sides of divided Nicosia can see each other. Photography, as is to be expected, is prohibited.

🏛 Arabahmet Mosque (Arabahmet Cami)

Salahi Sevket Sokagi.

Standing at the centre of the Arabahmet district is the Arabahmet Cami, covered with a vast dome. Built in the early 17th century on the site of a former Lusignan church, it was remodelled in 1845. The mosque was named after the Turkish military commander, Arab Ahmet Pasha.

The floor is paved with medieval tombstones taken from the church that formerly stood on this site. In the courtyard is a fountain and several tombs, including that of Kemal Pasha, Grand Vizier of the Ottoman Empire. The mosque holds a relic – a hair believed to come from the beard of the Prophet Mohammed – that is shown to the faithful once a year.

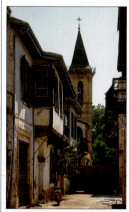

The Arabahmet district with its traditional Ottoman houses

Lysi (Akdoğan) ❷

Road map D3. 12 km (7.5 miles)
southwest of Dörtyol (Prastio).

A small farming village in
the southeastern part of the
Mesaoria plain, Lysi lies close
to the "Green Line". Its most
interesting historic site is the
unfinished Byzantine-style
church decorated with Neo-
Gothic architectural elements.

Environs
Along the road to Ercan
airport are the remains of
Ottoman aqueducts. The
surrounding area is home to
several neglected Orthodox
churches, including Agios
Themonianos, Agios Synesios,
Agios Andronikos and Moni
Agiou Spyridona monastery in
Erdemli (Tremetousha). The
latter is guarded, and visitors
should not approach it.

**The unfinished Neo-Byzantine
church in Lysi**

Enkomi-Alasia ❸

Road map E3. 🕐 Jun–Oct:
9am–2pm daily; Nov–May:
9am–1pm, 2–4:45pm daily. 🖾

Remains of a Bronze Age
town have been found near
the village of Enkomi-Alasia.
Archaeologists estimate that
Alasia was founded in the
18th century BC. The town
grew rich on trading in
copper, which was excavated
on the island and exported to
Anatolia, Syria and Egypt.
Alasia was the capital of
Cyprus and its main town –
its name synonymous with
the entire island. In the
12th century BC, when the
Mycenaeans arrived here, the

**Ruins near the village of Enkomi, a
few kilometres west of Salamis**

town's population numbered
an impressive 15,000. Following an earthquake in the
11th century BC, the town
was deserted and its inhabitants moved to Salamis.
Excavation works conducted
since 1896 have unearthed
the ruins of a Late Bronze
Age settlement, with low
houses lining narrow streets.
The Alasia ruins yielded a
tablet with Cypriot-Minoan
writing, not yet deciphered,
and the famous bronze statue
of the Horned God, dating
from the 12th century BC,
which is now kept in the
Cyprus Museum in Nicosia.
Strolling around the excavation site you will come across
the Horned God's sanctuary
and the "House of Bronzes",
where many bronze objects
were discovered.

Environs
Along the road to Famagusta
is the village of Enkomi
(Tuzla). Next to the shop is
a white platform, known as
the **cenotaph of Nikokreon**.
It contains the remains of
Nikokreon – the last King of
Salamis. Refusing to surrender
to the Hellenic king of Egypt,
Ptolemy I, Nikokreon

committed suicide by setting
fire to the royal palace. He
perished, along with his entire
family, in the flames that day.

Royal Tombs ❹

Road map E3. 🕐 9am–1pm,
2–4:45pm (9am–7pm in summer). 🖾

The royal necropolis by the
side of the road leading to
St Barnabas monastery has
over 100 tombs from the 8th
and 7th centuries BC. Some
have been given names, and
others designated numbers.
Almost all of the tombs are
opened to the east. Each one
was approached by a slanting
corridor known as a *dromos*,
on which the most interesting
artifacts were found.
Most of the tombs were
looted in antiquity, but some,
in particular numbers 47 and
49, contained a multitude of
objects that could be useful
to the royals in the next
world. The most famous finds
include the ivory inlaid royal
bed and throne, showing
clear Phoenician and Egyptian
influences. The Kings of
Salamis were buried with
their servants and horses.
Tomb number 50, the so-
called "St Catherine's prison",
was built during Roman
times on top of older tombs.
According to legend, the
Alexandrian saint, a native of
Salamis, was imprisoned by
her father, the Roman governor, for refusing to marry the
man chosen by him. The
tomb's walls bear the remnants
of Christian decorations.
The site also features a
small museum with plans and
photographs of the tombs,
and a reconstructed chariot
used to carry the kings of
Salamis on their final journey.

Royal Tombs from the 8th and 7th centuries BC, west of Salamis

St Barnabas Monastery, built near the tomb of the apostle Barnabas

St Barnabas Monastery ❺

Road map E3. ◯ *9am–1pm, 2–4:45pm (9am–7pm in summer).* 🈺

The monastery of St Barnabas was erected in 477 on the western end of the Constantia (Salamis) necropolis, near the spot where the apostle's grave was discovered. The construction of the church and monastery was financed by the Byzantine Emperor Zeno himself.

Two centuries later, it was demolished in one of the devastating Arab raids on Cyprus. All that remains of the original Byzantine edifice are the foundations. The present church and monastery were constructed in 1756 on the orders of Archbishop Philotheos, during Ottoman rule. The three-aisled church is covered with two flat domes resting on high drums. It now houses an **Icon Museum**.

Much more interesting, however, is the small **Archaeological Museum** occupying former monks' cells around the courtyard of the monastery. Displayed in a series of rooms are Neolithic tools and stone vessels, as well as a large number of ceramic items such as amphorae, jugs, vases and cups. Among the more curious items are a polished

A terracotta figurine, Archaeological Museum

bronze mirror, swords, hatchets and spearheads, made of the same metal. There are also terracotta figurines of people and animals, including an unusual horse with wheels instead of hooves, and clay baby rattles shaped like boars.

Other interesting exhibits are the black-glazed ceramics imported from Attica. These are decorated with intricate motifs of animal and human figures, including lions, wild boars and hares. There is also gold jewellery, a collection of Roman glass, and a stone figure of a woman holding a poppy – probably the goddess Demeter. The Classical period is further represented by sphinxes, showing the Egyptian influence, and carved lions.

A short distance east of the monastery stands a small **Byzantine-style church**. This rectangular, domed chapel was erected over the tomb of the apostle Barnabas. A stone staircase leads down to two chambers hewn into the rock where, according to legend, St Barnabas was buried. The saint was killed near Salamis for preaching Christianity, and his body was cast into the sea. His disciples fished the body out, and he was buried with St Matthew's gospel on his chest, under a lonely breadfruit tree to the west of Salamis.

From 1971 until the Turkish occupation of 1974, the St Barnabas Monastery was inhabited by the last three monks, the brothers Barnabas, Chariton and Stephen, who made a humble living by selling honey and painting icons.

SAINT BARNABAS

Born in Salamis, Barnabas accompanied St Paul on his missionary travels around Cyprus and Asia Minor. After parting from his master, Barnabas continued to promote Christianity on the island, for which he was killed in the year 57 AD. St Mark buried the body in secret.

St Barnabas acquired fame following a miracle that occurred after his death, when he revealed the site of his burial to Anthemios, the Bishop of Salamis. The discovery of the saint's relics, and the prestige they brought, helped preserve the autonomy of the Cypriot Church.

The tomb of St Barnabas

Salamis ⑥

Gymnasium Statue

The former Roman Salamis, which later became Byzantine Constantia, was the island's main port and capital for a thousand years. Destroyed by the Arabs in 648, Salamis is still the largest and the most interesting archaeological excavation site on Cyprus. The unearthed relics date from the Roman and Byzantine periods. Allow a full day for a visit, including a relaxing break on the nearby beach.

★ Caldarium
The hot bath chamber, fitted with a central heating system, had walls decorated with abstract mosaics.

Sudatorium
The Greek-Roman baths complex included a steam bath, which was also decorated with mosaics. An underfloor heating system is in evidence.

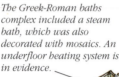

Latrines
This semicircular colonnaded structure contained a latrine which could be used by 44 people simultaneously.

Two pools with cold water were located beyond the east portico.

★ Gymnasium
A colonnade surrounded the rectangular palaestra of the gymnasium, which was devoted to the training of athletes.

STAR SIGHTS
★ Gymnasium
★ Caldarium
★ Roman Theatre

For hotels and restaurants in this region see pp164–5 and pp176–7

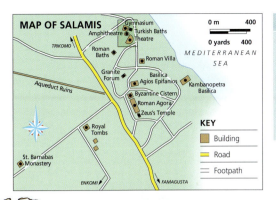

MAP OF SALAMIS

Gymnasium
Turkish Baths
Amphitheatre
Theatre
TRIKOMO
Roman Baths
Roman Villa
Granite Forum
Aqueduct Ruins
Basilica
Agios Epifanios
Kambanopetra Basilica
Byzantine Cistern
Roman Agora
Zeus's Temple
Royal Tombs
St. Barnabas Monastery
ENKOMI
FAMAGUSTA

MEDITERRANEAN SEA

0 m   400
0 yards   400

KEY

- Building
- Road
- Footpath

VISITORS' CHECKLIST

Road map E3. 8 km (5 miles) N of Famagusta. *0392 366 2864*. **Archaeological site** winter: 9am–1pm & 2–4:45pm; summer: 9am–7pm. **Necropolis** 1 km (0.6 mile) W of Salamis. **Tel** *0392 378 83 31.* winter: 9am–1pm & 2–4:45pm; summer: 9am–7pm.

Aqueduct
To the east of the gymnasium are the stone cisterns and other remains of an aqueduct that used to supply the baths and the pools with water.

★ Roman Theatre
Built 2,000 years ago, during the reign of Emperor Augustus, this auditorium could hold 15,000 spectators. Today the restored theatre serves as a venue for summer performances.

Amphitheatre
Built by the Romans in the early years of the modern era, it was destroyed by an earthquake in the 6th century.

Backstage area, with dressing rooms for the actors.

Famagusta (Ammochostos/ Gazimağusa) ❼

Atatürk monument

Once the world's wealthiest city, present-day Famagusta (Ammochostos in Greek and Gazimağusa in Turkish) presents a somewhat depressing sight. Yet within the mighty fortifications that kept out the Turkish army for nearly a year, and amid the many derelict buildings, are true gems of Gothic architecture. Former magnificent churches have been destroyed or turned into mosques. South of the city lies deserted Varosha, once Cyprus's biggest resort.

Namik Kemal Square, once the site of the Venetian Palace

Exploring Famagusta

Virtually all of Famagusta's major historic sites are found within the Old Town, surrounded by the Venetian fortifications. The best way to enter the city is through the Land Gate, leaving your car behind. The tourist information office is located by the gate. The city is not large; it is possible to explore it on foot.

🇨 Lala Mustafa Pasha Mosque

Namik Kemal Meydoni.
⬜ 24 hours daily.
This former cathedral was built between 1298 and 1312 to a Gothic design modelled on the Reims cathedral in France. It was here that Lusignan royalty, after the coronation in Nicosia, received the symbolic title of "King of Jerusalem".

Following the capture of the city in 1571, the victorious Turks converted the cathedral into a mosque and named it after the commander of the besieging army – Lala Mustafa Pasha. They also added a minaret to the left tower. The building is still a functioning mosque; visitors are admitted only outside the hours of prayer with the purchase of a ticket.

The white interior has 12 columns to support the Gothic vaulting. There is a modest *minbar* (pulpit) in the right aisle. The façade with its unusual window and enormous rosette, basking in the light of the setting sun, is one of the most beautiful sights in Cyprus.

🔒 Agia Zoni & Agios Nikolaos

Hisar Yolou Sokagi.
This small, excellently preserved Byzantine-style church, decorated with wall paintings, dates from about the 15th century.

Gothic portal of Lala Mustafa Pasha Mosque

It stands in an empty square, surrounded by a handful of palm trees. Close by is the larger Church of St Nicholas, now partly demolished.

🏛 Fountain and Jafar Pasha Baths

Naim Effendi Sokagi.
Located northwest of Namik Kemal Square, the fountain and baths were built in 1601 in the Ottoman style by the Commander of the Sultan's Navy and the Turkish Governor of Cyprus.

Jafar Pasha ordered the building of the aqueduct in order to supply the city with water. Both the aqueduct and the original town fountain have been destroyed. The current fountain has been reconstructed using fragments salvaged from the original.

🇨 Sinan Pasha Mosque

Abdullah Paşa Sokagi. ⬛ to visitors.
The former church of Saints Peter and Paul was turned into a mosque after the capture of the city by the Turks. This beautiful Gothic edifice, built of yellow stone and maintained in excellent condition, now houses the municipal library collection.

A former church turned into the Sinan Pasha Mosque

🏛 Venetian Palace

Namik Kemal Meydani.
⬜ 24 hours daily.
Not much remains of the former palace of the Lusignan kings and Venetian governors, built during Lusignan times. The area marked by its jutting stone walls is now a car park.

On the side of Namik Kemal Square stands a triple-arched façade supported by four granite columns from Salamis. Above the central arch is the coat of arms of Giovanni Renier – the Venetian military commander of Cyprus.

Remains of the Venetian Palace

VISITORS' CHECKLIST

Road map E3. 🚍 28,000.
ℹ️ Land Gate, 0392 366 28 64.
🚌 Gazi Mustafa Kemak Boulv.
🚢 east of the Sea Gate (for
tickets, call 0392 366 45 57).
🎭 Famagusta International
Festival (Jun–Jul).

Between 1873 and 1876, the left section of the building was used as a prison in which Turkish poet and playwright, Namik Kemal, was locked up on the Sultan's order. Now it houses his museum.

🔒 Nestorian Church

Somoundjouoglou Sokagi.
🔒 to the public.
Syrian merchant Francis Lakhas built this church in 1338 for Famagusta's Syrian community. The façade is adorned with a lovely rose window. Inscriptions inside are in Syrian, the language of the Nestorian liturgy.

Later, the church was taken over by Greek Cypriots and renamed Agios Georgios Exorinos. The word *exorinos* means "exiler". Greeks believe that dust taken from the church floor and sprinkled in the house of an enemy will make him die or leave the island within a year.

🔒 Churches of the Knights Templar and Knights Hospitaller

Kißla Sokagi. 🔒 to the public.
These two adjacent medieval churches are known as the twins. On the north façade, above the entrance, you can still see the carved stone coats of arms of the Knights

Romantic ruins of the Gothic Church of St John (Latin)

Hospitaller. In the early 14th century, following the dissolution of the Knights Templar order, their monastery and the Chapel of St Anthony were handed over to the order of St John of Jerusalem (the Knights Hospitaller). The Hospitallers' chapel, featuring a lovely rose window in the façade, now houses a theatre and an art gallery.

🔒 Church of St John (Latin)

Cafer Paşa Sokagi. 🕐 9am–1pm, 2–4:45pm (9am–7pm in summer).
Built in the late 13th century, during the reign of the French king Louis IX, the Church of St John was one of Famagusta's ealiest churches, and a splendid example of Gothic architecture. Now largely in ruins, the original north wall with the presbytery and tall Gothic windows remains standing. The capital of the surviving column is decorated with floral motifs and winged dragons.

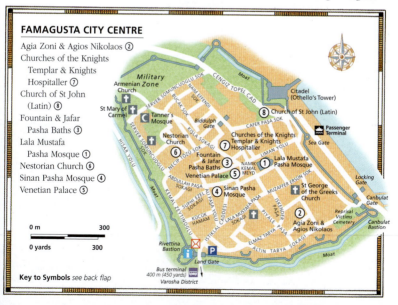

FAMAGUSTA CITY CENTRE

Agia Zoni & Agios Nikolaos ②
Churches of the Knights
  Templar & Knights
  Hospitaller ⑦
Church of St John
  (Latin) ⑧
Fountain & Jafar
  Pasha Baths ③
Lala Mustafa
  Pasha Mosque ①
Nestorian Church ⑥
Sinan Pasha Mosque ④
Venetian Palace ⑤

0 m   300
0 yards   300

Key to Symbols *see back flap*

🔒 Agios Ioannis

Varosha (Maraş). Polat Pasa Bulvari.
⬜ 9am–1pm, 2–4:45pm (to 2pm in summer). **Icon Museum** ● for restoration. 📷

The Neo-Byzantine Church of St John stands in the Varosha (Maraş) district of Famagusta, where the Turkish army is currently stationed. The renovated church houses a museum of icons, mostly from the 18th century, that were gathered from many destroyed Greek Orthodox churches.

The Varosha area, controlled by Turkish and UN forces, has been uninhabited for more than 30 years, ever since the expulsion of the Greek Cypriots. It is forbidden to photograph the crumbling houses or dozens of decaying beachfront hotels, dating from the 1960s.

Iconostasis in Agios Ioannis Church

🏛 Canbulat Bastion

Tel 0392 366 28 64. ⬜ 9am–1pm, 2–4:45pm (9am–5pm in summer). 📷

The bastion at the southeast corner of the Venetian defence walls was once called the Arsenal. Today it bears the name of the Turkish commander, Canbulat, who charged his horse at the Venetian war machine, which was studded with spinning knives, during the siege of Famagusta. Canbulat perished, cut to shreds, but his desperate attack put the machine out of action, and the Turks regard him as a hero. The bastion contains his tomb and a small museum with a collection of artifacts dating from antiquity and the Ottoman era.

🏛 Venetian City Walls

Famagusta's Old Town is encircled by huge defence walls erected by the Venetians, who felt threatened by the

Ruins of the Citadel (Othello's Tower)

Ottoman Empire's expansion into the eastern Mediterranean. The walls, 15 m (49 ft) high and up to 8 m (26 ft) thick, are reinforced with 15 bastions. The two gates leading to the town are the Land Gate and Sea Gate, which was constructed by the Venetian, Nicolo Prioli. His name, coat of arms, construction date (1496) and the Lion of St Mark have been carved in the marble brought from the ruins of Salamis.

To the right of the entrance are two marble statues of lions. Legend has it that one night the larger of the two will open its mouth, and the person who sticks his head in at that moment will win a fortune.

The entrance to the Old Town from the opposite side leads over a stone bridge that spans the moat. It is defended by the massive Rivettina (Ravelin) Bastion, which the Turks call Akkule ("White Tower"). It was here that the Venetians hoisted the white flag following the 10-month siege of

Famagusta in 1571 by the Turkish army. From the Old Town side you can see wall paintings and the coats of arms of the Venetian commanders.

The passageway features a small shrine. The restored rooms beyond the gate now house the tourist information bureau. Under the Rivettina Bastion are subterranean casemates. In 1619, a small mosque was built for the Muslim guards.

🏛 Citadel (Othello's Tower)

Cengiz Topel Caddesi (adjacent to the Sea Gate). ⬜ 9am–1pm, 2–4:45pm (to 7pm in summer). 📷

The Citadel was erected in the 12th century by the Lusignan Kings, to defend Famagusta Harbour from attack. Carved in marble above the gate are the Lions of St Mark (symbolizing Venice) and the name of Nicolo Foscari, who supervised the rebuilding of the fortress in 1492. This was a vast structure for its time, and it included a system of fortifications and subterranean casemates.

The Citadel is popularly known as Othello's Tower, after Shakespeare's play *Othello*, which was set largely in Famagusta. The empty interiors, Gothic rooms and gloomy casemates are now inhabited by pigeons, and the floors littered with discarded bullets and fragments of broken sculptures.

The Citadel walls afford a magnificent view over old Famagusta and the harbour.

The massive Venetian defence walls

🔒 St George of the Greeks Church

Mustafa Ersu Sokagi. ⬜ *24 hours daily.*
Erected in the 15th century, in Gothic-Byzantine style, just a shell remains of this church. The east apse still shows the fragments of wall paintings. The steps in the nave are typical of early Christian basilicas.

The roof was brought down by Turkish bombardment in the siege of Famagusta. To this day, the walls bear pockmarks of cannonballs. Legend says that a treasure belonging to St Epifanos (Archbishop of Salamis) lies under the floor.

Abutting the church to the south is the smaller church of Agios Symeon (St Simon's).

Ruins of St George of the Greeks Church

Biddulph Gate – a remnant of a Venetian merchant's home

🏛 Biddulph Gate

Naim Effendi Sokagi.
⬜ *24 hours daily.*
This Renaissance gate standing in a side street is a remnant of a medieval merchant's house. It was named in honour of Sir Robert Biddulph, British High Commissioner, who saved it from being pulled down in 1879. Departing from the usual custom of demolishing old structures, Biddulph pioneered the protection of Famagusta's historic sites.

Another interesting relic found along Naim Effendi Sokagi is an old, intact merchant's house, an excellent example of secular Renaissance architecture.

🔒 Churches in North Famagusta

The area at the north end of old Famagusta, around the Martinengo, San Luca and Pulacazara bastions, was previously occupied by the Turkish army. Now some of its historic sites are open to visitors. Among them is the rectangular **Church of St Mary of Carmel**, built of a yellow stone. It may be viewed only from the outside. The adjacent **Armenian Church** was built in the 16th century, when the Armenians had their Bishops in Nicosia and Famagusta. The interior is covered with paintings and Armenian inscriptions. A short distance away, in the direction of the Moratto bastion and beyond the Tanner's mosque, stands the splendidly preserved medieval **Church of St Anna**, featuring an unusual belfry rising above the façade; unfortunately it is closed to visitors.

🕌 Medresa

Liman Yolu Sokagi.
The single-storey domed building to the north of the Lala Mustafa Pasa mosque was once a college of Islamic studies, attached to an Ottoman mosque. Nowadays it would be difficult to discern any particular style in it, although it is often cited as an example of classic Ottoman architecture. The two granite columns brought from Salamis, and placed in front of the building, add to the overall impression of architectural chaos.

Coat of arms, Church of St Mary of Carmel

The stone plinth opposite the entrance bears the bust of Namik Kemal, a 19th-century Turkish poet and playwright, who, on orders of the Sultan, was imprisoned in the Venetian Palace opposite. To the right are two domed Turkish tombs, one with an interesting wrought-iron gate.

After serving as a college, the former medresa was later used as offices, and then as bank premises. Today the building stands empty.

🕌 Tanner's Mosque

Somoundjouoglou Sokagi.
This small, yellow limestone building was erected in the late 16th century as a church. In 1571, following the capture of Famagusta by the Turks, it was converted into a mosque. Clay pots were built into its vaults, intended to improve the general acoustics of the building. The mosque was later abandoned and left to decay. Since 1974 the building has been contained within a fenced-off compound used by the Turkish army; it now serves as a depot.

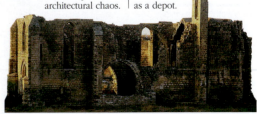
Ruins of St Mary of Carmel Church seen at sunset

Trikomo (İskele) **8**

Road map E2.

This small town lies close to the base of the Karpas peninsula. At its centre, right by the roundabout, stands the tiny Dominican **Church of St James** (Agios Iakovos). Intricately carved in stone, it resembles an encrusted jewellery box. At the western end of the town stands the two-aisled, single domed **Church of Panagia Thetokos**, which was erected in the 12th century. The church was restored in 1804, when it was also given its marble-panelled belfry. Inside you can still see the original wall paintings dating from the 12th century.

The **Icon Museum**, opened here in 1991, houses a collection of icons removed from the local Greek churches. The images are modern and of little artistic merit, yet the museum is worth visiting for its lovely interior frescoes.

🏛 **Icon Museum**
Panagia Theotokos Church.
🕐 9am–1pm, 2–4:45pm
(to 6:45pm in summer). 🎟

A mosque in Trikomo, a town at the base of the Karpas peninsula

Bogazi (Boğaz) **9**

Road map E2. On the road leading to the Karpas peninsula.

At this little fishing port on Famagusta Bay you can watch the fishermen returning with their catch, and also buy fresh fish each morning. Fishing trips are available for visitors, as are lessons in scuba diving. There are beautiful long,

The imposing walls of Kantara Castle, overlooking Famagusta Bay

sandy beaches in this area. A half-dozen local restaurants specialize in fish and seafood. European cuisine is also on offer at Moon Over the Water, an English-run seaside restaurant 2 km (1 mile) south of Bogazi.

Kantara Castle **10**

Road map E2. 🕐 9am–1pm, 2–4:45pm (9am–4:45pm in summer). 🎟

Kantara Castle is the easternmost medieval fortress of North Cyprus. It lies 630 m (2,068 ft) above sea level, at the base of the Karpasia peninsula, on a spot affording views of both Famagusta Bay and the shores of Asia Minor. This was already the site of a castle in Byzantine times. It was here that the English King Richard the Lionheart finally caught up with his adversary, Byzantine governor Isaac Komnenos, in 1191 and forced him to capitulate.

The castle rooms were mostly torn down by the Venetians, but the mighty walls survive in excellent condition. The route to the castle leads through a barbican with two towers; the vast southeastern tower has a water cistern at its base, also used as a dungeon. The two adjacent former army barracks are in good condition. The southwestern wing

of the castle features a secret passage that enabled the defenders to sneak out and launch a surprise attack on the besiegers. The north towers and the bastions afford magnificent views of the surrounding area.

Environs
A dozen or so kilometres (7.5 miles) west of the castle, close to the sea, is the lonely late Byzantine **Church of Panagia Pergaminiotissa**.

Karpasia Peninsula **11**

Road map E2, F1–2. 🛈 Yialoussa, 374 4984. 🕐 9am–5pm daily.

This long, rocky spit is the least developed part of the island, with sandy beaches on its north and south coast, and a scattering of historic Christian churches, including the monastery of Apostolos Andreas, which is awaiting restoration, to be funded by the UN and the EU. Known as Karpaz

Picturesque Panagia Pergaminiotissa

Yarimadasi (sometimes Karpas) to the Turks, this quiet peninsula has rolling hills, where wild donkeys roam, fringed by empty beaches, which provide nesting grounds for sea turtles. The eastern part of the peninsula is a nature reserve, home to birds and donkeys.

The best starting point for exploring the peninsula is the fishing village of **Bogazi**. A few kilometres to the left of the main road, near the village of **Komi** (Büyükkonuk), stands a small Byzantine church with beautiful 6th-century mosaics. The church is surrounded by the ruins of a Roman town. Only the apse remains of the 5th-century Church of Panagia Kanakaria, on the edge of **Boltaşli** (Lythrangkomi), east of Ziyamet (Leonarisso); the mosaics that used to decorate it can be seen in the Makarios Museum, in Nicosia. The rest of the church dates from the 11th century, except the tamboured dome which was added in the 18th century. The church is now closed.

The last petrol station is in **Yialousa** (Yenierenköy). Further south is the village of **Sipahi** (Agia Trias) with a three-aisled early Christian basilica. Dating from the 5th century, it was discovered by archaeologists in 1957, and is noted for its handsome floor mosaics. The marble-encrusted, cruciform font in the baptistry is the biggest in the island.

Beyond the small village of **Agios Thyrsos** stands Hotel Theresa, with the best accommodation on the peninsula.

Dipkarpaz (Rizokarpaso) is the peninsula's biggest, if somewhat neglected, village. It has a population of 3,000, comprised mainly of immigrants from Anatolia. Some 3 km (1.8 miles) to the north are the ruins of the 5th-century Church of **Agios Philon**, standing amid the ruins of the Phoenician town of Karpatia. The 10th-century basilica was later replaced by a chapel; just the south wall and the apse remain.

North of Agios Philon stands an ancient stone breakwater. A narrow road running along the coast leads to **Aphendrika**, with the ruins of an ancient harbour, a Hellenic necropolis and a fortress erected on bare rock. It also has three ruined churches: the partly domed Agios Georgios dating from the Byzantine period; the 12th-century Romanesque Panagia Chrysiotissa; and Panagia Assomatos, the best preserved of all three. On the opposite side of the peninsula is the beautiful Nangomi Beach.

Apostolos Andreas – the monastery of St Andrew

Apostolos Andreas ⑫

Road map F1. ☐ *24 hours daily.*

Near the tip of the Karpasia peninsula stands the monastery of St Andrew (Apostolos Andreas), an irregular edifice of yellow stone with a white bell tower. According to legend, it was here that the Saint's invocation caused a miraculous spring to appear, whose water cures epilepsy and ailments of the eyes, and grants pilgrims their wishes. During the Byzantine period, a fortified monastery occupied the site; some historians believe that it was here, rather than in Kantara, that Richard the Lionheart caught up with Isaac Komnenos.

In the early 20th century the monastery gained a reputation for its miracles, and became the target of mass pilgrimages. After 1974, the site was taken over by the Turkish army. Today it is once again open to visitors.

The 19th-century church has been stripped of its icons, but on the Feast of the Assumption (15 August) and St Andrew's Day (30 November), services are held for the pilgrims arriving from southern Cyprus.

In the crypt beneath the church the holy well, famed for its healing properties, still gushes the "miraculous" water. The site is regarded as holy by Greeks and Turks alike.

Environs
Less than 5 km (3 miles) from Apostolos Andreas monastery is **Zafer Burnu**, the furthest point of the Karpasia peninsula. This cave-riddled rocky cape was a Neolithic settlement known as Kastros, one of the earliest places of known human habitation in Cyprus. In ancient times it became the site of a temple to the goddess Aphrodite.

The offshore **Klidhes islets** (the "Keys" islets) are a haven for a variety of sea birds.

Turtle Beach in the Karpasia peninsula

Antifonitis Monastery ⑬

Road map D2. 29 km (18 miles) E of Kyrenia via Esentepe (Agios Amvrosios). ☐ *summer: 9am–2pm; winter: 9am–1pm, 2–4:45pm.* 🖼

In a pine-covered valley on the northern slopes of the Pentadaktylos mountains, some 8 km (5 miles) south of Esentepe, stands the disused 12th-century monastery church of Antifonitis. This was once the most important Byzantine church in the mountains of North Cyprus. Its Greek name, meaning "He who responds", is associated with a legend about a pauper who met a wealthy man and requested a loan. When the rich man asked who would vouchsafe the loan, the pauper replied, "God will". At this moment they both heard a voice from heaven. The monastery was built on the site of this miracle.

The church was built in the 7th century; the narthex and gallery date from the Lusignan period and the loggia was added by the Venetians. The church was originally decorated with magnificent frescoes, but since 1974 these have been defaced and damaged.

Buffavento Castle ⑭

Road map D2. ☐ *summer: 9am–4:45pm; winter: 9am–1pm, 2–4:45pm.* 🖼

Built on the site of a Byzantine watchtower remodelled by the Lusignans, this castle perches 950 m (3,117 ft) above sea level. The date of its construction is unknown,

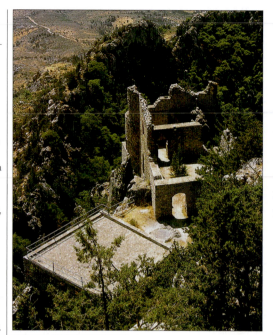

Buffavento, the highest castle in Cyprus

but this mountain stronghold was captured in 1191 by the Frankish king Guy de Lusignan. The castle was used for years as an observation post and political prison. Under Venetian rule the castle lost its importance and was abandoned.

Steep stairs lead from the gate to the top of the tallest tower, where a magnificent view awaits. In fine weather it is possible to see Kyrenia, Nicosia and Famagusta, as well as the Troodos mountains and the coast of Turkey.

Cold winter wind blowing from Anatolia explains the name of the castle, meaning the "wind blast". In old days bonfires lit on top of the tower served as means of communication with the garrisons stationed at St Hilarion and Kantara castles.

A marble monument by the car park commemorates the passengers and crew of a Turkish aircraft that crashed in fog in February 1988 on its approach to Ercan airport.

Environs

West of the castle, on the southern slopes of the juniper-covered mountains, stands the 12th-century Byzantine **Panagia Apsinthiotissa monastery**. It was restored in the 1960s, but after 1974 the monks were forced to abandon it. Its church is crowned with a vast dome; on its north side is a lovely original refectory.

The site is reached by turning off the Kyrenia-Nicosia highway and passing through Asagi Dikmen (Kato Dikomo) and Tasken (Vouno) villages.

Along the way is a giant stone flag erected by Turkish Cypriot refugees from Tochni (*see p74*) where, in the 1960s, the Greek EOKA organization murdered all the Turkish men.

The breathtaking view from Buffavento castle

◁ **View of the Old Harbour in Kyrenia**

Bellapais ⑮

Road map C2. 7 km (4.3 miles)
SE of Kyrenia. **Tel** 0392 815 75 40.
Abbey ☐ *summer: 9am–4:45pm;*
winter: 9am–1pm, 2–4:45pm. 🖾

One of the most beautiful
villages in Cyprus, Bellapais
lies amid citrus groves on
the northern slopes of the
Pentadaktylos mountains.
It features the splendidly
preserved ruins of a Gothic
abbey, to which the village
owes its name. It is thought
to be derived from the
French *Abbaye de la Paix*
(Peace Abbey).

The first monks to settle
here were Augustinians from
Jerusalem, forced to flee the
city after its capture by
Saladin. The first buildings
were erected in the early 13th
century, but the main section
of the abbey was built during
the reign of the Lusignan
kings, Hugo III and Hugo IV.
The abbey was destroyed by
the Turks, following their
conquest of the island.

Bellapais is one of the
loveliest Gothic historic sites
in the Middle East. The oldest
part of the abbey is its well-
preserved church, built in
the French Gothic style.

A spiral staircase in the
western end of the garth (the
garden close) leads to the
roof, affording a magnificent
view of the sea and the
mountains. The remaining
parts include the living
quarters, the kitchen, and the
old refectory illuminated by
the light entering through the

Splendidly preserved ruins of Bellapais abbey

vast windows facing the steep
crag. The garth cloisters once
contained a carved marble
sarcophagus and a lavatory,
where the monks washed
their hands before entering
the refectory. Now they are
used for concerts during
music festivals.

The English writer
Lawrence Durrell
lived in Bellapais
from 1953–6, and
described the
struggles of the
EOKA fighters in his
novel *Bitter Lemons*.
The house in which
he lived bears a
commemorative plaque.

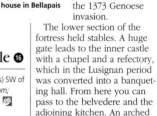

**Sign from Durrell's
house in Bellapais**

St Hilarion Castle ⑯

Road map C2. 7 km (4.3 miles) SW of
Kyrenia. ☐ *summer: 9am–5pm;*
winter: 9am–1pm, 2–4:45pm. 🖾

The best-preserved mountain-
top stronghold in North
Cyprus, this magnificent castle
bristles with turrets from its
walls built on sheer rock. It

was named after the monastic
saint from Palestine, who came
to Cyprus in search of solitude,
dying here in 372. The Byzantines built the church and
monastery in his memory.

The outer defence wall was
erected by the Lusignans.
The castle played an
important role in the
1228-31 struggle
for the domination
of Cyprus between
German Emperor
Frederick II of
Hohenstaufen and
Jean d'Ibelin; and in
the 1373 Genoese
invasion.

The lower section of the
fortress held stables. A huge
gate leads to the inner castle
with a chapel and a refectory,
which in the Lusignan period
was converted into a banqueting hall. From here you can
pass to the belvedere and the
adjoining kitchen. An arched
gate leads to the upper castle.

The south part of the castle
has the Gothic "queen's
window", with a spectacular
view over Karmi village.

Ruins of St Hilarion Castle, on top of a steep rock

For hotels and restaurants in this region see pp164–5 and pp176–7

Kyrenia (Girne) ⑰

Enjoying a picturesque location flanked by a range of craggy hills and the sea, Kyrenia is built around a charming harbour – the most beautiful in Cyprus – guarded by a mighty medieval castle. Its compact Old Town is full of bars, tavernas and restaurants, yet remains a tranquil place. The nearby seashore is lined with the best hotels in North Cyprus. Home to a sizeable expatriate community until 1974, there is still a small number of expats living here today.

Town hall building with the forecourt fountain

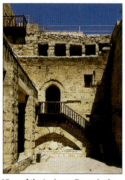
View of the Lusignan Tower in the castle (see pp148–9)

Exploring Kyrenia

Once you arrive in Kyrenia, it is best to leave the car at the large car park near the town hall, and then continue exploring on foot. Most of Kyrenia's historic sites are clustered around the old harbour. The tourist information office is housed in the former customs house. The town's main attractions – the harbour, castle and small museums – can be explored in a day.

🏛 Byzantine Tower

Ziya Rizki Caddesi and Atilla Sokagi. ◯ daily. Summer: 9am–7pm; winter: 9am–1pm, 2–4:45pm.

This massive stone defence structure, with walls several metres thick, once formed part of the town's defence walls. It now houses an art gallery selling local handicrafts, including rugs, paintings and other souvenirs. Strolling down Atilla Sokagi

you will come across a similar, but more derelict tower; also a number of Greek and Roman tombs.

🏛 Market

Canbulat Sokagi. ◯ 8am–7pm. The covered town bazaar, where fish, meat, fruit, vegetables and spices are sold, stands along Canbulat street leading towards the shore. This fairly dilapidated building is currently being renovated with funding provided by the UN.

🏛 Folk Art Museum

The old harbour. ◯ summer: 9am–2pm; winter: 9am–1pm, 2–4:45pm.

Set in a centuries-old Venetian house midway along the harbour, this museum houses a modest collection of traditional village costumes, household implements, furniture and tools. Also on display is an interesting giant olive press made of olive wood.

Art gallery inside the Byzantine Tower

🏛 Town Hall

This modern single-storey building stands on a small square, just a stone's throw from the Old Town. Standing in the forecourt is a unique fountain with three huge birds carved in white stone.

The nearby Muslim cemetery is full of the distinctive tombs – *baldaken turbe*.

☪ Djafer Pasha Mosque (Cafer Paşa Camii)

In the Old Town, close to the castle and the harbour. ◯ 24 hours daily. This small mosque with a stocky minaret was erected in 1589 by Djafer Pasha, commander of the Sultan's army and navy, and three times the Turkish governor of Cyprus. The founder's body rests in the small stone tomb to the right of the entrance. The simple prayer hall is lined with carpets.

About a dozen metres (40 ft) west of the mosque is the small, abandoned Chysospiliotissa church which was erected by the Lusignans in the early 14th century.

⚓ Harbour

Kyrenia's once important harbour was the safest haven along the north coast of Cyprus, so heavily fortified was it. In ancient times the Romans built a defence castle here; later on the Lusignans and the Venetians rebuilt it, creating a vast fortress. In the Middle Ages the harbour entrance was protected by a strong iron chain. Evidence of its former importance are the medieval stone lugs that were used to fasten the mooring lines of large ships.

Now the old harbour is devoted exclusively to yachts and pleasure boats, ready to take visitors on cruises along the coast. It is lined with an array of dining spots, particularly fish restaurants, with tables set close to the water's edge. The harbour looks particularly enchanting at night, when the calm waters reflect myriad sparkling lights.

🔒 Archangelos Church & Icon Museum

Near the harbour. ☐ summer: 9am–7pm daily; winter: 9am–1pm, 2–4:45pm daily. 📷

The former church of the Archangel Michael, standing on top of a hill close to the old harbour, now houses the Icon Museum.

This white edifice with its slender belfry was built in 1860. Some of its original

The distinctive white silhouette and belfry of the Archangelos church

furnishings remain, including the exquisite carved wooden iconostasis and pulpit. The walls are now hung with over 50 icons, dating from the 18th-20th centuries, that were

removed from local churches. One of the oldest was painted in 1714. Other objects on display are sacral books and a carved crosier. Outside are marble sarcophagi, dating from the Byzantine period.

During summer, Catholic mass is celebrated in the late-Gothic **Chapel of Terra Santa**, situated further west, in Ersin Aydin Sokagi. The only other Christian place of worship in Kyrenia is the Anglican **Church of St Andrew**, which was built in 1913 close to the castle and the Muslim cemetery.

🏛 Fine Arts Museum

☐ summer: 9am–7pm; winter: 9am–1pm, 2–4:45pm. 📷

This museum is housed in a somewhat ostentatious villa built in 1938 in the western part of Kyrenia. Its collection comprises a variety of unrelated exhibits, from anonymous paintings (both oil and watercolour) to European porcelain, to Oriental jewellery.

Kyrenia's natural horseshoe harbour, the most beautiful in Cyprus

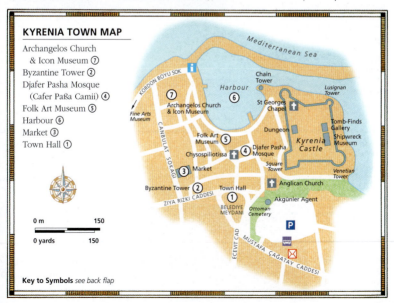

KYRENIA TOWN MAP

Archangelos Church
& Icon Museum ⑦
Byzantine Tower ②
Djafer Pasha Mosque
(Cafer Paşa Camii) ④
Folk Art Museum ⑤
Harbour ⑥
Market ③
Town Hall ①

Mediterranean Sea

KORDON BOYU SOK
Harbour
Chain Tower
Lusignan Tower
⑦ Archangelos Church & Icon Museum
⑥
St Georges Chapel
Fine Arts Museum
CANBULAT SOKAGI
Folk Art Museum ⑤
Chysospiliotissa ④ Djafer Pasha Mosque
③ Market
Byzantine Tower ②
Town Hall ①
ZIYA RIZKI CADDESI
BELEDIYE MEYDANI
Dungeon
Kyrenia Castle
Tomb-Finds Gallery
Shipwreck Museum
Square Tower
Venetian Tower
Anglican Church
Akgünler Agent
Ottoman Cemetery
ECEVIT CAD
MUSTAFA CAGATAY CADDESI

0 m   150
0 yards   150

Key to Symbols *see back flap*

Kyrenia Castle and Shipwreck Museum

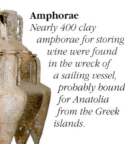

Ancient amphora

Kyrenia Castle was built by the Byzantines on the site of a Roman fort and later extended by the Lusignans. The Venetians turned it into a vast fortress occupied by the Turks in 1570. The castle was never taken by force.

Today it houses a Tomb-Finds Gallery and a Shipwreck Museum, with the wreck of an ancient vessel dating from the days of Alexander the Great. The magnificent view from the city walls encompasses the harbour and St Hilarion castle.

Amphorae
Nearly 400 clay amphorae for storing wine were found in the wreck of a sailing vessel, probably bound for Anatolia from the Greek islands.

★ Shipwreck Museum
On display here is what remains of a merchant vessel that sank in a storm some 2,300 years ago.

★ The Lusignan Tower
Arranged in the vaulted rooms of the two-storey tower are figures of medieval soldiers standing by the guns.

The Tomb-Finds Gallery comprises a reconstructed late Neolithic dwelling and tombs from both Kirini and Akdeniz (Agia Irini).

The Courtyard
Surrounded by stone walls, the large courtyard has a series of stone balls lying around and a quern (millstone) of volcanic rock.

The Venetian Tower
The southeast section of Kyrenia Castle includes the Venetian Tower. Arranged in its gloomy casements are figures of resting soldiers and Venetian gunners in action.

Defence Walls
Once powerful castle fortifications are now severely dilapidated.

Square tower

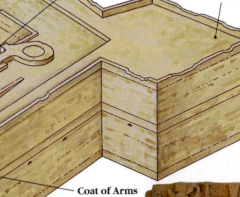

Coat of Arms
A medieval knight's stone-carved coat of arms is preserved in the castle walls.

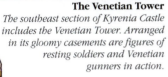

West wall

Entrance
The castle is reached via a narrow bridge spanning a moat, once filled with sea water.

STAR SIGHTS

★ Lusignan Tower

★ Shipwreck Museum

Lapithos (Lapta) – a popular destination for daytrips from Kyrenia

Lambousa (Lambusa) ⑱

Road map C2. Situated on the coast, 1.5 km (1 mile) from the village of Alsançak (Karavas).

On a small, rocky peninsula near Cape Acheiropitios, Lambousa was one of several ancient Cypriot kingdoms. This cosmopolitan city-state was inhabited by the Greeks, Phoenicians, Romans and Byzantines, as well as the Hittites and Franks. The earliest inhabitants arrived in the 13th century BC. In the 8th century BC Lambousa was conquered by the Phoenicians, but its most glorious times were in the Roman and Byzantine periods.

In the course of excavation works carried out in the early 20th century, archaeologists discovered on this site a 6th-century Byzantine treasure consisting of gold and silver artifacts. Some of these are now on display in the Cyprus Museum in Nicosia (*see p123*), with the rest divided between the British Museum in London, the Metropolitan Museum in New York and the Dumbarton Oaks Collection in Washington, DC.

Only the eastern portion of ancient Lambousa is open to the public. It includes a dozen rock tombs and a series of vast tanks for keeping freshly caught fish alive.

Lapithos (Lapta) ⑲

Road map C2. 18 km (11 miles) west of Kyrenia.

This picturesque village, with its isolated dwellings scattered around mountain slopes, is a popular day-trip destination from Kyrenia.

The abundant water supply made this a natural supply base for ancient Lambousa, until the threat of Arab raids in the 7th century caused the inhabitants to move to a safer site inland. The settlement was once famous for its silks and exquisite ceramics.

Lapithos was formerly inhabited by both Cypriot communities living in concord; they left behind seven churches and two mosques. In 1963–4 the local Turks were forced to leave the village. After 1974 it was the Greeks' turn to leave.

Now, in addition to Turkish Cypriots, Lapithos' population includes settlers from Anatolia and a handful of foreigners.

Environs
Karman (Karmi) is one of the loveliest Cypriot villages, with whitewashed houses built on hillsides. The small church has a collection of icons removed from the abandoned Greek churches. Nearby is a necropolis dating from 2,300–1,625 BC. The village is now inhabited almost exclusively by British and German expatriates.

Larnaka tis Lapithou (Kozan) ⑳

Road map C2.

This village enjoys a scenic location on the southern slopes of Selvii Dag (Kiparis-sovouno), the peak of the Kyrenian range at 1,024 m (3,360 ft). It makes an excellent base for hikes and bicycle trips around the neighbouring mountains. The local church was turned into a mosque, while the nearby monastery, Panagia ton Katharon, was sacked after 1974.

Kormakitis village, the capital of the Cypriot Maronites

Kormakitis (Koruçam) ㉑

Road map B2. 9 km (6 miles) west of Camlibel (Myrton).

Kormakitis is the capital of the Cypriot Maronite Christian sect. In the 1960s this was a prosperous small town with a

Fragments of ruins from the ancient city-state of Lambousa

Views from the Kormakitis peninsula

population of over 1,000. Now it has dwindled to about one tenth of that number. Although the Maronites tried to stay impartial in the Greek-Turkish conflict, after 1974 many were forced by Turkish persecution to leave their homes and emigrate. The current residents of the village are mostly elderly, and despite living through those difficult times, the people are unfailingly kind, cheerful and hospitable.

Daily mass is still celebrated in the local church, **Agios Gregorios**, which is now far too large for the needs of its current congregation. To visit the church you should contact the nearby convent or go to the next-door coffee-house to enquire about the church being opened. **Profitis Ilias**, standing close to the village, is the main Maronite monastery on the island.

Environs

Next to the village of Akdeniz (Agia Irini), which lies close to the Güzelyurt (Morfou) bay, is an interesting archaeological site believed to date from the late Bronze era to the Archaic era. A reconstruction of a tomb that was discovered here can now be seen in the Kyrenia Castle museum.

Just off the road leading to Nicosia stands a Bronze Age shrine – the Pigadhes sanctuary. Its stone altar is decorated with geometric reliefs and crowned by a pair of bull horns, indicating the Minoan influence.

Cape Kormakitis (Koruçam Burnu) ㉒

Road map B2.

Cape Kormakitis, called Koruçam Burnu by the Turks, is the northeasternmost part of Cyprus. In terms of landscape and wildlife, it is similar to the Karpasia and Akamas peninsulas; together they are the wildest and least accessible parts of the island. The few villages that existed in this areas have now been largely deserted. The North Cyprus authorities plan to turn this area into a nature reserve.

A rough track running among limestone hills covered with Mediterranean vegetation leads from the Maronite village of Kormakitis towards the small village of Sadrazamköy (Livera). From here, a 3.5-km (2.2-mile) unmade but serviceable road runs towards Cape Kormakitis.

Waves breaking off Cape Kormakitis

The cape lies in a desolate area of dreary rocks, a handful of deserted dwellings and an unmanned lighthouse at the very tip. The nearby rocky island of Nissi Kormakitis lies a mere 60 km (37 miles) from Cape Anamur on the Anatolian coast of Turkey.

For centuries, the cape has been inhabited by Maronites, a Christian sect that originated in Syria and Lebanon in the 7th century. This Eastern Christian sect, whose members proclaim themselves to be Catholic and to recognize the supremacy of the Pope, arose from a dispute between Monophysites (who postulated a single, divine nature of Jesus) and Christians (who believed Jesus to be both divine and human). The Maronites took their name from the 4th- or 5th-century Syrian hermit, St Maron. They arrived on Cyprus in the 12th century, with the Crusaders, whom they served during their campaigns in the Holy Land.

ENDANGERED SEA TURTLES

The legally protected green turtle (Chylonia mydas)

Both the loggerhead (*Caretta caretta*) and green (*Chylonia mydas*) species of sea turtle that nest on the beaches of Cyprus are endangered species subject to conservation programmes. Their nesting season lasts from mid-May to mid-October. The female digs a hole 30–60 cm (12–24 in) into the sand, in which she deposits her eggs. The hatchlings emerge after 55–60 days and head for the sea. Those that survive will return after 30 years to the same beach to breed. Only one in 40 turtles succeeds.

Morfou (Güzelyurt) ㉓

Road map B3.
🎪 *Orange Festival (May).*

The Turkish name Güzelyurt means "beautiful place". And, indeed, the local citrus groves and picturesque bay add to the lovely scenery here.

It was close to the town that archaeologists discovered the earliest traces of human habitation in Cyprus, dating from the Neolithic and Early Bronze eras when copper was produced and exported.

The best historic site in Güzelyurt is the **church and monastery of Agios Mamas**, built during the Byzantine period on the site of a former pagan temple. In the 15th century it acquired Gothic embellishments, and in the 18th century a dome.

The interior features the throne of St Mamas, a Gothic window carved in stone, an iconostasis and a marble sarcophagus of the saint.

Until 1974 swarms of pilgrims streamed to Agios Mamas from all over Cyprus, but after the Turkish invasion it was shut and used to store icons brought here from the nearby Orthodox churches. It is now an **Icon Museum**.

Other than Agios Mamas, the town has few tourist attractions. Next to the church is the **Archaeology and Natural History Museum**. Besides several exhibits of stuffed animals and birds, and a collection of ancient

Monastery buildings of Agios Mamas in Morfou

Atatürk's statue in Lefke

ceramics, the museum also houses an exhibition of Late Bronze Age objects found in the course of excavations conducted in Töumba and Skourou.

> 🏛 **Icon Museum & Archaeology and Natural History Museum**
> Agios Mamas. ⬜ *summer: 9am–7pm; winter: 9am–1pm & 2–4:45pm.* 📷

Léfka (Lefke) ㉔

Road map B3.

Inhabited for over 400 years by Turks, Lefke is a major centre of Islam on the island. The central square sports a huge equestrian statue of Atatürk. A few hundred metres further on stands the early 19th-century mosque of **Piri Osman Pasha**, built in the Cyprian style. The garden surrounding the mosque contains the tomb of Vizier Osman Pasha, who was supposedly killed by poison – a victim of a palace intrigue. His marble sarcophagus is one of the loveliest surviving works of its kind from the Ottoman period.

Lefke European University, one of five universities in North Cyprus, trains students from many countries of the Middle East and Central Asia. The pleasant **Lefke Gardens Hotel** occupies a renovated 19th-century inn *(see p165)*. Lefke is also the seat of Kibrisli Syke Nazim, the *murshid* or

Logo of the university in Lefke

spiritual leader of the Naqshbandi order of Sufism, who decides on all spiritual aspects of life of the faithful.

Environs
In the nearby coastal town of Gemikonagi (Karavostasi) is the excellent **Mardinli** restaurant, standing on a beach surrounded by a garden and orchard that provide its kitchen with fruit and vegetables. On the other side of town, between the road and the sea, stands an imposing monument to a Turkish pilot killed during the 1974 invasion.

Soloi (Soli Harabeleri) ㉕

Road map B3. 20 km (12.5 miles) W of Güzelyurt. ⬜ *summer: 9am–7pm; winter: 9am–1pm, 2–4:45pm.* 📷

Soloi, a one-time city-state of Cyprus, was supposedly founded at the suggestion of the Athenian law-giver Solon, who persuaded King Philocyprus of Aepea to build a new capital close to the river Ksero. In his honour, the town was named Soloi.

The reality, however, was probably quite different. As long ago as Assyrian times (c.700 BC) a town called Sillu stood on this site. It was a stronghold of Greek culture, and was the last town to fall to the Persians.

The town gave its name to the entire region of Solea, on the northern slopes of the Troodos mountains, where Cypriot copper was mined near the present-day town of Skouriotissa. The extraction and export of this metal spurred the growth of Soloi, particularly during Roman times. There was a good harbour, needed for the export of copper, and abundant water.

It was in Soloi that St Mark converted a Roman named Auxibius to Christianity; he later became bishop of Soloi.

Stones taken from the ruins of the ancient town were used by the British and the French in the building of the Suez Canal and the coastal town of Port Said. It was only in the late 1920s that Swedish archaeologists unearthed a theatre, and in 1964 a Canadian team uncovered the basilica and part of the agora (market place).

The Roman theatre was built for an audience of 4,000 people, and had a lovely view over the sea. It has been restored and during summer is often used as a venue for shows and concerts.

Above the theatre the archaeologists uncovered remains of palaces and a temple to Athena. The famous 1st-century marble statuette of Aphrodite, found nearby, can now be seen in the Cyprus Museum in Nicosia (see p122). Lower down are the ruins of the 5th-century Byzantine basilica, which was destroyed in the course of the 632 Arab raid.

Displayed under a makeshift roof are some fairly well-preserved mosaics from the temple floor, featuring geometric and animal motifs. The most interesting mosaics depict water birds surrounded by dolphins. Another small medallion features a swan.

Unearthed to the north of the ruined basilica is a poorly preserved agora.

Soloi is surrounded by vast burial grounds, dating from various periods of antiquity.

Ruins of the ancient palace in Vouni

Vouni
(Vuni Sarayi) ㉖

Road map B3. 27 km (17 miles) west of Güzelyurt. ☐ summer: 10am–5pm; winter: 9am–1pm & 2–4:45 pm. 🖼

Mosaic from Soloi

This magnificent, some-what mysterious palace stands atop a coastal hill, 250 m (820 ft) above sea level. The site is extraordinarily beautiful, with panoramic views over the North Cyprus coast and the Troodos mountains to the south. The palace was likely built by a pro-Persian king of Marion (a city near present-day Polis), as evidenced by its Oriental architectural details.

Occupying a strategic spot, the residence was probably intended to intimidate the nearby pro-Athenian town of Soloi. Following an anti-Persian insurrection, Vouni (which means "mountain" in Greek) was taken over by the supporters of Greece. Having occupied the palace, they rebuilt it, adding a temple to Athena, among other things. When the reversal of military fortunes resulted in the Persians returning to power, the palace was burned down in 380 BC.

Today the ruins are reached via a new, narrow and winding road. Above the car park are the scant remains of a temple to Athena, dating from the late 5th century BC. The stairs on the opposite side lead to the palace court-yard, which features a guitar-shape stone stele with a hole in it and an unfinished face of a woman, probably a goddess. The adjacent cistern was used to supply water to the luxuri-ous baths in the northwestern portion of the palace, which reputedly had 137 rooms.

Environs
The small rocky island off the west coast, visible from Vouni palace, is **Petra tou Limniti**. This is the oldest inhabited part of Cyprus, colonized as early as the Neolithic era.

Remains of the ancient agora, in Soloi

TRAVELLERS' NEEDS

WHERE TO STAY

Cyprus has a choice of places to stay that is every bit as wide as its portfolio of visitor attractions and holiday activities, with accommodation to suit all budgets. Its climate attracts holidaymakers throughout the year, and most of its hotels and guesthouses are also open year round. Accommodation ranges from simple, family-run guesthouses and small apartment complexes to large resort hotels with an array of facilities for families, luxury villas with private pools, and stylishly restored village houses. Hotels in the three- and four-star categories are generally more luxurious than similar hotels in other Mediterranean countries, and Cyprus has a well-deserved reputation for affordable comfort.

Logo of the Grekosun Hotels chain

The fabulous swimming pool of an exclusive Cypriot resort

INFORMATION

Most hotels in the popular resorts are block-booked by holiday companies, making it difficult for independent travellers to find good accommodation on arrival. Booking a holiday package (which includes flights and hotel) is the best and usually cheapest option. In low season, bargains may be found on the Internet. The **Cyprus Hotel Association** also has booking desks at Larnaka airport.

HOTELS

Most of the island's hotels are clustered along the coast on either side of Larnaka and Limassol, and in the resorts of Pafos, Agia Napa and Protaras. Few stretches of the island's coastline, however, are without a scattering of places to stay. In the Larnaka and Limassol areas most hotels are compact high-rise blocks, while many hotels in the Pafos and Agia Napa regions are low-rise resort complexes with swimming pools and play areas for children. There are also small hotels and apartment complexes in these resorts, though most are reserved by tour operators. Visitors looking for a tranquil setting can head to some of the lesser-known places inland.

All major hotels are modern and well equipped, with air conditioning. The **Cyprus Tourism Organization (CTO)**, and the Turkish tourism ministry in the occupied North, grade hotels from one to five stars. Those rated one or two stars are likely to be slightly shabby, with few facilities. Upper-end hotels may offer a wide range of activities, from watersports, riding, tennis and golf to cabaret, traditional music and dancing, and discos.

RATES

Rates vary depending on the season, with bargains available outside the peak spring and summer months. Rates are highest during Easter (both Greek Orthodox and non-Orthodox Easter), for the two weeks around Christmas, and from June to September.

Most larger hotels offer a choice of bed and breakfast, half-board or full-board pricing. Smaller hotels may not include breakfast in the rate. Make sure the quoted rate includes local taxes.

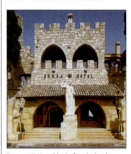
Roman II Hotel in Pafos, imitating an ancient Roman building *(see p158)*

PRIVATE ACCOMMODATION

It is not easy to find accommodation in private homes, and when you do find it, such accommodation does not usually offer a high standard of comfort or facilities, or a

Bellapais Gardens hotel, with its inviting swimming pool *(see p164)*

◁ A lovely sandy beach in Agia Napa

A camping site near the Baths of Aphrodite

competitive rate. However, the **CTO** can provide a list of small bed-and-breakfast establishments.

Lodgings in monasteries were once a popular option, but today are available only to Orthodox pilgrims.

AGROTOURISM

Visitors who prefer the charm of a quiet, rural village to the hustle and bustle of a tourist resort can opt for agrotourism accommodation. You book your stay in a village, usually in a restored traditional house, and have the opportunity to participate in some of the traditions of this village. This is especially popular in the mountains, with Cypriots as well as visitors from abroad.

Village houses usually feature modern kitchens and bathrooms, but you must be prepared for the occasional cut in the water and power supplies. These houses almost always have a garden, where you can enjoy such delights as oranges fresh from the tree. Basic home-made food-stuffs, such as bread, fresh honey or jam, can be bought from neighbours; other supplies can be brought from the larger towns.

HOSTELS AND CAMPSITES

Hostel beds are in short supply, but there are some in Nicosia, Larnaka, Pafos and in the Troodos mountain resorts. None offer a high standard of comfort. The few youth hostels in South Cyprus that once belonged to the International Youth Hostel Association are no longer in operation. You can obtain information about budget hotels and apartments on the Internet by keying in "Hostels in Cyprus".

There are five officially designated camping sites at Governor's Beach (Limassol district), Geroskipou, Pegeia and Polis (Pafos district), and at Troodos, run by the **CTO** and intended mainly for urban Cypriots seeking an inexpensive holiday. Governor's Beach and Pegeia are open all year round; the others from spring through to October. Facilities are basic, but include shower and toilet facilities, and a simple bar-restaurant.

RESERVATIONS

Arriving in Cyprus without a hotel reservation is inadvisable, as most hotels have been built to meet demand from package holiday companies and are block-booked by them. In resorts, including Pafos, Agia Napa and Protaras, few affordable and acceptably comfortable hotel rooms are available to independent travellers. However, the

Tochni, the most popular agro-tourism village in Cyprus (*see p161*)

CTO supplies a directory of hotels of all categories and independent travellers can book directly with hotels by phone, fax or e-mail, or with specialist hotel booking sites via the Internet. In the North, where good-quality hotels are far fewer, booking ahead is even more essential.

DISABLED TRAVELLERS

Most newer, larger hotels in the South are wheelchair-accessible (some even have ramps leading to the beach) and hotels here are working to meet European accessibility norms. Cheaper, smaller hotels, village houses and villas are unlikely to offer wheelchair access. In the North, hotels are far less likely to be wheelchair-accessible. Ask your hotel, travel agent or tour operator to confirm accessibility details in writing, by fax or e-mail.

DIRECTORY

INFORMATION

Cyprus Tourism Organization (CTO)

Leoforos Lemesou 19, 1390 Nicosia.

Tel 22 691 100.

Fax 22 331 644.

www.visitcyprus.com

Cyprus Hotel Association

Andreas Araouzos 12, 1303 Nicosia.

Tel 22 452 820.

Fax 22 375 460.

www.cyprushotelassociation.org

AGROTOURISM

Cyprus Agrotourism Company

Leoforos Lemesou 19, PO Box 24535, 1390 Nicosia.

Tel 22 340 071.

Fax 22 334 764.

www.agrotourism.com.cy

Choosing a Hotel

Hotels have been selected across a wide price range for facilities, good value and location. All rooms have private bath and are wheelchair accessible unless otherwise indicated. Most have Internet access, and some form of fitness facilities. The hotels are listed by area. For map references, see the road map on the inside back cover.

PRICE CATEGORIES
The following price ranges are for a twin room with bath or shower including service and tax, in euros.

€ Under €50
€€ €50–€100
€€€ €100–€150
€€€€ €150–€200
€€€€€ Over €200

WEST CYPRUS

CHLORAKAS Azia Beach   €€€€
Akamas Road, Chlorakas, 8099 **Tel** *26 845 100* **Fax** *26 845 200* **Rooms** *299*   **Road Map** A4

With a cool mint-green and white decor complemented by palms in the foyer, the Azia Beach is a refined, elegant hotel. Rooms follow the same colour scheme and have amenities that include a luxury bathroom. The hotel has its own swimming pool and spa complex, and is situated next to a beach close to Pafos. **www.aziaresort.com**

CORAL BAY Crown Resorts Horizon   €€€
Coral Bay Avenue, Coral Bay, Pafos, 8068 **Tel** *26 813 800* **Fax** *26 813 888* **Rooms** *210*   **Road Map** A3

The large, bright foyer of this hotel immediately makes guests feel at home. The four-star Horizon is family-oriented, with numerous facilities for children, including a playground and club. There are also tennis courts, a health centre and a pool complex. The hotel lies in the pretty Coral Bay area of Pafos. **www.crownresortsgroup.com**

CORAL BAY Coral Beach Hotel   €€€€
Coral Bay Avenue, Coral Bay, Pafos, 8099 **Tel** *26 881 000* **Fax** *26 621 742* **Rooms** *421*   **Road Map** A3

With its own pleasure-craft harbour, dining terraces, restaurants, children's facilities and sports amenities, including an Olympic-sized swimming pool where athletes train, this hotel offers everything a family might need for the perfect holiday. Rooms are spacious and attractive, and most have sea views. **www.coral.com.cy**

GEROSKIPOU Ledra Beach   €€€
Theas Aphrodites Avenue, Geroskipou, 8101 **Tel** *26 964 848* **Fax** *26 964 611* **Rooms** *261*   **Road Map** A4

Located right on the seafront in the village of Geroskipou, a few kilometres from Pafos, this modern hotel offers well-presented rooms with many amenities, such as balconies and TVs; not all have sea views, however. Communal facilities include a private marina for small pleasure craft, restaurants and a gym. **www.louishotels.com**

LATSI (LATCHI) Anassa   €€€€€
Baths of Aphrodite Road, Neo Chorio, Latsi, 8830 **Tel** *26 888 000* **Fax** *26 322 900* **Rooms** *177*   **Road Map** A3

Situated in an idyllic spot overlooking the Chrysochou Bay near Polis, this beautiful hotel, the most luxurious on the island, is truly something special. Elegant and secluded, it offers every amenity, including its own spa treatment centre, tennis courts and gardens full of bougainvillea. It also caters for children. **www.thanoshotels.com**

PAFOS Kissos Hotel   €
Verenigis Street, Pafos, 8102 **Tel** *26 936 111* **Fax** *26 945 125* **Rooms** *144*   **Road Map** A4

Centrally located close to the Tombs of the Kings, the Kissos is an attractive three-star hotel with well-presented rooms, some of which overlook a lagoon-style swimming pool. A sauna and gymnasium, tennis courts, mini golf and even a giant-sized chess board are among the amenities for guests. **www.kissoshotel.com**

PAFOS Roman II Hotel   €
Tombs of the Kings Road, Pafos, 8102 **Tel** *26 944 400* **Fax** *26 946 834* **Rooms** *87*   **Road Map** A4

Love it or hate it, you can't ignore the wonderful Roman II Hotel, sister of the Roman Hotel and a landmark building in central Pafos. Both are designed to resemble ancient temples – inside and out. Relax in the rooftop pool, dine on the terraces or enjoy the gardens or health club while surrounded by colourful frescoes. **www.romanhotel.com.cy**

PAFOS Venus Beach   €€
Coral Bay Road, Pafos, 8102 **Tel** *26 949 200* **Fax** *26 949 224* **Rooms** *216*   **Road Map** A4

With an orange and lemon colour scheme throughout, the Venus Beach is a bright, welcoming five-star hotel right on the seafront between Pafos and Coral Bay. It offers restaurants, a health club, children's facilities and even volleyball and tennis for those seeking exercise. **www.venusbeachhotel.com**

PAFOS Alexander the Great   €€€
Poseidon Avenue, Pafos, 8102 **Tel** *26 965 000* **Fax** *26 965 100* **Rooms** *202*   **Road Map** A4

Step inside this seafront hotel surrounded by lush gardens, and its exuberant Old World decor will immediately capture your imagination. Rooms are lavishly presented, too. The hotel offers elegant restaurants serving Cypriot and international cuisine, waterside terraces, pools, a spa and a health centre. **www.kanikahotels.com**

Key to Symbols *see back cover flap*

PAFOS Paphos Amathus Beach   €€€
Poseidon Avenue, Pafos, 8098 **Tel** *26 883 300* **Fax** *26 883 333* **Rooms** *272*   **Road Map** *A4*

A luxurious hotel nestling in extensive landscaped gardens along the seafront, the Paphos Amathus Beach welcomes families and couples alike. Its facilities include a spa, pools and tennis courts. The restaurants use herbs grown in the hotel gardens and serves breads and pastries made in the on-site bakery. **www.amathus-hotels.com/paphos**

PAFOS Pioneer Beach Hotel   €€€
Poseidon Avenue, Pafos, 8101 **Tel** *26 964 500* **Fax** *26 964 370* **Rooms** *254*   **Road Map** *A4*

A resort-style complex that hugs the seafront, the Pioneer Beach offers well-presented rooms that include a fridge, minibar, satellite TV and bathrobes. The hotel also has a pleasant health club, mat-bowling rings and a floodlit tennis court for the energetic, as well as restaurants to suit most tastes. **www.pioneer-cbh.com**

PAFOS Queen Bay Hotel   €€€
Coral Bay Road, Pafos, 8102 **Tel** *26 946 600* **Fax** *26 946 777* **Rooms** *200*   **Road Map** *A3*

Tucked away down a long leafy drive, this seafront hotel specializes in catering for families with small children in tow and offers a paddling pool, adventure playground, children's menu and babysitting services. A snooker room, bars, darts and a health club are available to keep the adults entertained. **www.queensbay.com.cy**

PAFOS St George   €€€
Coral Bay Road, Pafos, 8063 **Tel** *26 845 000* **Fax** *26 845 800* **Rooms** *245*   **Road Map** *A4*

Characterized by the traditional red-roofed St George Chapel that stands in an elevated position at its entrance, this luxury seafront hotel offers elegant yet informal surroundings. Pools and a leisure centre will appeal to those seeking an active holiday, while the lawns offer a place to sit quietly and relax. **www.stgeorge-hotel.com**

PAFOS Annabelle   €€€€
Poseidon Avenue, Pafos, 8102 **Tel** *26 885 000* **Fax** *26 945 502* **Rooms** *198*   **Road Map** *A4*

Guests can relax in luxurious surroundings at the Annabelle, a five-star hotel right on the Pafos seafront. Along with beautifully decorated guest rooms, its Amorosa, Fontana and Mediterraneo restaurants serve fine cuisine (formal dress required), while a health and beauty centre offers a range of treatments. **www.theannabellehotel.com**

PAFOS Elysium Beach Resort   €€€€€
Queen Verenikis Avenue, Pafos, 8107 **Tel** *26 844 444* **Fax** *26 844 333* **Rooms** *249*   **Road Map** *A4*

A modern hotel complex, the Elysium is lavishly presented, refined and relaxing. It is close to Pafos centre and all the attractions of the area. On-site facilities include fine dining and alfresco eateries, the Opium health centre, pools and a children's theme park. The hotel even has its own Byzantine chapel. **www.elysium-hotel.com**

POLIS Bougainvillea Apartments   €
Verginas Street, Polis **Tel** *26 812 250* **Fax** *26 322 203* **Rooms** *28*   **Road Map** *A3*

Located along one of the long roads that lead from the town centre to a pine forest, campsite and secluded beach on the Polis coastline, the Bougainvillea offers apartments and villas that are ideal for those who want to get away from it all. The accommodation is well presented. **www.bougainvillea.com.cy**

POLIS Natura Beach Hotel   €€
Christodoulou Papanilopoulou Street, Polis, 8830 **Tel** *26 323 111* **Fax** *26 322 822* **Rooms** *60*   **Road Map** *A3*

It would be rare to find such a welcoming family-run hotel in a better position than the Natura Beach. Literally steps from the beach and water's edge, along a quiet coastal road, the hotel offers rooms and chalets with outstanding views of the bay. The restaurant uses fresh produce from its own garden. **www.natura.com.cy**

SOUTHERN CYPRUS

AGIA NAPA Limanaki Beach Hotel   €€
1 October Street, Agia Napa, 5330 **Tel** *23 721 600* **Fax** *23 722 345* **Rooms** *70*   **Road Map** *E3*

One of the most popular smaller hotels in Agia Napa, not least because of its superb location right on the seafront, the Limanaki Beach offers delightful rooms with many facilities and a pleasant restaurant *(see p172)* serving Cypriot and international cuisine. It has a terrace and a wonderful sea view. **www.ayianapahotels.net**

AGIA NAPA Grecian Bay Hotel   €€€
32 Kryo Nero, Agia Napa, 5330 **Tel** *23 842 000* **Fax** *23 721 307* **Rooms** *271*   **Road Map** *E3*

Set among landscaped gardens and lush greenery, this five-star hotel is part of the Grecian Park Hotel complex and, as such, has access to even more leisure facilities than those on-site. The rooms are beautifully presented and each one has a private balcony, although you must specify if you want a sea view. **www.grecianbay.com**

AGIA NAPA Nissi Beach   €€€€
Nissi Avenue 5330, Nissi Beach, Agia Napa, 5343 **Tel** *23 721 021* **Fax** *23 721 623* **Rooms** *270*   **Road Map** *E3*

The Nissi Beach is a sprawling hotel housed in a landmark building in the centre of Agia Napa. It is the resort's most luxurious accommodation, with every amenity – from live dancing and music most evenings, to top-quality restaurants, sports facilities and exotic gardens. **www.nissi-beach.com**

AMATHOUS Amathus Beach Hotel

Amathous Avenue, Limassol, 4044 **Tel** *25 832 000* **Fax** *25 832 540* **Rooms** *244*   **Road Map** *C4*

The luxurious foyer of this seafront hotel is a taster of the exquisite decor that continues throughout the building. The main restaurant and terrace overlook the gardens and the sea, while the hotel's facilities include a spa and well-being centre, pools, tennis courts and suites with private pools. **www.amathus-hotels.com/limassol**

AMATHOUS Grand Resort

Amathous Avenue, Limassol, 3724 **Tel** *25 634 333* **Fax** *25 636 945* **Rooms** *255*   **Road Map** *C4*

Dominating the skyline, the Grand Resort is one of the landmark hotels in Limassol's Amathous district. It is large and sprawling, and yet its palm-tree-fringed swimming pools and gardens provide intimate areas to relax and unwind. Amenities include fine restaurants, a health centre and tennis courts. **www.grandresort.com.cy**

EPISKOPI Episkopiana Hotel

Kremastis Street, Episkopi, 3505 **Tel** *25 935 093* **Fax** *25 935 094* **Rooms** *100*   **Road Map** *B4*

With children's facilities that include playgrounds, a pool, babysitting services and a programme of events, the Episkopiana is an ideal base for a family. Lying between Pafos and Limassol in Episkopi village, it offers the chance to get away from it all, but many tourist attractions are still only a short drive away. **www.episkopiana.com**

LARNAKA Faros Village

Faros Avenue, Pervolia, Larnaka, 6305 **Tel** *24 422 111* **Fax** *24 422 114* **Rooms** *134*   **Road Map** *D3*

The Faros Village lives up to its name, with numerous facilities for day-to-day life, including shops, a restaurant *(see p172)*, tennis courts, children's playgrounds and even a mini-golf course. Its guest rooms are well presented and housed in low buildings close to its swimming pool and extensive exotic gardens. **www.farosvillage.com**

LARNAKA Boronia Hotel Apartments

Dhekelia Road, Larnaka, 7040 **Tel** *24 646 200* **Fax** *24 644 120* **Rooms** *19*   **Road Map** *D3*

The Boronia Hotel Apartments have an excellent location only 500 metres from the water's edge. There are also shops and a good selection of tavernas close by. With a small complex of apartments centred around a pool, the resort is quiet and has its own restaurant serving European fare.

LARNAKA Lenios Beach Hotel

Dhekelia Road, Larnaka, 7040 **Tel** *24 646 100* **Fax** *24 647 104* **Rooms** *54*   **Road Map** *D3*

Located on a sandy beach close to Larnaka's main attractions, the Lenios Beach is a modern, attractive hotel with a wealth of facilities for guests. These include a Mediterranean-themed restaurant and a garden eatery, a health suite with a sauna, a pool and well-presented guest rooms. **www.lenioshotel.com**

LARNAKA Svetlos Hotel

Oroklini Road, Oroklini, 7040 **Tel** *24 824 900* **Fax** *24 824 901* **Rooms** *46*   **Road Map** *D3*

With facilities that include a health club, tennis courts, children's play areas and a Mediterranean-style restaurant, the Sveltos is ideal for family relaxation. It is also great for exploring Larnaka, thanks to its proximity to the major sights of the city, such as the medieval fort and the Pierides-Marfin Laiki Bank Museum.

LARNAKA Louis Princess Beach Hotel

Dhekelia Road, Oroklini, Larnaka, 7041 **Tel** *24 645 500* **Fax** *24 645 508* **Rooms** *138*   **Road Map** *D3*

The long sweep of whitewashed buildings surrounded by palm trees and a lagoon-style swimming pool make the Louis Princess Beach a relaxing venue for a long- or short-stay holiday. A fitness suite complete with a gymnasium and a spa, as well as a range of restaurants are available to all guests. **www.louishotels.com**

LARNAKA The Golden Bay Beach Hotel

Dhekelia Road, Pyla, Larnaka, 7080 **Tel** *24 645 444* **Fax** *24 645 451* **Rooms** *193*   **Road Map** *D3*

Set beside the gorgeous sandy beach of Golden Bay, this contemporary hotel has its own Greek village-style taverna, The Ouzeri, and an à la carte restaurant, Les Etoiles. There's a piano bar, a health centre, pools and children's playground facilities, too. Guest rooms offer plenty of amenities. **www.lordos.com.cy**

LARNAKA Lordos Beach Hotel

Dhekelia Road, Pyla, Larnaka, 7080 **Tel** *24 647 444* **Fax** *24 645 847* **Rooms** *175*   **Road Map** *D3*

Specializing in facilities for all age groups – including paddling pools and playgrounds for the little ones, and a solarium, billiards rooms, tennis courts and watersports for the grown-ups – the Lordos Beach is a good choice for a family holiday. It lies next to a long, sandy beach and is close to town. **www.lordos.com.cy**

LARNAKA Palm Beach Hotel

Dhekelia Road, Oroklini, Larnaka, 7040 **Tel** *24 846 600* **Fax** *24 846 601* **Rooms** *228*   **Road Map** *D3*

Close to Larnaka centre, this seafront hotel is set in extensive gardens with more than 700 mature palm trees and native shrubs. A beach and a coastal walkway are just a few metres' walk from the breakfast restaurant. Guest rooms, decorated in the Mediterranean-style, have hi-tech gadgets and TVs. **www.palmbeachhotel.com**

LIMASSOL Pefkos Hotel

Kavazoglou and Misiaouli 70, Limassol, 3608 **Tel** *25 660 066* **Fax** *25 577 083* **Rooms** *97*   **Road Map** *C4*

Centrally located right near the Old Town of Limassol, the shopping complexes and the hub of evening eateries, the Pefkos Hotel offers a good base for a lively holiday. It has its own pool, restaurant and games rooms, and accommodation is well presented, with satellite TVs and other features. **www.pefkoshotel.com**

Key to Price Guide *see p158* **Key to Symbols** *see back cover flap*

LIMASSOL Aquarius Beach   €€
*Amathous Avenue, Mouttagiaka, Limassol, 4531 **Tel** 25 326 666 **Fax** 25 430 666 **Rooms** 33   **Road Map** C4*

Standing right on the Limassol seafront, beside a clean sandy beach, and featuring a restaurant that frequently hosts local musicians playing traditional Cypriot music, the Aquarius Beach is a popular establishment. Guests can enjoy the private swimming pool and the lush gardens. **www.aquarius-cy.com**

LIMASSOL Golden Arches   €€
*Amathous Avenue, Limassol, 3721 **Tel** 25 322 433 **Fax** 25 325 835 **Rooms** 110   **Road Map** C4*

The Golden Arches takes its name from the arches that form part of its façade, giving this hotel a distinctive look. Facilities include lavish gardens, swimming pools and even a nightclub with live music, along with a restaurant. All the rooms have been decorated in a Mediterranean style. **www.goldenarcheshotel.com**

LIMASSOL Arsinoe Beach Hotel   €€€
*62 Amathous Avenue, Limassol, 4532 **Tel** 25 321 444 **Fax** 25 329 908 **Rooms** 179   **Road Map** C4*

With sports facilities that include a gymnasium, tennis, watersports, swimming pools and a health suite, the seafront Arsinoe Beach is popular with active families. Evenings can be spent in its piano bar or restaurants, and the hotel arranges special Cyprus Nights, with live music and dancing. **www.arsinoe-hotel.com**

LIMASSOL Four Seasons   €€€€€
*Amathous Avenue, Limassol, 3313 **Tel** 25 858 000 **Fax** 25 310 887 **Rooms** 287   **Road Map** C4*

The bronze glass-front façade of this five-star hotel on the coastal road makes an impact at first glance – and inside it just gets better. From its extensive health and spa centre to its fine à la carte restaurants, landscaped gardens and lavish guest rooms, this hotel is one of the finest on the island. **www.fourseasons.com.cy**

LIMASSOL Le Meridien Spa and Resort   €€€€€
*Coast Road, Limassol, 3308 **Tel** 25 862 000 **Fax** 25 634 222 **Rooms** 339   **Road Map** C4*

A sprawling hotel in lush gardens and with a seemingly endless array of amenities for families, Le Meridien is noted for having one of the largest indoor and outdoor thalassotherapy centres in the Mediterranean. The rooms have been decorated beautifully, and all have a private bathroom and a TV. **www.lemeridien.com**

LIMASSOL Londa   €€€€€
*72 George I Avenue, Limassol, 3509 **Tel** 25 865 555 **Fax** 25 320 040 **Rooms** 68   **Road Map** C4*

A chic boutique-style hotel, the Londa offers a beachside location and many amenities, including its Caprice of Mykonos restaurant (formal dress required), patisserie and bar, a stylish pool and extensive conference facilities. Rooms are effortlessly elegant and contemporary, while the gardens are lavishly planted. **www.londahotel.com**

LIMASSOL Mediterranean Beach   €€€€€
*Amathous Avenue, Limassol, 3310 **Tel** 25 311 777 **Fax** 25 324 754 **Rooms** 291   **Road Map** C4*

This is a contemporary building with large expanses of glass that make it bright and airy. The extensive gardens are complete with stone features and bridges that cross to islands in the middle of the swimming pools. The hotel's exclusive restaurants, spa and guest rooms are pure five-star luxury. **www.medbeach.com**

LIMASSOL St Raphael Resort   €€€€€
*Amathous Avenue, Limassol, 3594 **Tel** 25 634 100 **Fax** 25 636 394 **Rooms** 272   **Road Map** C4*

A bright, fresh family-oriented hotel, the five-star St Raphael Resort is located in luxurious surroundings. Many of its rooms boast a sea view and are equipped with balconies and flat-screen TVs. Restaurants (formal dress) and bars, pools, sports facilities and a spa combine to make this a great place to stay. **www.raphael.com.cy**

PANO LEFKARA Lefkarama   €
*Pano Lefkara village centre, 7705 **Tel** 24 342 154 **Fax** 24 342 154 **Rooms** 10   **Road Map** C4*

The family-run Lefkarama is housed in a beautiful traditional Cypriot stone-cottage building complete with stone arches and bougainvillea in the courtyard. It offers a homely base to explore the village, which is famous for its lace-making, and the surrounding mountainside.

PISSOURI Bunch of Grapes Inn   €
*Ioamou Erotokritou Street, Pissouri, 3779 **Tel** 25 221 275 **Fax** 25 222 510 **Rooms** 11   **Road Map** B4*

Located in the heart of the pretty hilltop village of Pissouri, in a small street of traditional Cypriot stone cottages, this small family-run hotel offers its guests the chance to immerse themselves in village life, but remains well positioned for travelling further afield to see the island. The restaurant specializes in home-made local dishes.

PISSOURI Columbia Beach Hotel & Resort   €€€€€
*Coastal road, Pissouri Bay, 3779 **Tel** 25 833 333 **Fax** 25 221 505 **Rooms** 129   **Road Map** B4*

Overlooking the beautiful Pissouri Bay and set within a complex that has been architecturally designed to resemble a traditional Cypriot village, the Columbia Beach features sophisticated restaurants, a health spa and fitness suite, and extremely comfortable guest rooms. There is also an on-site chapel. **www.columbia-hotels.com**

TOCHNI Cyprus Villages   €
*Various venues **Tel** 24 332 998 **Rooms** 80   **Road Map** C4*

Cyprus Villages is the collective name for several holiday complexes in the villages of Tochni, Kalvassos, Skarinou and Psematismenos. Packages include a range of activities, such as cookery and horse riding, although not all venues have pools, fitness and children's facilities or restaurants on-site. **www.cyprusvillages.com.cy**

TROODOS MOUNTAINS

KAKOPETRIA Krystal Hotel
Gr Digenis Street, Kakopetria, 2810 **Tel** *22 922 433* **Fax** *22 923 678* **Rooms** *29*   **Road Map** *B3*

The Krystal is a small, privately run hotel set in its own gardens and located a short walk from the centre of the village of Kakopetria. Its attractive restaurant has been decorated with traditional stone features and serves a mixture of typical Cypriot cuisine and international dishes. A babysitting service is also available.

KAKOPETRIA Makris Hotel
Kakopetria village, 2810 **Tel** *22 922 419* **Fax** *22 923 367* **Rooms** *52*   **Road Map** *B3*

Set in a pine forest in the heart of the Troodos Mountains, in the popular resort of Kakopetria, the Makris is the place for a relaxing break. Facilities include a swimming pool, tennis courts and organized excursions. The hotel is ideally situated for visitors seeking refreshing walks in the summer and snow in winter. **www.makrishotel.com**

KAKOPETRIA The Mill Hotel
Mylou 8, Kakopetria, 2810 **Tel** *22 922 536* **Fax** *22 813 970* **Rooms** *13*   **Road Map** *B3*

Housed within a former mill building in the heart of Kakopetria, this hotel is renowned for its good restaurant *(see p173)*, specializing in trout. Features include guest rooms and suites with satellite TV and Internet connection, along with a team that will organize guides for trips into the Troodos Mountains. **www.cymillhotel.com**

PEDOULAS Mountain Rose
Pedoulas village, 2850 **Tel** *22 952 727* **Fax** *22 953 295* **Rooms** *15*   **Road Map** *B3*

A cosy hotel in the centre of Pedoulas village, the Mountain Rose has its own restaurant, which serves Cypriot cuisine, as well as the occasional international dish. Produce is usually fresh from the village itself. The well-presented rooms have private bathrooms and television. **www.mountainrosehotel.com**

PEDOULAS Health Habitat Hotel
Pedoulas village, 1306 **Tel** *22 952 283* **Fax** *22 314 017* **Rooms** *30*   **Road Map** *B3*

A health and slimming resort, this complex offers a consultation upon arrival to devise a specially tailored diet that will be served in the à la carte restaurant. A programme of sauna, gym and exercise is provided, along with suggestions for relaxation. Guests can enjoy cycling and treks into the Troodos Mountains.

PEDOULAS Two Flowers
Filoksenias 26, Pedoulas, 2850 **Tel** *22 952 372* **Fax** *22 952 235* **Rooms** *14*   **Road Map** *B3*

Surrounded by trees and with views towards Mount Olympus, the highest point on the island, this small hotel is a great place to stay and unwind. Housed in a period property, its guest rooms are well presented with features such as beams and stone walls. Classic local dishes are served in its elegant restaurant. **www.twoflowershotel.com**

PLATRES Petit Palais Hotel
Pano Platres, Platres, 4825 **Tel** *25 422 723* **Fax** *25 421 065* **Rooms** *32*   **Road Map** *B3*

The Petit Palais Hotel serves home-made Cypriot dishes in its pretty little restaurant and open-air café. A terrace on the first floor provides a great place to sit and enjoy the scenery of the Troodos Mountains. Its guest rooms have balconies with fine views, too, along with facilities that include TVs. **www.petitpalaishotel.com**

PLATRES Spring Hotel
Psilo Dentro, Platres, 4820 **Tel** *25 421 330* **Fax** *25 421 330* **Rooms** *14*   **Road Map** *B3*

Standing in the foothills of the Troodos Mountains, the Spring Hotel offers panoramic views from almost all the guestroom balconies. It is pleasingly furnished and homely throughout. Guests can enjoy traditional, home-cooked meals and drinks on the terrace, or follow one of the nearby hiking trails into the forest. **www.spring-hotel.net**

PLATRES Edelweiss Hotel
53 Spyrou Kyprianou Street, Platres, 4820 **Tel** *25 421 335* **Fax** *25 422 060* **Rooms** *22*   **Road Map** *B3*

The Edelweiss is an attractive whitewashed hotel with wooden shutters that give it enormous charm. Its guest rooms are beautifully presented and include private bathrooms and balconies, along with satellite TV. The hotel restaurant's terrace affords diners some wonderful views. **www.edelweisshotel.com.cy**

PLATRES Forest Park Hotel
62 Spyrou Kyprianou Street, Platres, 4825 **Tel** *25 421 751* **Fax** *25 421 875* **Rooms** *137*   **Road Map** *B3*

The largest and most luxurious of all the hotels in the Troodos Mountains, the Forest Park has a large range of amenities available for its guests. There's a health suite with sauna and fitness room, swimming pools, tennis courts and restaurants. Guest rooms are well presented, with fabulous views. **www.forestparkhotel.com.cy**

PLATRES New Helvetia Hotel
Helvetia Street, Platres, 4820 **Tel** *25 421 348* **Fax** *25 422 148* **Rooms** *32*   **Road Map** *B3*

Located in the heart of Platres, close to the town's tavernas, walking routes and cycling trails, the New Helvetia is ideal for activity-break enthusiasts. It offers guests the use of a gymnasium, a mountain-bike station and a relaxation area. Other features include a restaurant, lounge bar and breakfast terrace. **www.newhelvetiahotel.com**

Key to Price Guide *see p158* **Key to Symbols** *see back cover flap*

PLATRES Pendeli Hotel €€

Pano Platres, Platres, 4825 **Tel** *25 421 736* **Fax** *25 421 808* **Rooms** *81* **Road Map** *B3*

An attractive hotel with a heated outdoor swimming pool and lovely gardens, the Pendeli is popular with visitors who enjoy a rural location. The restaurant serves fine cuisine, including a range of local dishes, while its fitness facilities allow guests to work off any excess calories consumed. **www.pendelihotel.com**

TROODOS Jubilee Hotel €

Troodos village, 1504 **Tel** *25 420 107* **Fax** *22 673 991* **Rooms** *37* **Road Map** *B3*

The highest hotel in Cyprus at 1,727 m (5,666 ft) above sea level, the Jubilee is the only hotel in Troodos village itself. Stylishly presented, it offers fine cuisine in its restaurant, a children's play room and a whole host of activities – from skiing, hiking and rambling, to birdwatching and cycling. **www.jubileehotel.com**

CENTRAL CYPRUS

AGROS Vlachos Hotel €

Agros village, 4860 **Tel** *25 521 330* **Fax** *25 521 890* **Rooms** *18* **Road Map** *C3*

This attractive and compact hotel in the village of Agros, in the heart of the island, offers well presented and comfortable rooms. A babysitting service is available for parents who may wish to enjoy the cosy bar or linger over the extensive menu in the restaurant *(see p175)*.

AGROS Rodon Hotel €€

Rodou 1, Agros, 4860 **Tel** *25 521 201* **Fax** *25 521 235* **Rooms** *155* **Road Map** *C3*

Situated in a mountainside location overlooking olive groves and the river, the Rodon is a large, bright hotel offering many amenities for its guests. Among its facilities are a restaurant *(see p175)* serving fine local cuisine and dishes with a European flavour, a gymnasium, a health centre and tennis courts. **www.rodonhotel.com**

ASKAS Evgenia's House €

77 Gregori Afxentiou, Askas 2752 **Tel** *22 642 344* **Fax** *22 643 122* **Rooms** *4* **Road Map** *C3*

Housed in a stone building dating from around 1800, Evgenia's House is part of an island-wide agrotourism project that renovates period homes in villages, providing accommodation for visitors. Features include wooden beams, traditional reed ceilings, balconies and stone floors. No meals are provided but there are tavernas in Askas village.

LYTHRODONTAS Avli Georgallidi Hotel €€

3 M Drakos, Lythrodontas, 2565 **Tel** *22 543 236* **Fax** *22 517 172* **Rooms** *5* **Road Map** *C3*

A traditional style hotel in its own gardens, surrounded by the Machairas Forest, the Avli Georgallidi makes a great place to escape the fast lane and is an ideal base for visits to the ancient sites at Tamassos and Idalion. Guest rooms are cosy and there's a restaurant that specializes in using home-grown produce. **www.avli.com.cy**

SOUTH NICOSIA

SOUTH NICOSIA Asty Hotel €€

Prince Charles 12, Nicosia, 2373 **Tel** *22 773 030* **Fax** *22 773 311* **Rooms** *52* **Road Map** *C3*

Just a short walk from the Agios Dometicos Church and within easy reach of the Cyprus Museum, the Asty is conveniently located for those intending to explore the city. It offers a restaurant serving a wide choice of international dishes, along with pretty gardens and mini golf. **www.astyhotel.com**

SOUTH NICOSIA Averof Hotel €€

19 Averof Street, Nicosia, 1702 **Tel** *22 773 447* **Fax** *22 773 411* **Rooms** *25* **Road Map** *C3*

The Averof is a small yet attractive establishment that is within easy reach of the main attractions of Nicosia. It is pleasingly presented throughout, and despite not having many facilities for guests other than a cosy bar and restaurant, it is a good base from which to explore the island's capital. **www.averof.com.cy**

SOUTH NICOSIA Classic Hotel €€€

94 Regaena Street, Nicosia, 1010 **Tel** *22 664 006* **Fax** *22 670 072* **Rooms** *57* **Road Map** *C3*

Situated within the city walls of the Old Town, the Classic is a stylish hotel with a range of executive rooms, each with facilities that include satellite TV and a minibar. It is close to Nicosia's main attractions, and features an up-market restaurant that serves traditional cuisine and wine. **www.classic.com.cy**

SOUTH NICOSIA Castelli Hotel €€€€

38 Ouzounian Street, Nicosia, 1504 **Tel** *22 712 812* **Fax** *22 680 176* **Rooms** *46* **Road Map** *C3*

With a hint of colonial styling in its appearance, and featuring rich wood panelling, glass in abundance and lavish flooring and furnishings, the Castelli is an elegant if small hotel. It is located just inside the walls of the city and has a large restaurant that serves a range of classic dishes.

SOUTH NICOSIA Holiday Inn Nicosia
🛜 🍽 ≋ 🏋 📺 🍴 📶 **P**   €€€€
70 Regaena Street, Nicosia, 1504 **Tel** *22 712 712* **Fax** *22 673 337* **Rooms** *140*   **Road Map** *C3*

Ideal as a base for exploring Nicosia, the Holiday Inn is located within the city walls and just minutes from the famous Ledra Street. Its full complement of amenities includes beautifully presented guest rooms, several themed restaurants serving international cuisine and lots of leisure facilities. **www.holiday-inn.com**

SOUTH NICOSIA Cleopatra Hotel
🛜 🍽 ≋ 🏋 📺 🍴 📶 **P**   €€€€€
8 Florina Street, Nicosia, 1065 **Tel** *22 844 000* **Fax** *22 844 222* **Rooms** *90*   **Road Map** *C3*

An elegant four-star hotel, the Cleopatra is within easy walking distance of the city walls and the main shopping and commercial areas of the city. There is also a vast selection of tavernas close by. The hotel has its own swimming pool and terraces, along with a fine-dining restaurant, a gym and a health centre. **www.cleopatra.com.cy**

SOUTH NICOSIA Hilton Cyprus
🛜 🍽 ≋ 🏋 📺 🍴 📶 **P**   €€€€€
Archbishop Makarios III Avenue, Nicosia, 1077 **Tel** *22 377 777* **Fax** *22 377 788* **Rooms** *298*   **Road Map** *C3*

The only five-star hotel in Nicosia and, without any doubt, the most luxurious, the Hilton offers every amenity to its guests – from pools, a health spa and fitness facilities, to fine dining, live music and beautifully presented rooms. It stands in exotic gardens, just minutes from the city centre. **www.hilton.com**

SOUTH NICOSIA Hilton Park Nicosia
🛜 🍽 ≋ 🏋 📺 🍴 📶 **P**   €€€€€
Grivas Digenis Avenue, Nicosia, 2413 **Tel** *22 695 111* **Fax** *22 351 918* **Rooms** *194*   **Road Map** *C3*

Located in the commercial heart of the city, the Hilton Park is geared towards the business traveller, but it is equally suitable for holiday-makers keen to be in the thick of city life. It has every comfort you could wish for – from tasteful rooms to an à la carte restaurant and an exotic palm-tree-filled lobby. **www.hilton.com**

NORTH CYPRUS

BELLAPAIS Ambelia Village
🍽 ≋ 🏋 🍴 📶 **P**   €€
PO Box 95, Bellapais **Tel** *0392 815 36 55* **Fax** *0392 815 77 01* **Rooms** *50*   **Road Map** *C2*

The Ambelia Village is an attractive collection of self-catering studios and villas in either a poolside or landscaped garden location; all have air conditioning. The hotel itself has a Mediterranean-themed restaurant and is just five minutes' walk from the centre of Bellapais and its abbey ruins. **www.cyprus-ambelia.com**

BELLAPAIS Bellapais Gardens
🍽 ≋ 🏋 🍴 📶 **P**   €€
Beylerbeyi, Crusader Road, Bellapais **Tel** *0392 815 60 66* **Fax** *0392 815 76 67* **Rooms** *17*   **Road Map** *C2*

Housed in a dramatic building on the hillside close to the abbey, the Bellapais Gardens complex is run by a family who pride themselves on their hospitality. Their restaurant has a menu that uses the finest local ingredients and features regional delicacies. The hotel has a pool and a bar. **www.bellapaisgardens.com**

FAMAGUSTA (GAZIMAĞUSA) Mimoza Beach
🍽 ≋ 🏋 📺 🍴 📶 **P**   €€
Famagusta **Tel** *0392 378 82 19* **Fax** *0392 378 82 09* **Rooms** *51*   **Road Map** *E3*

Standing alongside a sandy beach, with every guest room enjoying a sea view from the balcony, the Mimoza Beach is popular with holidaying families. It has children's play areas, along with a lagoon-style pool, gardens and a restaurant where Cypriot Nights are held, with live music and dancing. **www.mimozabeachhotel.com**

FAMAGUSTA (GAZIMAĞUSA) Park Hotel
🍽 ≋ 🏋 📺 🍴 📶 **P**   €€
Salamis Road, Famagusta **Tel** *0392 378 82 13* **Fax** *0392 378 91 11* **Rooms** *93*   **Road Map** *E3*

With tennis courts, windsurfing and a large swimming pool available, the Park Hotel is a magnet for travellers keen on exercise. It stands beside a sandy beach not far from Salamis, and has many guest rooms offering sea views. Among its facilities is a restaurant serving local and international cuisine.

FAMAGUSTA (GAZIMAĞUSA) Portofino Hotel
🍽 ≋ 🏋 🍴 📶 **P**   €€
Fevzi Cakmak Avenue, Famagusta **Tel** *0392 366 43 92* **Fax** *0392 366 29 49* **Rooms** *53*   **Road Map** *E3*

The Portofino is not the most inspiring-looking hotel, but step inside and a bright, airy foyer awaits. Its guest rooms are equally pleasing and come complete with a lounge area and balcony. Turkish and Cypriot cuisine is on offer at its roof bar and restaurant, which both afford great views. **www.portofinohotel-cyprus.com**

FAMAGUSTA (GAZIMAĞUSA) Salamis Bay Conti Resort Hotel
🛜 🍽 ≋ 🏋 📺 🍴 📶 **P**   €€€
Famagusta **Tel** *0392 378 82 00* **Rooms** *392*   **Road Map** *E3*

The Salamis Bay Conti Resort is one of the largest and most luxurious complexes on the east coast of the island. It has every facility for guests, including restaurants, numerous bars, swimming pools, children's play areas and a health spa, along with sports such as basketball. **www.salamisbay-conti.com**

FAMAGUSTA (GAZIMAĞUSA) Palm Beach Hotel
🛜 🍽 ≋ 🏋 📺 🍴 📶 **P**   €€€€
Deve Limani, Famagusta **Tel** *0392 366 20 00* **Fax** *0392 366 20 02* **Rooms** *108*   **Road Map** *E3*

With a bright cream and peach decor and lots of outdoor dining areas, this contemporary hotel situated right on the beach is popular with families as well as couples. It has its own casino, and room amenities include balconies or terraces, private bathrooms and multichannel TV. **www.northernpalmbeach.com**

Key to Price Guide *see p158* **Key to Symbols** *see back cover flap*

KARAVAS (ALCANCAK) Merit Crystal Cove Hotel 🖼 🍴 🏊 🛅 📺 📋 🅿   €€€

Karavas, Kyrenia **Tel** *0392 821 23 45* **Fax** *0392 821 87 74* **Rooms** *307*   **Road Map** *C2*

Perched high on the rocks of the coastline and overlooking a sweep of sandy beach, the Merit Crystal Cove is one of the most luxurious hotels in the area. It offers beautiful comfortable guest rooms and a range of extras including its own casino, watersports, a health spa and a beauty centre. **www.meritcrystalcove.com**

KYRENIA (GIRNE) Acapulco Beach Club 🖼 🍴 🏊 🛅 📺 📋 🅿   €

Acapulco Holiday Village, Catalkoy, Kyrenia **Tel** *0392 824 44 49* **Fax** *0392 824 44 55* **Rooms** *470* **Road Map** *C2*

A family-oriented seaside resort, the Acapulco is big in both size and character. Whatever the hour, there is almost always something to do. Numerous sports are offered, such as tennis and golf, and guests can enjoy some of the finest Mediterranean-style cuisine in one of the resort's numerous restaurants. **www.acapulco.com.tr**

KYRENIA (GIRNE) British Hotel 🖼 🍴 📋 🅿   €

Eftal Akca Street, Yacht Harbour, Kyrenia **Tel** *0392 815 22 40* **Fax** *0392 815 27 42* **Rooms** *18*   **Road Map** *C2*

Located beside the pretty harbour, the British Hotel couldn't be better placed for exploring Kyrenia. A tall, narrow building, it has rooms over four floors, all with private facilities and most with balconies and views of the harbour. The hotel also has its own restaurant and roof terrace. **www.britishhotelcyprus.com**

KYRENIA (GIRNE) Club Lapethos 🖼 🍴 🏊 🛅 📺 📋 🅿   €€

Maresai Fevri Cakmak Avenue, Kyrenia **Tel** *0392 821 86 69* **Fax** *0392 821 89 66* **Rooms** *230*   **Road Map** *C2*

An 800 sq m (8,610 sq ft) swimming pool, a pool garden of similar proportions and an indoor pool will keep even the most ardent swimmer content for days. Many other sporting activities are available at the Club Lapethos, too. Guest rooms are well presented, and there are many restaurants and children's play areas. **www.lapethosresort.com**

KYRENIA (GIRNE) Dome Hotel 🖼 🍴 🏊 🛅 📺 📋 🅿   €€

Kordonboyu Avenue, Kyrenia **Tel** *0392 815 24 53* **Fax** *0392 815 27 72* **Rooms** *160*   **Road Map** *C2*

Arguably the most famous hotel in Kyrenia, the Dome has seen many changes since it first opened its doors to travellers in 1939. Located right on the seafront and having undergone a sophisticated refurbishment, the hotel today is stylish as ever. **www.dome-cyprus.com**

KYRENIA (GIRNE) Onar Holiday Village Hotel 🍴 🏊 🛅 📺 📋 🅿   €€

PK 736, Kyrenia **Tel** *0392 815 58 50* **Fax** *0392 815 58 53* **Rooms** *64*   **Road Map** *C2*

Situated in the foothills of the Five Finger mountain range overlooking Kyrenia, the Onar Holiday Village is a peaceful base for long or short family breaks. Its whitewashed villas, designed to resemble traditional Cypriot cottages, stand in lush gardens and have many amenities, including air conditioning. **www.onarvillage.com**

KYRENIA (GIRNE) The Colony 🖼 🍴 🏊 🛅 📺 📋 🅿   €€€€

Ecevit Avenue, Kyrenia **Tel** *0392 815 15 18* **Fax** *0392 815 59 88* **Rooms** *94*   **Road Map** *C2*

Kyrenia's most luxurious hotel can provide elegant evening cocktails or relaxation in the hot tub depending on your mood. Sumptuous furnishings can be seen everywhere, rooms are gloriously lavish and there are lots of places to escape the fast lane, such as the Piazza courtyard. **www.parkheritage.com**

KYRENIA (GIRNE) Jasmine Court Hotel 🖼 🍴 🏊 🛅 📺 📋 🅿   €€€€

Naci Talat Cad, Kyrenia **Tel** *0392 444 77 70* **Fax** *0392 650 00 70* **Rooms** *192*   **Road Map** *C2*

Looking out over the sea off Kyrenia, the sprawling Jasmine Court is an elegant five-star beachside complex. Its restaurants, including the Babacakka Restaurant and Café de Paris, serve fine cuisine from around the world. Guests can also enjoy its fitness suite, casino, pools and regular themed entertainment. **www.jasminecourthotel.com**

LAPITHOS (LAPTA) LA Hotel & Resort 🍴 🏊 🛅 📺 📋 🅿   €

Maresai Fevzi Cakmak Cad, Lapithos **Tel** *0392 821 89 81* **Fax** *0392 821 89 92* **Rooms** *180*   **Road Map** *C2*

Set in the historic village of Lapithos, a short distance from Kyrenia, the LA Hotel & Resort is a sprawling complex of well-presented and equipped villas and restaurants designed in a style befitting the Mediterranean location. The buildings stand in mature gardens that surround a pool and sun terraces. **www.la-hotel-cyprus.com**

LAPITHOS (LAPTA) Manolya Hotel 🖼 🍴 🏊 🛅 📺 📋 🅿   €

Maresai Fevri Cakmak Cad, Lapithos **Tel** *0392 821 84 98* **Fax** *0392 821 81 24* **Rooms** *61*   **Road Map** *C2*

An attractive hotel nestled on a rocky stretch of seashore with the Besparmak Mountains as a backdrop, the Manolya is ideal for exploring the area's rugged coastline. It is beautifully presented throughout, with guest rooms and restaurants, and even the children's play areas, all affording great views. **www.manolyahotel.com**

LÉFKA (LEFKE) Lefke Gardens Hotel 🍴 🏊 🛅 📋 🅿   €

Léfka, Guzelyurt **Tel** *0392 728 82 23* **Fax** *0392 728 82 22* **Rooms** *21*   **Road Map** *C2*

With its pretty courtyard dining area and pool, the Lefke Gardens Hotel in the heart of Léfka village has a relaxing feel. Housed in a renovated period property, it also oozes character. Guest rooms are decorated in traditional Cypriot style and offer facilities such as a minibar, bathroom and TV.

NORTH NICOSIA (LEFKOŞA) Saray Hotel 🖼 🍴 🛅 📺 📋   €€

Ataturk Meydani, North Nicosia **Tel** *0392 228 30 02* **Fax** *0392 228 48 08* **Rooms** *72*   **Road Map** *C3*

This centrally located hotel affords guests the chance to spend evenings under the stars in its rooftop bar and restaurant, admiring the view of Nicosia while dining on Turkish Cypriot-inspired cuisine. The Saray has well-presented guest rooms, a disco, an American bar and a casino.

WHERE TO EAT

Signboard of a Cypriot tavern

The range of restaurants in Cyprus is wide enough to satisfy even the most discerning gastronome. The predominant type of eatery is the small, inexpensive bar; the most popular serving local cuisine. The true atmosphere of a Cypriot banquet can be experienced in a traditional *taverna*, while smart restaurants are more likely to serve European cuisine. Greek-style *tavernas* and Turkish-style restaurants *(meyhane)* guarantee an evening with a great Cypriot atmosphere, often featuring folk performances and music. In general, the further you go from the popular resorts, the more authentic the cuisine.

A traditional Cypriot *taverna* in Nicosia

CHOOSING A RESTAURANT

A vast selection of eating establishments exists in Cyprus. This is particularly evident in the popular resorts, where there are tavernas and restaurants on every street, serving a range of local and international cuisine. In addition to the traditional *tavernas*, serving Greek and Turkish-influenced dishes, there are French, Italian, Mexican, Chinese, Thai, Indian, Middle Eastern, Russian and even Japanese restaurants.

There are also hundreds of cafés and snack bars, as well as a growing number of inter-national fast-food restaurants

Most restaurants are casual, without a dress code. In terms of value, restaurants in town are usually cheaper than hotel restaurants. Look out for establishments frequented by the locals – these tend to serve good-value, tasty food.

On the whole, eating out in Cyprus is reasonable. Do bear in mind, however, that imported wines are much more expensive than locally produced wines.

WHEN TO EAT

Breakfast is usually eaten between 7:30 and 10am. Most budget and inexpensive hotels serve a Continental breakfast, consisting of tea or coffee, fruit juice, toast, white bread, jam, honey and butter. Upscale hotels usually provide guests with a self-service bar, stocked with light salads, a selection of cheeses, scrambled eggs and sausages. In North Cyprus it is custom-ary to serve the traditional Turkish breakfast of bread, jam, white cheese and olives.

Lunch is usually eaten between noon and 2:30pm.

Menu boards outside a fish restaurant

There are hundreds of cafés and snack bars selling Cypriot specialities such as *souvlaki* and doner kebabs, as well as sand-wiches, burgers and pizzas.

Dinner, the most celebrated meal of the day, is eaten between 8pm and late into the night. An evening around the table is a social event, and can last several hours, so it is worth selecting a table with a good view. The meal usually starts with a selection of *mezedhes* (appetisers), fol-lowed by a meat or fish main course accompanied by wine.

A popular waterfront bar on one of Kyrenia's beaches

WHAT TO EAT

The exquisite cuisine of Cyprus is famous for the simplicity of its ingredients and its ease of preparation. Traditional local recipes tend to be influenced by modern European trends – British cuisine plays a major role here.

The most important items on a Cypriot menu are the starters – called *mezedhes* – a vital element of a meal in any Mediterranean country, accompanied by traditional Cypriot bread baked on a hotplate. A decent restaurant will always include *halloumi* (grilled goat cheese), roast

Preparing pizza in one of Nicosia's pizzerias

courgettes, and the real delicacy – *koupepia* – stuffed vine leaves. Other specialities include *hummus* (chickpea dip), *tahini* (sesame sauce) and *kleftiko* (lamb roasted in a clay stove).

For main courses, the Cypriot menu is dominated by lamb and seafood, and an array of vegetables, usually served with rice or roast potatoes. Dishes of lamb are superbly complemented by strong Cypriot wines.

Fish is the most expensive item on the menu, although at coastal locations it is generally very fresh and tasty, so well worth the expense. Chicken is usually the cheapest meat dish available.

Happily for visitors, there should be no problem choosing from the menu, as the names of dishes are usually translated.

VEGETARIANS

Cypriot cuisine is based on essentially healthy Mediterranean produce and includes many vegetarian dishes, traditionally eaten in Cypriot homes during the Lenten period and other Orthodox fasts, when meat is shunned. As well as huge "village salads" *(choriatiki)* of tomatoes, cucumber, onions, peppers, olives and feta cheese, there is plentiful fresh fruit and a good array of grilled and fried vegetable dishes, based on aubergines (eggplant), courgettes (zucchini), artichokes, peppers and tomatoes, and lots of tasty dips based on chickpeas, fava beans and

other pulses. Cypriot cheeses are also worth recommending, especially the traditional fried *halloumi* cheese.

However, there is little understanding in Cyprus of the pure vegetarian diet, and it is not easy to find a restaurant that will prepare true vegetarian meals to order – even many so-called vegetable dishes may contain meat stock. In resorts vegetarians may find their choices limited to cheese, omelettes, fruit and salads.

ALCOHOL

As far back as ancient times, Cyprus has produced good wines, helped by the fertile soil and warm, mild climate. The quality of local wine has been maintained to this day, thanks to the careful nurturing and traditional methods of wine production.

Wine-tasting sessions are held in wineries all over the island. Between them, these wineries produce nearly 40 varieties of wine, sherry and brandy. In the villages at the foot of the mountains you can try home-made liqueurs, which, in terms of quality and flavour, are often as good as branded products.

The best known product is the sweet dessert wine, Commandaria. Nicknamed the "Cypriot sun", this fortified wine with a raisin-like flavour makes an excellent digestive to round off a traditional Cypriot dinner, and a good souvenir to take home. The

strong, dry *zivania* apéritif is classified by the European Union as eau-de-vie.

The locally produced beers have a good flavour and are also inexpensive. In North Cyprus you should try cold Efes; in the south, try KEO or the island-bottled Carlsberg.

Tables set on the panoramic terrace of a restaurant in Bellapais

PRICES

The highest prices are charged by restaurants in fashionable resorts. Here the best-value meals are generally the chef's recommended dishes of the day. Set menus may be substantially cheaper than a selection of à la carte items. Seafood dishes are particularly expensive.

You can eat more reasonably at restaurants in town – especially those frequented by the locals.

The total bill always includes VAT and usually a service charge of around 10 per cent. Most restaurants accept credit cards nowadays.

The romantic terrace of a dining establishment overlooking Coral Bay

The Flavours of Cyprus

Cypriot food is a mixture of Greek and Turkish cooking, along with some British influences, and features all the rich flavours typical of Mediterranean produce. Fruit such as oranges, lemons, cherries and figs are all grown locally, and the island's grapes are made into delicious wines. Vegetables, herbs and olives (to eat and for oil) grow in abundance. Meat is predominantly lamb, pork and chicken, and fresh seafood is plentiful along the coast. A good way to try a selection of local food is with a platter of *mezedhes* (*meze* for short), which may comprise of up to 20 dishes.

Oregano and thyme

Cypriot fisherman preparing his catch for sale

SOUTHERN CYPRUS

The cuisine of the south is inspired by the flavours of the Mediterranean area. Popular ingredients include olives and fresh herbs from the rich soils of the foothills of the Troodos mountains, and lemons from the groves found largely in the western region near Pafos. Locally made cheeses such as feta and halloumi give a distinctive taste to many dishes. Most meals start with a selection of dips made using recipes that have been handed down from generation to generation for centuries. These recipes have their roots in Greek cuisine, and are generally served with a freshly baked "village" loaf. Bread plays an important part in the diet of southern Cypriots. A flattish-domed loaf, village bread, is usually plain white but may also be flavoured with cheese or olives. Main courses tend to be meat-based rather than fish, although swordfish, in particular, is caught fresh everyday and almost always is served grilled with lemon. Chickens, pigs and goats are reared in most rural areas and provide meat that is usually cooked with herbs and served with potatoes grown in the red soil found in the Larnaka area. A

Pita breads

Roasted red peppers

Grilled halloumi

Dolmades (kupepia)

Taramosalata

Olives

Tzatziki

Selection of typical Cypriot *mezedhes*

REGIONAL DISHES AND SPECIALITIES

Dishes of the south include *afelia* (pork simmered in red wine with coriander) and *kleftiko*. Moussaka and *dolmades* (stuffed vine leaves) are among the dishes drawn from Greek cuisine. Dips include *taramosalata* (puréed salted mullet roe) and *tzatziki* (yoghurt, cucumber, garlic and mint).

Sweet pastries

The cuisine of northern Cyprus includes dishes such as *imam bayildi* (tomato-and onion-stuffed aubergines), *borek* (cheese-filled pastries) and *bamya bastisi*, a tomato and okra stew. Meat dishes include *doner* kebabs of sliced, spiced roast lamb, *iskender* or *bursa* (kebabs in a thick, spicy tomato sauce) and *adana*, a length of minced lamb bound together with red pepper flakes and cooked on a skewer.

Souvlakia *are small chunks of pork, marinated in lemon juice, herbs and olive oil, grilled on skewers.*

Local grocer offering a wide range of fresh and dried produce

"village salad" *(choriatiki salata)*, made of lettuce, cabbage, tomatoes, olives and feta cheese is a typical accompaniment to the main course. Bananas, oranges and cherries are among the many fruits grown in this part of the island and, along with sweet cakes, generally complete a meal.

NORTHERN CYPRUS

Cuisine in north Cyprus takes its influences from the island itself and the Turkish mainland, where many of the staple dishes were inspired by Middle-Eastern and central Asian cooking. Spices such as saffron and paprika, along with garlic, chillies and peppers, are used extensively; these ingredients give a colourful hue and a spicy kick to

traditional northern dishes. Most meals are based around meat, usually chicken or lamb, and vegetables grown on the flat plains south of the Pentadaktylos mountain range and along the coast. Many recipes come from the

Cypriot coffee, served strong and black with pastries

days of the Ottoman Empire and are characterized by their spicy tomato, yoghurt and cream based sauces. Meze-style meals, usually for large groups of friends or family, are a staple on the menu too, but differ slightly from those found in the south in that they are more often inspired by Turkish cuisine. Main courses are generally served with rice, boiled potatoes and salad accompaniments, and are usually followed by sweet pastries, such as sticky *baklâva*, or milk puddings and fresh fruit, especially citrus fruits, which grow prolifically in the north of the island.

WHAT TO DRINK

Cyprus offers the ideal climate and geography for growing grapes for winemaking, and production can be traced back to around 2000 BC. Of the over 40 varieties, the most famous is Commandaria, a sweet wine dating from the time of Richard the Lionheart. Zivania vodka and ouzo (along with Cyprus brandy used to make the island's signature cocktail, the Brandy Sour) are popular drinks too, as is sherry. Freshly squeezed fruit juices are also very good, and inexpensive. Cyprus, however, is above all the land of the coffee shop and villagers, mostly men, will spend hours over a strong Cypriot coffee, which is always served with a glass of cold water.

Scharas *means "from the grill". Here, swordfish has first been marinated in lemon juice, olive oil and herbs.*

Kleftiko *is usually goat meat wrapped in paper and cooked so that the juices and flavours are sealed in.*

Giaourti kai meli *(yoghurt with honey) is served in speciality "milk shops", to be eaten there or taken home.*

Choosing a Restaurant

The following restaurants have been selected across a wide range of price categories for their good value, exceptional food and/or interesting location. The restaurants are listed by area, starting with West Cyprus, and then alphabetically by town. For map references, see the road map on the inside back cover.

PRICE CATEGORIES
The following price ranges are for a three-course meal for one including a half-bottle of wine, tax and service, in euros.
€ Under €25
€€ €25–€35
€€€ €35–€45
€€€€ €45–€50
€€€€€ Over €50

WEST CYPRUS

KATHIKAS Yiannis Tavern   €
11 Georgiou Kleanthous, Kathikas, 8573 **Tel** *26 633 353*   **Road Map** *A3*

Yiannis and his team provide truly excellent Cypriot and international cuisine that is beautifully served and accompanied by fine wines. Be sure to leave enough room for one of their delectable desserts. With subtle lighting and music playing in the background, the atmosphere in this village stone eatery is pleasant and relaxed.

KATHIKAS Petradaki Tavern   €€
Kato Vrisi 45, Kathikas, 8573 **Tel** *99 596 528*   **Road Map** *A3*

An elegant restaurant decorated in creams and whites, Petradaki is as popular with the local community as it is with visitors. It has a large outside terrace for dining alfresco. The menu is classic Cypriot, with meat and fish dishes cooked with herbs and sauces, followed by a choice of delicious desserts. It also has a good wine list.

LATSI (LAKKI/LATCHI) Faros Restaurant   €
Latsi coastal road, Latsi, 8840 **Tel** *26 321 304*   **Road Map** *A3*

This lively taverna offers quiz nights, the Sky Sports channel, pool and karaoke, along with a menu of classics such as chicken and fish served with salads, vegetables and chips. Run by Bambos and his family, this is a welcoming and informal venue, situated right on the harbourside at Latsi, overlooking the boats.

PAFOS Demokritos   €
1 Dionysos Street, Kato Pafos, 8041 **Tel** *26 933 371*   **Road Map** *A4*

Acknowledged as the oldest restaurant in Kato Pafos, Demokritos has been entertaining and serving guests since 1971. Live music, energetic dancers and an extensive menu of Cypriot and international dishes such as *souvlaki* make a visit here a truly memorable experience.

PAFOS Petra Tou Romiou   €
Pafos-Limassol coastal road, Petra Tou Romiou **Tel** *26 999 005*   **Road Map** *A4*

Specializing in grilled meat dishes, such as *souvlaki* pork kebabs and chicken served with herbs and delicious salads, the Petra Tou Romiou restaurant is popular with visitors to the landmark Birthplace of Aphrodite, not far from Pafos. It lies on the coastal road, overlooking the sea, and is bright and informal.

PAFOS Roman Tavern   €
Tombs of the Kings Road, Pafos, 8102 **Tel** *26 944 400*   **Road Map** *A4*

A fun themed restaurant styled as if it were a Roman temple, complete with columns and colourful frescoes, the Roman Tavern offers the chance to dine inside or alfresco, around its swimming pool. The menu features grilled and barbecued meats and fish, *meze* and a good selection of desserts.

PAFOS Theo's Seafood Restaurant   €
Apostolou Pavlou Avenue, Pafos, 8046 **Tel** *26 932 829*   **Road Map** *A4*

Housed in a delightful stone building overlooking the fort and the bustling Pafos harbour, Theo's is widely known for its excellent fish and seafood menu. A family-run restaurant, it serves classic dishes made from traditional recipes handed down through the generations. Its swordfish and sea bass are particularly delicious.

PAFOS Cavallini   €€€€
Poseidon Avenue, Pafos, 8098 **Tel** *26 964 164*   **Road Map** *A4*

With home-made pasta dishes, desserts and ice cream on the menu, not to mention an extensive selection of classic Italian specialities and wines to choose from, Cavallini's is a magnet for anyone who adores the flavours of Italy. Elegant and refined, it offers alfresco dining on a palm tree-fringed terrace.

PAFOS O'Neills Irish Bar and Grill   €€€€
Tombs of the Kings Road, Pafos, 8102 **Tel** *26 935 888*   **Road Map** *A4*

Visitors could be forgiven for thinking they have stepped into a real Irish pub when entering O'Neills. This lively bar and grill serves a wide selection of hearty food and drinks, with Irish beers a speciality. A large plasma screen dominates the pub, keeping everyone up to date with the latest sport results.

Key to Symbols *see back cover flap*

PAFOS Phuket Chinese
Tombs of the Kings Road, Pafos, 8102 **Tel** *26 936 738*   €€€€   **Road Map** *A4*

An elegant Oriental-themed restaurant complete with dark bamboo-style chairs and white linens, Phuket has wholeheartedly adopted the feng shui principles. Its menu is classic Thai and Chinese à la carte, and set menus with Peking duck are a speciality. Fine wines are available to complete the dining experience.

PAFOS Artio
Piramou Street, Pafos, 8102 **Tel** *26 942 800*   €€€€€   **Road Map** *A4*

Artio's delivers a fine à la carte brasserie-style menu against a backdrop of orange, cream and brown minimalist interior decor. This centrally located restaurant serves delicious Cypriot and internationally inspired light meals and evening dinners, with a good selection of fine wines.

PAFOS Chloe's
Poseidon Avenue, Pafos, 8102 **Tel** *26 934 676*   €€€€€   **Road Map** *A4*

Chloe's is beautifully decorated in an Oriental style, with authentic artifacts and a red, brown, black and white colour scheme. The menu is à la carte and uses organic vegetables; the Peking duck and various sweet-and-sour dishes are the house specialities. Staff are very attentive.

PAFOS Kouyiouka Watermill Restaurant
Pafos–Polis Chrysochou Road, Giolou village **Tel** *26 632 847*   €€€€€   **Road Map** *A3*

Housed in a beautifully restored 19th-century listed watermill with timber beams and stone walls is this restaurant in the village of Giolou, 20 minutes' drive from Pafos. It serves traditional Cypriot cuisine and its wood ovens are used to bake bread, which is sold in the shop. The Watermill Museum tells the story of traditional village life.

POLIS Archontariki Tavern
Makarios Avenue, Polis, 8830 **Tel** *26 321 328*   €€€   **Road Map** *A3*

Archontariki is a quiet and peaceful restaurant that provides the opportunity to dine alfresco. This old townhouse has a pretty courtyard that is set back from the road. On the menu are fresh fish and seafood dishes, along with meat and vegetable fare with an European flavour.

POLIS Sabuneri
Skouli to Simou road, Simou, 8812 **Tel** *99 683 177*   €€€   **Road Map** *A3*

Sabuneri describes itself as a traditional village stone taverna, which conjures up the image of a tiny eatery. In fact, it is a sprawling restaurant in an extraordinary location, overlooking the Evretou Dam and a deserted village. Its menu consists largely of *mezes*. Special themed evenings are often held here.

POMOS Kanalli Restaurant
Pomos Harbour, Pomos village **Tel** *26 342 191*   €€€€   **Road Map** *A3*

Overlooking the dramatic coastline of Pomos and its delightful fishing harbour, Kanalli Restaurant is as popular with locals as it is with visitors on a day out from nearby Polis or Pafos. Its menu is traditional Cypriot, including dishes like *souvlaki*, *afelia* (pork in red wine) and, of course, *mezes*.

SOUTHERN CYPRUS

AGIA NAPA Odyssos
Nissi Avenue, Agia Napa, 5343 **Tel** *99 244 880*   €   **Road Map** *E3*

The Odyssos restaurant is easily found: it is right opposite the long stretch of beach at Nissi Bay and has tall palm trees on its terrace. Its menu offers burgers and grilled-meat dishes, along with fish such as swordfish and local delicacies like *halloumi* and *meze*. It is usually a hive of activity, so get there early.

AGIA NAPA Captain Andreas
37 Evagorou Street, Agia Napa, 5340 **Tel** *23 722 162*   €€   **Road Map** *E3*

Specializing in fish, often caught by Captain Andreas who can be seen bringing his catch ashore some mornings, this family-run taverna is a popular eatery in the centre of Agia Napa. Dishes are priced by the weight of fish they contain and include swordfish cooked with lemon, calamari rings and fish *meze*.

AGIA NAPA Vassos Fish Harbour Tavern
Makariou 51, Agia Napa, 5342 **Tel** *23 721 884*   €€   **Road Map** *E3*

Located on the harbourside of Agia Napa, Vassos is something of an institution. Founded in 1962, it is a firm favourite with local residents as well as visitors, and it serves the freshest fish possible caught by Captain Vassos's own nets. Choose a lobster from the tanks, fish from the display cabinet or a wide-ranging seafood *meze*.

AGIA NAPA Maistralia Beach Restaurant
Kryou Nerou 42, Agia Napa, 5342 **Tel** *23 723 754*   €€€   **Road Map** *E3*

Located in the heart of Agia Napa, close to all the town's attractions and with a great view of the beach and sea, the Maistralia Beach serves local Cypriot dishes such as *afelia* and *souvlaki*, along with international fare. The emphasis tends to be on fish and seafood, but meat eaters will also find plenty of choice.

AGIA NAPA Limanaki Fish & Grill   €€€€
1 October Street, Agia Napa, 3322 **Tel** *23 721 600*   **Road Map** *E3*

With a superb location right on the seafront of Agia Napa and a splendid terrace where diners can eat alfresco while gazing at the sea, the Limanaki is a popular restaurant housed within the Limanaki Beach Hotel *(see p159)*. The menu offers a wide choice of Cypriot and international dishes, with fish *meze* a speciality.

AGIA NAPA Sage Restaurant and Wine Bar   €€€€
Kryou Nerou 10, Agia Napa, 5342 **Tel** *23 819 276*   **Road Map** *E3*

Beautifully presented dishes – such as smoked salmon with avocado or prawns to start; prime steak, fresh fish or pasta to follow; and tempting desserts – are the order of the day at Sage, an upmarket restaurant that is ideal for a romantic meal or a special event. It is in a prime location, too, right in the heart of the town.

LARNAKA Art Café 1900   €€
6 Stasinou Street, Larnaka, 6305 **Tel** *24 653 027*   **Road Map** *D3*

Housed in a renovated townhouse dating from 1900, Art Café 1900 is run by Marios and Maria, who have created a charming bistro with paintings, period furniture and subtle lighting. The menu shows the couple's gastronomic flair, with chicken in orange, thyme and garlic the highlight among the specialities.

LARNAKA The Coral Inn   €€€
Dhekelia Road, Larnaka, 7040 **Tel** *24 646 200*   **Road Map** *D3*

Characterized by its Native American interior decor, with lots of greenery and wood, the Coral Inn is located near the sea and is popular with both guests of the Boronia Hotel Apartments and local residents alike. The menu is traditional European and includes fish, chicken and meat dishes, pastas and desserts.

LARNAKA Faros Restaurant and Pool Bar   €€€
Larnaka Road, Larnaka, 6305 **Tel** *24 422 111*   **Road Map** *D3*

As part of the Faros Village complex *(see p160)*, this bright restaurant and nearby pool bar offer a wide range of international cuisine. There's an à la carte menu, accompanied by a wine list, with a selection of cheeses and fresh fruit to complete the meal. The pool bar offers lighter dishes and live music.

LIMASSOL Pizza Plus   €
Promachon Eleftherias 13, Limassol, 4101 **Tel** *25 311 555*   **Road Map** *C4*

A town-centre restaurant that celebrates the flavours of Italy, Pizza Plus is much more than your average pizzeria and takeaway. Its menu of Italian specialities is extensive, with authentic recipes and carefully selected ingredients. Diners can see their pizza being prepared for them, before it is baked in a coal-fired oven.

LIMASSOL Bono Gourmet   €€
Anexartisias Street, Limassol, 3036 **Tel** *25 378 800*   **Road Map** *C4*

In addition to a menu of light snacks, including salads, pasta dishes and sandwiches prepared with ingredients from the on-site delicatessen, this chic bistro/restaurant offers a great choice of pâtés, terrines, coffees and cheeses from around the world to take home. It is situated in the heart of Limassol.

LIMASSOL Caballeros Restaurant   €€
Old Town, Limassol **Tel** *25 878 982*   **Road Map** *C4*

A landmark restaurant located opposite the medieval castle in Limassol, Caballeros makes an atmospheric place to enjoy a light lunch or an evening meal. Sit outside and admire the view or inside in stylish surroundings. The menu is classic Cypriot with some international favourites.

LIMASSOL Incontro Café   €€
Agios Nikolaos Makariou Street, Limassol **Tel** *25 377 519*   **Road Map** *C4*

A stylish café in central Limassol, Incontro Café combines big comfy sofas, antique-style furniture and crisp white linens with contemporary wall prints. It makes a relaxing place to meet with friends and enjoy its great coffee, sandwiches with a twist and tossed salads.

LIMASSOL Karatio Restaurant   €€
Old Carob Mill Factory, Limassol, 3025 **Tel** *25 820 469*   **Road Map** *C4*

Housed in the Old Carob Mill Factory close to Limassol's medieval castle, this café lounge is full of period atmosphere and yet it retains a contemporary feel. While its stone walls and decor are historic, its choice of metal, cream leather and light-wood furnishings and its menu of bistro-style dishes are pure 21st century.

LIMASSOL Longmen Restaurant   €€
Akademias Avenue, Limassol, 3076 **Tel** *25 318 844*   **Road Map** *C4*

The Longmen has been a popular Chinese restaurant in Limassol for around 15 years, largely because it serves high-quality cuisine in an authentic Oriental style. Its prawn, chicken and duck dishes, with complementing wines, are its specialities. The Far Eastern decor adds to the dining experience.

LIMASSOL St Ermogenis Valley   €€
Episkopi village, Limassol **Tel** *25 933 939*   **Road Map** *C4*

Occupying a glorious location next door to the historic church of St Ermogenis and a few minutes' walk from the amphitheatre in Kourion, this restaurant in a village 14 km (9 miles) from Limassol makes an ideal stop while sightseeing. Set under shady mature trees, it serves a wide choice of Cypriot and international dishes.

Key to Price Guide *see p170* **Key to Symbols** *see back cover flap*

LIMASSOL Artima Stretto Restaurant   €€€

Old Carob Mill Factory, Limassol, 3025 **Tel** *25 820 466*   **Road Map** *C4*

Artima is a red and white themed Italian and Mediterranean restaurant that is open for informal lunches, as well as stylish evening dining. Its menu features stuffed tortelloni pasta with porcini mushrooms and other pasta dishes to start; delicious meat and seafood specialities to follow; and amazing ice creams to finish.

LIMASSOL Cleopatra Lebanese Restaurant   €€€

John Kennedy Street, Limassol **Tel** *25 586 711*   **Road Map** *C4*

Fresh, authentic ingredients are used in the Lebanese à la carte dishes served at this town-centre restaurant. Also on the menu are *meze* plates of salads, small pies and local delicacies. Stylish and welcoming, Cleopatra is open from around 10am to midnight for lunches and evening dining.

LIMASSOL Famagusta Nautical Club   €€€

Beach Road, Limassol, 3507 **Tel** *25 324 056*   **Road Map** *C4*

This club is situated right on the beach in Limassol. It is open daily for breakfast and serves Mediterranean-style meals until around midnight, allowing diners to enjoy views of the sea by day and of the stars by night. There is also a children's menu, extensive vegetarian options and a buffet on Sundays.

LIMASSOL Il Sapore   €€€

Amathous Avenue, Limassol, 3606 **Tel** *25 313 184*   **Road Map** *C3*

Il Sapore is a small slice of Italy in the heart of Limassol. With a menu of pasta dishes, meat specialities and salads, this lively restaurant uses ingredients that are authentically Italian. One of the highlights is the signature dish of *scallopine di vitello* (tender veal). There is an extensive Italian wine list, too.

LIMASSOL Salaminia   €€€€€

Amathous Avenue, Limassol, 3724 **Tel** *25 634 333*   **Road Map** *C4*

Situated in the plush surroundings of the Hawaii Grand hotel, Salaminia is a beautifully presented restaurant that is ideal for special-occasion dining. It has two menus: an à la carte list that features a wide selection of international dishes, and a table d'hôte that changes daily. There is also a comprehensive fine wine list.

PISSOURI Dionysos   €€€€

Coastal road, Pissouri Bay, 3779 **Tel** *25 833 791*   **Road Map** *B4*

The Dionysos is a pleasant restaurant with a refined atmosphere. Inside the decor is elegant, while the outside terrace overlooks a long pool and the Mediterranean. Live music plays gently in the background, and the menu is classic Cypriot with an international twist, accompanied by fine wines.

PROTARAS Polyxenia Isaak   €€

Coastal road, Protaras, 5310 **Tel** *23 832 929*   **Road Map** *E3*

With a location by the beach, views out to sea, a lively atmosphere and a friendly team always keen to please, the traditional-style Polyxenia Isaak is a popular dining place with locals and visitors alike. Its menu features some Cypriot classics such as *halloumi*, *sheftalies* and *keftedes* (meatballs), washed down with local wines.

PROTARAS Sfinx   €€

Cavogreko 381, Protaras, 5310 **Tel** *23 831 277*   **Road Map** *E3*

Situated in the heart of Protaras, the Sfinx bar has plasma screens tuned to the latest live matches and other sporting events from around the world. Live music is also a feature. It serves beers and lighter beverages until late, along with a menu of hearty dishes, such as *moussaka*, kebabs and burgers.

ZYGI Captain's Table Fish Tavern   €€€

Zygi harbour, between Larnaka and Limassol, 7739 **Tel** *24 333 737*   **Road Map** *C4*

Fresh lobster, octopus, cuttlefish, sea bass and calamari are just some of the fish and seafood you can expect to find on the menu at the Captain's Table. All are either served with a variety of delicious sauces or simply with lemon. The restaurant is right on the seafront of Zygi, a fishing bay along the south coast.

TROODOS MOUNTAINS

KAKOPETRIA Pine Hill Lodge   €

Nicosia to Troodos road, Kakopetria, 2800 **Tel** *22 923 142*   **Road Map** *B3*

Pine Hill Lodge is a spacious, modern and welcoming restaurant. The location, high in the Troodos mountains, affords great views of the pine forests that surround the lodge. Diners have the choice of eating indoors or alfresco, on the large terrace. The menu consists primarily of traditional Cypriot fare.

KAKOPETRIA Mill Restaurant   €€€

Mylou 8, Kakopetria, 2800 **Tel** *22 922 536*   **Road Map** *B3*

Renowned for its excellent à la carte menu, the Mill Restaurant is popular with guests staying at the adjoining Mill Hotel *(see p162)*, but also with diners from further afield, who make a special trip to sample its famous fresh trout dishes. It is housed in a former mill building that has plenty of character.

LANEIA Platanos Tis Lanias Tavern
Laneia village, 4744 **Tel** *25 434 273*
Road Map B3

The Platanos Tis Lanias Tavern in the heart of Laneia village offers a welcome stop to those touring in the Troodos Mountains and in need of some refreshment. It is traditional in style and hospitality, with a menu comprised almost entirely of delicious Cypriot dishes cooked to original recipes, including *moussaka*, *afelia* and *souvlaki*.

LANEIA Lania Tavern
Laneia village, 4744 **Tel** *25 432 398*
Road Map B3

Located in the centre of Laneia, a pretty village just north of Limassol and known locally for its large number of artistic residents, the Lania Tavern is open for lunch every day and for evening dining on Friday and Saturday. The menu is classic Cypriot. Ask for a table on the terrace so you can take in the view of the village.

MONIATIS Andreas Makris Restaurant
Moniatis village, 4747 **Tel** *25 421 275*
Road Map B3

The large terrace of this village-centre restaurant is the scene of much singing and dancing to traditional Cypriot music, especially on festival days and bank holidays, when villagers come out to enjoy the sunshine. The menu is largely grills and barbecue dishes, all made to age-old local recipes.

MONIATIS Paraskeuas Restaurant
Moniatis village, 4747 **Tel** *25 433 626*
Road Map B3

Paraskeuas is a traditional restaurant where a vine-covered terrace forms the centrepiece of a garden full of exotic-looking plants. It offers diners a choice of Cypriot dishes – from *kleftiko* cooked for around eight hours in a special outdoor oven, to *sheftalies* delivered fresh from the kitchen the minute they are cooked.

PLATRES Psilo Dendro
Pano Platres, Platres, 4825 **Tel** *25 421 350*
Road Map B3

There may be few frills at the Psilo Dendro, but if it's pure rustic country charm and delicious trout that you are after, then this restaurant will provide them. It occupies a beautiful setting in the forest, not far from the waterfalls that dominate the area, and it runs its own trout farm. Fish is, unsurprisingly, the main ingredient on the menu.

PLATRES Belvetere Restaurant
62 Spyrou Kyparianou Street, Platres, 4825 **Tel** *25 421 751*
Road Map B3

A bright, attractive restaurant, the Belvetere is housed within the Forest Park Hotel complex *(see p162)*, deep in the forests of the Troodos Mountains. It offers a range of contemporary Cypriot and international dishes, including a kosher menu; it also hosts theme nights, live music and dancing events.

PRODROMOS Louis Restaurant Kebab Coffee Bar
Prodromos village, 4840 **Tel** *25 462 049*
Road Map B3

This modern bar and coffee shop has, in fact, quite a traditional atmosphere. The place is always buzzing, largely because of the many visitors who find it on their way to visit the Kykkos Monastery. A good stop for a light meal, Louis serves grilled-meat dishes, kebabs and Cypriot fare.

TRIMIKLINI JR Restaurant
Trimiklini village, 4730 **Tel** *25 432 212*
Road Map B4

Situated in the heart of this pretty little village set on a hillside deep in the Troodos Mountains, JR offers diners the chance to take a seat on the unusual arcade-style terrace and enjoy fine food, local wines and an outstanding view. Most dishes on the menu are made to traditional Cypriot recipes using local produce.

TROODOS Dolfin Taverna
Troodos village, 1504 **Tel** *25 420 215*
Road Map B3

The Dolfin Taverna is a haven of tranquillity located in a renovated 1940s-style building that has lots of rustic character. Close to the centre of the village, the highest on the island at around 1,700 m (5,575 ft) above sea level, it offers a menu that includes a delicious *meze* starting with dips and finishing with fruit.

TROODOS Fereos Park Restaurant
Troodos village, 1504 **Tel** *25 420 114*
Road Map B3

An attractive little restaurant with wooden furniture, the Fereos Park, in the heart of Troodos village, has a welcoming atmosphere noticeable as soon as you step through the door. The aromas of grilling *souvlaki*, *kleftiko* fresh from its eight hours in the oven and *stifado* (stew) will tempt you to stay awhile.

VASA Ariadne Restaurant
Vasa village, 4505 **Tel** *25 942 185*
Road Map B4

Ariadne's stands among the pretty whitewashed houses with red roofs that characterize the village of Vasa, in the foothills of the Troodos Mountains. This attractive family-run taverna offers a menu of Cypriot classics such as *afelia* and *souvlaki*, along with fresh fruit in season from the trees that surround its courtyard.

VRETSIA Evagoras Vretsia Village Tavern
Vretsia village, 8644 **Tel** *99 636 195*
Road Map B3

This bright village tavern is set in the countryside in the foothills of the Troodos Mountains and is run by a friendly couple. It offers a good selection of traditional Cypriot dishes, such as a *meze* featuring dips and meat specialities. The tavern lies close to the Venetian bridges and the Routhkias and Dhiarizos rivers.

Key to Price Guide *see p170* **Key to Symbols** *see back cover flap*

CENTRAL CYPRUS

AGROS Rodon Hotel Restaurant

Agros village, 4860 **Tel** *25 521 201*

Road Map *C3*

With à la carte and table d'hôte menus featuring some of the finest international and Cypriot cuisine, as well as a good wine list, the Rodon Hotel Restaurant *(see also p163)* is popular with both hotel guests and passing diners. It is situated in a glorious position overlooking olive groves and the nearby river.

AGROS Vlachos Restaurant

Agros village, 4860 **Tel** *25 521 330*

Road Map *C3*

Forming part of the small complex of the Vlachos Hotel *(see p163)*, in the heart of Agros village, this restaurant is attractive, with traditional decorations on the walls. It has a pleasing atmosphere, and it's a real treat to spend time here, relaxing over a glass of wine and enjoying one of the menu's Cypriot dishes.

STROVOLOS Kavouri Fish Tavern

Strovolos 125, Strovolos, 1504 **Tel** *22 425 153*

Road Map *C3*

Kavouri Fish Tavern is ideally located for those exploring central Cyprus and heading towards Nicosia, since it is right on the outskirts of Strovolos. It is renowned as much for its striking decor as it is for the seemingly endless parade of dishes that arrive at your table as part of its speciality *meze*.

SOUTH NICOSIA

SOUTH NICOSIA Chillies Mexican

Hippocrates 46–49, Nicosia, 1015 **Tel** *22 671 647*

Road Map *C3*

With a decor of orange, yellow and red tones that suggests an image of a traditional Mexican home, this is a fun and lively restaurant close to the centre of Nicosia. The menu is one of the best in the city for authentic Mexican cuisine, and almost every dish is hot and spicy.

SOUTH NICOSIA Xefoto Live Music Taverna

Aeschylou 6, Laiki Geitonia, Nicosia, 1087 **Tel** *22 666 567*

Road Map *C3*

Housed in a lovely, traditional house in the Old Town of Nicosia, Xefoto is a large restaurant that has a wonderful atmosphere and in the evening becomes a lively place to sit and relax over a pleasant meal. It is known for its good range of live music. The menu is classic Cypriot with a European twist.

SOUTH NICOSIA Navarino the Wine Lodge

1 Navarino, Nicosia, 1057 **Tel** *22 780 775*

Road Map *C3*

Navarino has gained a reputation for its good European buffet menus and its extensive wine list. Housed in a colonial-style building, it caters for weddings, special live-music events and parties, as well as daily dining. It is usually packed with local residents and visitors alike.

SOUTH NICOSIA Rocket Diner

Diagorou 2, Nicosia, 1097 **Tel** *22 818 333*

Road Map *C3*

With a black, red and white colour scheme and furnishings straight out of the 1940s, the Rocket Diner is like stepping into an American time warp. It is close to the Cyprus Museum and serves a vast range of burgers, fries, steaks, hot dogs and shakes, as well as offering a great salad cart.

SOUTH NICOSIA Alexandros

Kostaki Pantelides, Nicosia, 1087 **Tel** *22 671 174*

Road Map *C3*

A traditional taverna-style restaurant, the Alexandros is situated on one of the main streets that lead to the Old Town area of the city, making it ideal as a coffee or lunch stop when out sightseeing. It serves a good breakfast, as well as Cypriot classics and pastries for light snacks.

SOUTH NICOSIA Brasserie Au Bon Plaisir

103 Gregory Afxentiou, Agios Dometiou, Nicosia, 2373 **Tel** *96 755 111*

Road Map *C3*

This is one of the best French restaurants in Nicosia. It is run by a French team and is well located for the main sights in the city. The dishes are prepared and cooked according to French methods, and the menu features meats and fish served with delicious sauces. A good French and Cypriot wine list is also available.

SOUTH NICOSIA Club Evohia and Restaurant

99 Makarios Avenue, Nicosia, 1516 **Tel** *22 376 219*

Road Map *C3*

With a moody decor of dark wood, exposed brickwork and red accessories, along with some fabulous Art Nouveau-inspired windows, the Club Evohia and Restaurant is certainly atmospheric. Dress is casual to formal, and the international menu is complemented by a good selection of wines, coffees and sumptuous desserts.

SOUTH NICOSIA Fanous Lebanese Restaurant
Solonos 7C, Old Nicosia, 1011 **Tel** *22 666 880*
       €€€
Road Map *C3*

Fanous is one of the best Lebanese restaurants in Cyprus. Located in the heart of Old Nicosia, this atmospheric eatery serves a lengthy menu of authentic dishes, including *fatoush*, a traditional Lebanese salad, and *tabouleh*, a mix of tomatoes and crushed wheat with lemon and parsley. Theme nights are a speciality.

SOUTH NICOSIA La Spaghetteria
31A Evagorou Avenue, Nicosia, 1066 **Tel** *22 665 585*
       €€€
Road Map *C3*

This bright, attractive eatery is popular with those who adore freshly made pasta and authentic Italian recipes, all of which are freshly prepared each morning. You can select a type of pasta and then choose a sauce to go with it plus a salad, or opt for a dish from one of the Italian regions. The wines are Italian, too.

NORTH CYPRUS

BELLAPAIS The Abbey Bell Tower
Bellapais centre **Tel** *0392 815 75 07*
       €
Road Map *C2*

The Abbey Bell Tower is situated directly opposite the beautiful Bellapais Abbey ruins; as such, it is always popular with visitors to this hillside town, as well as with local residents. Its decor is bright and fresh, and while its menu features a few classic Turkish dishes, such as *borek*, in the main it serves European dishes.

BELLAPAIS Ayna Restaurant Bar
Bellapais centre **Tel** *0392 821 86 61*
       €€
Road Map *C2*

Ayna is situated in the heart of Bellapais and makes for a good rest stop when sightseeing. It is a pleasingly presented restaurant with an extensive menu of traditional Turkish fare such as *karniyarik* (aubergines stuffed with spicy meat and beans), along with pasta dishes, sandwiches and salads.

BOGAZI (BOĞAZ) Bogaz Terrace Restaurant
Coastal road, Bogazi **Tel** *0392 371 25 58*
       €€
Road Map *E2*

The Bogaz Terrace is a popular restaurant just along the coastal road leading to north Karpasia. Its timber-roofed dining room and terrace overlook the beach and sea, and can usually be found full of local residents and visitors enjoying the freshly cooked local dishes. A disco is held for energetic diners.

FAMAGUSTA (GAZIMAĞUSA) DB Café
Namik Kemal Meydani 14, Famagusta **Tel** *0392 366 66 10*
       €€
Road Map *E3*

If pizzas are your passion, you'll love the selection at the lively DB Café. Everything from *halloumi* cheese and tomato to spicy peppers top the wide variety of thin- and thick-based pizzas available. There are salads to complement, along with steaks and some local dishes as an alternative.

FAMAGUSTA (GAZIMAĞUSA) Bedis Bar and Restaurant
Near Salamis ruins, Famagusta **Tel** *0392 378 82 25*
       €€€
Road Map *E3*

Looking out over the sea on the island's east coast, the Bedis Bar and Restaurant is a good place to refuel after a visit to the Salamis ruins. Diners can choose between the covered outside eating area and the cosy inside dining hall. The menu is an imaginative combination of local and international cuisine, with *meze* a speciality.

FAMAGUSTA (GAZIMAĞUSA) Petek Patisserie
Yeail Deniz 1, Famagusta **Tel** *0392 366 71 04*
       €€€
Road Map *E3*

Stepping into the Petek Patisserie in the Old Town comes as a pleasant surprise. Little indoor fountains combine with a delicately coloured decor, while a terrace gives diners an outstanding view of the harbour and the surrounding countryside. The menu includes Turkish and European specialities.

KYRENIA (GIRNE) Mirabelle
Ugur Mumen Road 2, Kyrenia **Tel** *0392 815 73 90*
       €
Road Map *C2*

Open from mid-morning through to the late evening, the palm tree-surrounded Mirabelle offers a good range of dishes for breakfast, lunch and early evening dining. The specialities on its international- and Turkish-inspired menu include fish grills and *meze*, with tasty desserts to follow.

KYRENIA (GIRNE) Altinkaya Fish Restaurant
Yavuz Cikarma Plaji, Alsancak, Kyrenia **Tel** *0392 821 83 41*
       €€
Road Map *C2*

The Altinkaya is a typical Turkish coastal restaurant with Mediterranean-style decor and a large terrace overlooking the long sweep of coastline. Its menu focuses on fresh fish, such as sea bream caught daily in the local waters and prepared to delicious traditional recipes. The fish *meze* is a speciality.

KYRENIA (GIRNE) Canli Balik
Kyrenia Harbour, Kyrenia **Tel** *0392 815 21 82*
       €€
Road Map *C2*

Do not miss the chance to sit and enjoy some delicious local cuisine and wines while looking out at the yachts moored in the picturesque harbour of Kyrenia. Canli Balik is one of the best local restaurants at which to do so. Its menu features fresh fish grilled to perfection.

Key to Price Guide *see p170* **Key to Symbols** *see back cover flap*

KYRENIA (GIRNE) Chinese House   €€
Karaoglanoglou Road, Kyrenia **Tel** *0392 815 21 30*   **Road Map** C2

Take a break from sightseeing around the Kyrenia coast by stopping at the Chinese House, which, as its name suggests, specializes in the finest dishes from China. Both recipes and decor are authentic, and its team offers a warm welcome. Don't pass up the opportunity to dine on the pretty terrace surrounded by greenery.

KYRENIA (GIRNE) Green Valley Bar Restaurant   €€
Alsancak Road, Kyrenia **Tel** *0392 821 88 49*   **Road Map** C2

Surrounded by lush gardens, palm trees and bougainvilleas, the Green Valley Bar Restaurant serves some very good European cuisine, local kebabs, *mezes* and fresh fish dishes. It has a lively atmosphere most evenings of the week, with regular themed nights based on belly-dancing and folk dancing.

KYRENIA (GIRNE) Jashan's   €€
Karaoglanoglou Road, Kyrenia **Tel** *0392 822 20 27*   **Road Map** C2

Authentic Indian cuisine – such as samosas with spiced potato-and-pea fillings, deep-fried *pakoras* served with mint chutney, mild and hot curries, tandoori and spicy *chaat* dishes – are prepared and served by Riaz and his team of chefs at Jashan's. Lovely desserts and a good wine list are also available in this popular, elegant restaurant.

KYRENIA (GIRNE) Laughing Buddha   €€
Ecevit Street, Nicosia Road, Kyrenia **Tel** *0392 815 87 15*   **Road Map** C2

Housed inside an old building with outstanding views and a pretty stream in the garden, the restaurant has an oriental theme in both the cuisine and decor. The setting and the atmosphere are full of fun at the Laughing Buddha, and there are almost 100 authentic dishes to choose from.

KYRENIA (GIRNE) Lemon Tree Fish Restaurant   €€
Catalcoy Road, Kyrenia **Tel** *0392 815 24 96*   **Road Map** C2

The Lemon Tree is one of the area's most popular fish restaurants, largely because of its idyllic location amid lemon groves and overlooking the beautiful Kyrenia coastline. Of course, the expertly prepared and cooked fresh fish also adds to its popularity. It is open for late-evening dining.

KYRENIA (GIRNE) Missina Fish and A La Carte Restaurant   €€
Omer Faydah Sk. 12, Karaoglanoglou, Kyrenia **Tel** *0392 822 38 44*   **Road Map** C2

With its elegant decor of creams and whites, interspersed with the deep blue of the Mediterranean, and with atmospheric lighting throughout, Missina is a popular à la carte restaurant in the heart of Kyrenia. Its outside terrace is large and ideal for spending refined evenings enjoying fine food under the stars.

KYRENIA (GIRNE) Niazi Restaurant   €€
Kordonboyn, Kyrenia **Tel** *0392 815 21 60*   **Road Map** C2

The Niazi Restaurant is a long-established eatery that stands in the heart of Kyrenia and is well located for visits to the castle and the pretty harbour. Its air conditioning also offers a welcome break from the heat. The speciality on the extensive menu is *meze*, which consists of numerous tiny portions of classic Turkish dishes.

KYRENIA (GIRNE) Set Fish Restaurant   €€
Yet Limani, Kyrenia **Tel** *0392 815 23 36*   **Road Map** C2

A delightfully rustic restaurant housed in a building that dates in part from the Venetian period, the Set Fish is an atmospheric venue for a romantic meal. It has a terrace with a great view and is situated close to the famous harbour of Kyrenia. Its menu consists mainly of classic fish and seafood dishes.

KYRENIA (GIRNE) Sez-I Fish Restaurant   €€
Kervansaray Karaoglanoglou, Kyrenia **Tel** *0392 822 30 60*   **Road Map** C2

A brightly coloured nautical-themed restaurant that capitalizes on its location in the heart of Kyrenia's lively beach-resort area, Sez-I Fish is popular with couples as well as holidaying families. Its menu combines excellent fish dishes, for which it is renowned, with international fare.

KYRENIA (GIRNE) The Carpenters   €€€
Karaoglanoglou, Kyrenia **Tel** *0392 822 22 51*   **Road Map** C2

The Carpenters is friendly, family-run and one of the longest established restaurants in Kyrenia. It is located a short distance from the town's famous harbour and serves both local dishes and international cuisine, accompanied by freshly baked bread from the village. The pretty, shaded garden offers a welcome retreat from the heat of the day.

NORTH NICOSIA (LEFKOŞA) Californian Restaurant   €
M Akif 74, Dereboyu, Nicosia **Tel** *0392 227 07 00*   **Road Map** C3

With a smart, elegant dining room upstairs and a fast-food type eatery downstairs, the Californian Bar Continental serves some delicious local cuisine inspired by the best Cypriot and Turkish recipes, along with European à la carte dishes. It is conveniently located, close to many of North Nicosia's main attractions.

NORTH NICOSIA (LEFKOŞA) Boghtalian Konak   €€
Salhi Sevket Sok, Arabahmet, Nicosia **Tel** *0392 228 07 00*   **Road Map** C3

Housed in a landmark building in the Arabahmet area of the city, Boghtalian Konak is an elegant restaurant that features an Ottoman-style banqueting hall, an atmospheric private dining room and a shaded courtyard dining area. Its food is pure Cypriot, with *meze* leading the way.

SHOPPING IN CYPRUS

Cyprus is famous for its handicrafts, especially the intricate laces and beautifully embroidered fabrics created by Cypriot women. Artisan food and drink, such as honey and jam as well as fruit- and herb-flavoured alcohol, are widely available. A variety of rose products, including oils, soap and perfume, are also gaining popularity.

Souvenir tray with a map of Cyprus

Other popular gifts are silver and copper jewellery based on traditional designs, and inexpensive leather goods. One of the pleasures of a trip to Cyprus is sampling the local food, whether in a market (where fresh fruit and spices abound) or bakery. *Halloumi* cheese, washed down with an inexpensive but enjoyable Cypriot wine, such as Othello, tastes delicious.

WHERE TO SHOP

Souvenirs can be bought anywhere on the island. Shops, boutiques and street stalls are found in abundance in the larger towns and along the promenades of the famous resorts. In the mountain villages, small family-run shops sell basic commodities, while home-made foodstuffs, such as orange marmalade, jam and excellent honeys, can be bought directly from their producers at tree-shaded roadside stalls.

Near every major historic site you will find a stall that sells typical local souvenirs, postcards and handicrafts. The most common items for sale are clay amphorae and jugs, baskets and traditional lace and embroidery.

Supermarkets and small local shops, which are usually open late, have the best prices for foodstuffs, but you can also buy a variety of cold drinks and snacks at the beach. The larger hotels have their own shops.

A shop selling handicrafts in the centre of Larnaka

OPENING HOURS

The peak holiday season is June to mid-September, when shops have the longest hours. They open from 7am to 8pm (7:30pm in winter), some with a 3-hour lunch break (1–4pm). On Wednesdays shops close between 1pm and 3pm, and on Saturdays at 5pm.

From April to May, and mid-September to October, the

shops are open between 8am and 7pm (8pm on Fridays).

From November to March, shops open from 8am to 7pm (8pm on Friday), except Wednesdays (to 1pm or 2pm) and Saturdays (to 3pm).

Markets are best seen early in the morning, when the choice of produce is largest.

HOW TO PAY

In small boutiques, beach shops and markets it is customary to pay by cash. Credit cards are widely accepted in larger establishments, including supermarkets, and souvenir and jewellery shops.

A stall with a variety of home-canned fruits and jams

MARKETS

An inherent feature of the Mediterranean scenery, markets are found in all larger towns of Cyprus. The most picturesque are the fruit and vegetable markets in Nicosia and Larnaka. They are held mainly for the benefit of the local community, so even in high season few articles intended for visitors are available; nevertheless, their local colour and character make them a great tourist attraction. Haggling is a common practice.

A typical Cypriot market, brimming with fresh produce

Most markets sell fresh fruit, vegetables and spices. Those in seaside resorts may also have interesting costume jewellery, flip-flops and beach bags. Printed T-shirts are another popular tourist item.

Markets that specialize in fresh local produce are best visited early in the morning. At that time of day, the air is cool and you can take a leisurely stroll between the rows of stalls, savouring the flavours and scents. Here you will find readily available fresh produce, including exotic fruit and vegetable varieties little known in mainland Europe. You can also buy traditional cheeses, sausages, many types of fish, and a variety of nuts and sweets. Sacks full of fragrant, colourful spices stand next to the stalls.

Every now and then you can also find antiques offered at reasonable prices.

FOOD

One of the island's specialist foods is *halloumi* – the traditional goat's cheese, which is excellent in salads and delicious when fried or grilled. Another tasty delicacy is *soujoukkos* – a sweet almond filling covered with thickened grape juice.

The best souvenir from Cyprus is the sweet "Cyprus sun" – the local full-bodied Commandaria wine with its rich, warm and truly sunny bouquet. Other noteworthy beverages include *ouzo*, also known in Greece and Turkey, and the very strong *zivania* (virtually pure grape alcohol) that will knock you off your feet, even in small quantities.

A well-stocked wine shop in Omodos, in the Troodos mountains

Other good food purchases include delicious dried fruit, and rose petal jam. The sweet fruit jellies – *loukoumia* – are the Cypriot version of Turkish delight. The highlanders produce exquisite herb-scented honey. The most popular spices are small, hot peppers.

The owner of a jewellery studio at work on a new piece

SOUVENIRS

A wide range of souvenirs is available in Cyprus, but the most popular are ceramics and wickerwork. The Cyprus Handicraft Service has shops and workshops in many towns and cities.

Traditional Cypriot lace is produced in the villages of Lefkara and Omodos, and makes a beautiful souvenir.

In North Cyprus you can buy embroidery based on traditional Turkish designs.

Exquisite icons are sold in the mountain monasteries, sometimes painted by the monks themselves.

Traditional copper pots and bowls, and attractive and inexpensive leather goods, are available throughout Cyprus and make good gifts.

DIRECTORY

MARKETS

Larnaka
Leontos Sofou Str. ◻ 6am–2pm Mon–Sat.
Dromolaxia Rd. ◻ 6am–2pm Sat.

Limassol
Central market. ◻ 6am–3pm Mon–Sat.
Town market, Makarios III Ave. ◻ 6am–1pm Sat.
Linopetra. ◻ 6am–2pm Sat.

Nicosia
Market square. ◻ 6am–5pm Sat.
Strovolos, Dimitri Vikellou Str. ◻ 6am–6pm Fri.
Ohi Square. ◻ 6am–5pm Wed.

Pafos
Agora Str. ◻ 6am–1pm Mon–Sat.

CYPRUS HANDICRAFT SERVICE

Larnaka
Cosma Lysioti 6. **Tel** *24 304 327.*

Limassol
Themidos 25. **Tel** *25 305 118.*

Nicosia
Leoforos Athalassas 186.
Tel *22 305 024.*

Pafos
Leoforos Apostolou Pavlou 64.
Tel *26 306 243.*

Beautifully embroidered, colourful shawls from Lefkara

What to Buy in Cyprus

Thanks to the centuries-long influence of a variety of cultures, Cyprus offers its visitors a wealth of souvenirs of every description, from beautiful icons in the south, to typical Turkish water pipes in the north. Some towns are famous for their unique lace designs, ceramics and exquisite jewellery. Leather goods are particularly attractive in the northern part of the island. The choice of souvenirs is truly astounding, and searching for that original item to take home with you is half the fun.

Icons

Icons, painted by Greek Orthodox monks, are very popular with tourists. They vary from simple to elaborate designs, some with robes depicted in silver or with golden floral motifs.

Madonna and Child icon

REPUBLIC OF CYPRUS

A beautifully embroidered tablecloth – a handsome gift

Textiles

Colourful stripes form the traditional pattern seen on tablecloths and rugs. The hand-woven fabric used in these articles is called lefkonika. *Its name comes from the town of Lefkonikon (now in North Cyprus) where the fabric was first produced.*

Woven rug with the distinctive striped pattern

Lace

The most famous Cypriot lace – lefkaritika – comes from Lefkara. The best-known motif is the Da Vinci pattern, which, according to legend, was passed on to local lace-makers by the famous Italian artist.

Exquisite lace

An original tin kettle

Tin and Copperware

Tin-plated kettles decorated with fine patterns are a practical, as well as a decorative present. Copper ornaments are also popular. The most beautiful of these include bracelets with traditional Greek designs.

A beautifully decorated silver trinket

Tray decorated with a map of Cyprus

Tourist Souvenirs

The most common souvenirs from Cyprus are plates, ashtrays, mugs and T-shirts

decorated with the image of Aphrodite or a map of the island. But the inventiveness of the souvenir producers knows no bounds, and stalls are loaded with fancy knick-knacks.

Silver

In addition to lace, Lefkara prides itself on its silver creations. Here, you can find the finest jewellery made to unusual designs, and intricately decorated trinkets.

Statuette of Aphrodite – the patron goddess of Cyprus

Alcoholic Beverages

One of the best souvenirs from the island is "Cyprus sun" – sweet local Commandaria wine, full-bodied, with a rich bouquet reminiscent of the famous Madeira wine. Other noteworthy beverages include ouzo and the strong zivania (grape spirit).

Bottle of white wine

"Cyprus sun" – the sweet Commandaria

Wicker basket

Wickerwork

Inexpensive wicker baskets can be bought in the markets of Nicosia, Limassol and Larnaka, or directly from their makers in the villages of Liopetri or Sotira, near Agia Napa.

Cypriot Music

Traditional Cypriot music is based on Greek motifs. The famous "Zorba's Dance" is a favourite with tourists.

CD of traditional Cypriot music

Pottery

Cypriot markets are full of clay jugs, bowls and other vessels, of all shapes and sizes, often richly ornamented.

Clay water jug

Local Delicacies

The outstanding local delicacy is halloumi – a goat's cheese. People with a sweet tooth should try soujoukkos – made of almonds and grape juice, or loukoumi (Cyprus delight).

Cypriot sweets

NORTH CYPRUS

Ceramics

A wide variety of ceramic products is on offer. Available in all shapes and sizes, they are decorated in traditional patterns. The loveliest and most popular with tourists are the traditional bowls and jugs.

A jug – a popular form of earthenware

Hookah (or narghile)

The hookah is a typical souvenir from the north. Tourists buy these water pipes, tempted by the fruity aroma of tobacco. The full set also includes charcoal and tobacco.

A hookah – a typical souvenir from North Cyprus

Tourist Souvenirs

The most popular souvenirs are hand-woven rugs and tablecloths, and plates decorated with pictures of popular historical sites, with commemorative inscriptions. The selection of souvenirs is not great, but prices are reasonable. Stalls selling souvenirs can be found at the main tourist sites.

A colourful souvenir plate

An encrusted wooden box with the popular game backgammon

Traditional knife with a beautifully decorated handle

ENTERTAINMENT IN CYPRUS

Every visitor to Cyprus, whether young or old, will find plenty of entertainment to enjoy. Hotels stage folk evenings, with traditional music and dancing. Guests can dance to the tune from *Zorba the Greek*, watch an unusual display in which a dancer places a tower of glasses on his head, or join in games of skill based on traditional Greek entertainment.

Having fun at one of the many water parks

In addition to this, every major resort has modern bars, pubs and clubs playing music mostly from the 1970s and 80s. Festivals, casinos and amusement parks provide even more diversions.

In Cyprus, European-style fun and games combine with traditional local entertainment, which is very popular with the tourists.

CTO office in Pafos

INFORMATION

Information on current cultural events can be obtained from tourist offices and hotel reception desks. Even before leaving for your trip, it's worth checking out Cyprus on the Internet, so that you can time your arrival to coincide with local festivals, such as the wonderful wine festivals, which are accompanied by free tastings. Leaflets handed out on the streets may contain interesting information on local events, as do posters displayed in public places.

CLUBS AND CAFES

The island has a thriving nightlife. The major resorts, full of noisy clubs, modern bars and crowded pubs, are the most popular places to enjoy a lively night out. People looking for all-night parties and dancing should stay in Limassol – the centre of entertainment on the island. In the resort of Agia Napa it is customary to take a refreshing morning swim in the Mediterranean Sea after a night on the town. Tickets to the largest clubs can be

booked in advance over the telephone or via the Internet.

Cultural life in Cyprus is not limited to bars, cafés, nightclubs or folk shows staged on hotel terraces. Larger towns also have theatres performing a classical repertory as well as modern plays in historic settings.

It is worth dropping into one of the stylish cafés in the pedestrianised Laiki Geitonia area of Nicosia, to taste Cypriot coffee. Served in small glasses, this strong and sweet coffee will revive you in no time at all.

HOTEL ENTERTAINMENT

Many hotel concierges and travel agents will arrange activities for visitors, including equipment hire for anything from tennis rackets or bicycles to a luxury yacht. They can also organize lessons for you. Their offers are displayed in hotels, where you can also book a boat cruise, an excursion or a diving course. Most hotels also sell tickets to

concerts, dance shows and other performances by local artists. In some venues, Cypriot orchestras entertain dinner guests nightly. Other traditional Cypriot evenings are popular and easy to book.

Children dressed up during the Flower Festival in Larnaka

FEASTS AND FESTIVALS

Traditional religious festivals in Cyprus coincide with those celebrated in Europe. On New Year's Day, Cypriots exchange presents and eat the traditional New Year cake – *vasiloptta*. Epiphany

Café-patisserie in Famagusta

is celebrated in the seaside towns with a swimming competition: the winner is the person who recovers the crucifix hurled out over the water. During Holy Week, an effigy of Judas is burned, and icons are covered with a pall. Anthestiria – the flower festival held in May, heralds the arrival of spring. In September the annual arts festival is held in Nicosia. The same month sees the Limassol wine festival.

The North celebrates mainly Muslim festivals. The most important widely celebrated of these is Eid-al-Fitr.

CASINOS

Gambling is not particularly popular in Cyprus, but there are some who enjoy casino games. Roulette and blackjack attract mainly tourists from Turkey. Casinos are found only in North Cyprus. Inhabitants of South Cyprus often cross the border to try their luck in one of the gambling dens. The best casinos are found in the larger, more upmarket hotels of Kyrenia and Famagusta.

A casino in the Colony hotel (see p165), located in Kyrenia

EXCURSIONS

Information about organized excursions and sightseeing bus tours can be obtained from hotel reception desks or tourist information centres. The most popular excursions are daytrips to major tourist attractions and historic sites, visits to traditional villages, and Cypriot evenings with traditional food, drink and dancing. Boat cruises along the coast are also available.

The colourful waterpark in Agia Napa

AMUSEMENT PARKS

Unlike most rival Mediterranean resorts, Cyprus has lots of purpose-built attractions for younger visitors. A visit to a waterpark or a mini-zoo is a must when on holiday with children. The vast waterparks, usually occupying several hectares, offer numerous amusements. In addition to swimming pool complexes, they have scenic routes that can be travelled by small boat, while admiring Greek ruins scattered along the shores. Large swimming pools have secret coves, artificial waves, thickets and diving sites. They vie with one another to provide the most unusual attractions, such as the Zenith Zeus slide with its 370 bends. The waterpark in Agia Napa, styled after ancient Greek designs, combines entertainment with a history lesson. Waterparks, being outdoor attractions, are open only during high season.

Educational parks and their collections of island fauna and flora are also sources of unforgettable delight and knowledge for youngsters.

In the summer the most popular parks are crowded. Every amusement park is virtually a small town in itself, with shops, restaurants and numerous attractions.

Those who fail to get their fill of fun during the daytime can take a stroll along the seaside promenades during the evening, and drop into a funfair for a ride on a carousel sparkling with flashing lights. Limassol (see pp68–73) and other large resorts have such funfairs.

DIRECTORY

EXCURSIONS

Airtour-Cyprus Sightseeing
Naxou 4, Nicosia. *Tel 22 452 777.*
www.airtourcyprus.com

Amathus Tours
Plateia Syntagmatos 2, Limassol.
Tel 77 778 277.

CitySightseeing Pafos
Harbour Coach Park, Pafos.
Tel 99 393 766.
◻ 10am–4pm daily.
www.cypruscitysightseeing.com

Salamis Tours Excursions
Salamis House, 28 Oktovriou,
Limassol. *Tel 25 860 000.*
http://salamisinternational.com

WATERPARKS

Aphrodite Waterpark
Geroskipou-Pafos, Poseidonos Ave.
Tel 26 913 638.
◻ daily. May & Jun: 10:30am–
5:30pm; Jul & Aug: 10am–6pm;
Sep & Oct: 10am–5pm.
www.aphroditewaterpark.com

Fasouri Water Mania Waterpark
Near Trahoni village, Limassol.
Tel 25 714 235.
◻ daily. May, Sep & Oct:
10am–5pm; Jun–Aug: 10am–6pm.
www.fasouri-watermania.com

Waterworld Waterpark
Agia Napa. *Tel 23 724 444.*
◻ daily. Apr & Oct: 10am–5pm;
May–Sep: 10am–6pm.
www.waterworldwaterpark.com

OUTDOOR ACTIVITIES

Contrary to popular belief, Cyprus offers much more in the way of recreation than splashing in the sea and sunbathing on the beaches. Certainly many visitors are drawn by the prospect of sunshine, peace and tranquillity. But the island's mild, warm climate, combined with its unique topography, attracts all types of outdoor enthusiasts. Visitors seeking an active holiday will find numerous facilities for sport, as well as excellent and professional coaching and instruction. You can enjoy a wide array of watersports, including snorkelling, diving and wind-surfing. On land there is excellent hiking, horse riding and cycling. In winter, you can even learn to ski or snowboard on the slopes of Mount Olympus.

Studying the map

Hiking in the Troodos mountains

HIKING

The island's best hiking areas are in the mountain regions. Clearly signposted walking trails and scenic nature trails, found mainly in the Troodos mountains and on the Akamas peninsula, help hikers to discover the most fascinating corners of Cyprus. The most enjoyable island hikes lead through nature reserves.

When hiking, you should always carry a detailed map of the region. And before setting off, it is important to pack appropriate warm clothing; even when it is hot on the coast, it can be quite chilly high up in the mountains. Also be sure to bring plenty of drinking water and sunblock.

CYCLING TRIPS

Virtually all tourist resorts on Cyprus have bicycles available for hire. The island's cycling routes are magnificent, particularly in the mountains, and this is a great way to enjoy the scenery. Maps showing the routes are available from tourist information centres, in every resort and larger town.

It is a good idea to carry a pump with the correct tip, and self-adhesive patches for inner-tubes in case of punctures. For more complicated repairs, you can ask for help from a specialist bicycle shop.

HORSE RIDING

Cyprus's beaches and gentle hills provide the ideal terrain for horse riding. Horse-lovers will appreciate a beautiful ride along the paths that wind their way gently through the pine-clad hills. An unhurried walk through a cypress grove, or a wild gallop over wooded hills, will be a memorable part of your holiday in Cyprus.

Virtually all you need to enjoy horse riding is a well-trained, docile animal. But for those who are nervous of horses, donkey rides are also widely available.

Snowboarder on the slopes of Mount Olympus

SKIING AND SNOWBOARDING

Depending on the weather, it is possible to ski and snowboard on the northeast slopes of Mount Olympus between December and mid-March. The island's highest mountain provides good snow conditions, with four ski lifts and an equipment hire centre for visitors. Individual and group tuition is available for both skiers and snowboarders to help novices negotiate the complexities of a downhill run.

A leisurely family cycling trip

If you are planning to engage in snow sports during your holiday in Cyprus, you can keep an eye on the weather forecast and snow conditions by checking on the Internet or teletext information service, or asking your tour operator.

TENNIS

Most top hotels have their own hard courts and tennis schools, and floodlit, all-weather public tennis courts can be found in most major towns. Aficionados will enjoy a game played at high altitude (above 1,500 m/ 4,921 ft), amid the pine and cedar woods. This is made possible by the location of one of the most scenic courts, near Troodos.

GOLF

Cyprus has perfect golfing weather for much of the year, though some may find July and August uncomfortably hot. There are several 18-hole courses, all offering golf clubs for hire. Particularly note-worthy is the Tsada Golf Club, situated near Pafos on the picturesque grounds of a 12th-century monastery. There are many other high-quality, scenically located golf courses of varying degrees of difficulty for golfers of every ability.

The north of the country has no public golf courses, but visitors may use the golf

Building sandcastles at the beach in Larnaka

course in Pentayia, which is located to the southwest of Morfou (Güzelyurt).

OTHER ACTIVITIES

Increasingly popular excursions in four-wheel-drive vehicles give visitors the chance to discover the lesser-known parts of the island and to admire its beauty away from the tourist centres.

Rock-climbers may head for the crags of Troodos, Droushia or Cape Greco, around Agia Napa. Novice climbers should always be assisted by an experienced instructor.

Cyprus is full of ancient relics, and among its main attractions are the archaeological sites. The ruins at Amathous, near Limassol, are partially flooded, so they can be viewed while swimming in the sea. Other important sights are Kato Pafos and Salamis, in the north.

DIRECTORY

Cyprus Airsports Federation
PO Box 28940, 2084 Nicosia.
Tel 22 339 771. Fax 22 449 873.
www.caf.org.cy

Cyprus Climbing Federation
Nicosia. *Tel 22 314 252.*
www.cyprusclimbing.com

Cyprus Cycling Federation
Amphipoleos 21, Strovolos, Nicosia.
Tel 22 449 870. Fax 22 449 871.
www.cypruscycling.com

Cyprus Equestrian Federation
Tel 22 872 172. Fax 22 872 170.
www.cyef.org.cy

Cyprus Golf Resorts Ltd.
PO Box 2290, 8062 Pafos.
Tel 26 642 774. Fax 26 642 776.
www.cyprusgolf.com

Cyprus Ski Club
Nicosia.
Tel 22 449 837. Fax 22 449 838.
www.cyprusski.com

Cyprus Tennis Federation
Ionos 20, Engomi, 2406 Nicosia.
Tel 22 449 860. Fax 22 668 016.
www.cyprustennis.com

Nicosia Race Club (horse riding)
Grigoriou Afxentiou, Nicosia.
Tel 227 82727. Fax 227 75690.
www.nicosiaraceclub.com.cy

CAR RALLIES

Drivers travelling around Cyprus will get enough excitement from driving the narrow streets of Nicosia or steep roads of the Troodos mountains. But if you want even more driving thrills, you can attend one of Cyprus' several car rallies, sprints or hill climbs. These are held at

Churning out clouds of dust at the popular International Rally of Cyprus

various locations including Limassol, Larnaka, Nicosia and Pafos. Further details, including the routes and the results of recent years, can be obtained from the website of the Cyprus Motor Sports Federation (www.cmf.org.cy) or from any of the individual towns' automobile clubs.

Watersports

The beaches of Cyprus are fun places for the whole family. Sunbathing, volleyball and all kinds of water-sports are available to keep you entertained. The numerous attractions include snorkelling, diving, windsurfing, waterskiing and sailing. Sea breezes moderate the high temperatures, and the clear water is ideal for swimming. There is no shortage of places to hire equipment, allowing you to practise even the most ambitious watersports or take a scuba-diving course.

Snorkelling in the clear blue waters near rock formations

DIVING

The clear, clean coastal waters of Cyprus simply beckon underwater explora-tion. Diving is extremely popular in Cyprus, and there are diving schools and centres in virtually every seaside resort in the island.

The greatest thrills can be experienced from underwater explorations in the regions of Larnaka and Agia Napa, famous for the island's loveliest beaches. Experienced divers may look for the local wrecks of cargo boats and naval vessels. This is quite a unique attraction since, unlike many countries, the Cyprus Tourism Organization does allow the exploration of vessels that have sunk off its coast.

Visitors will be flooded with offers from hundreds of diving clubs and schools. These organizations offer not only diving lessons for novices and children, but also sea cruises combined with diving. The initial lessons can often be taken in the hotel, since many of them run their own diving schools.

SNORKELLING

There is plenty to see underwater, even within a few metres of the shore if you are a beginner at this sport. The shallows teem with tiny fish, sea anemones and urchins clinging to the rocks. If you're lucky, you may even see an octopus slither past.

It's well worth heading out to the more rocky shores where there is more to see than on the sandy bottom. One of the best places for snorkelling is the north coast of the Akamas peninsula, where rocky coves and tiny offshore islands abound in a variety of sealife.

Many hotels hire out snorkel-ling equipment. You can also buy masks with snorkels and flippers at local sports shops; these do not cost much.

It is prohibited to collect sponges or any archaeological items found on the seabed.

WINDSURFING AND KITEBOARDING

Almost all the beaches run courses for windsurfing. The gentle afternoon breezes may not meet the expectations of the more competitive windsurfers. The best winds blow around the capes, between Agia Napa and Protaras, and in the region of Pafos. Kiteboarding, which involves being towed at high speeds by a giant parachute-like kite, is starting to catch on in Agia Napa.

Dozens of yachts moored in Larnaka marina

SAILING

Sailing is very popular in Cyprus, and the island's marinas play host to vessels from practically every European country. Skippered yachts can be chartered from island marinas (Larnaka and Limassol are the main centres) by the day or for longer cruises, and smaller dinghies and catamarans are available by the day or half-day from beaches around Agia Napa, Protaras, Limassol and Latsi. The many boat charter companies have their offices in coastal resorts, where you will also find sailing schools.

The waters around Cyprus offer magnificent sailing conditions, and the island is often referred to as a "sailor's paradise". Southwesterly

A diver exploring the sights under water

The Cypriot coast – an ideal destination for an active holiday

winds prevail in the summer. The delicate westerly breeze blowing in the morning changes gently around noon to a westerly wind of 15–20 knots. In the winter, the temperatures are milder and the sun less scorching. In December and January the winds are mainly 10–20 knots from the southeast. There can be occasional rain at this time, but the prevailing clear weather makes sailing conditions close to ideal.

From Cyprus you can sail to nearby Israel, Lebanon, Egypt, the Greek islands and Turkey.

BEACH SPORTS

For the most part, beaches are found close to hotels, and are watched over by lifeguards in the summer, making them peaceful and comfortable recreation grounds. The beautiful sandy beaches in small sheltered coves are particularly welcoming to those who are lured by the charm and appeal of Aphrodite's island.

Colourful inflatable rings for children

The delightful small rocky coves and beaches provide a quiet and charming spot for a refreshing dip. The best known of these scenic beaches is the rocky coast by Petra tou Romiou – the Rock of Aphrodite.

Private hotel beaches as well as public beaches become very crowded during peak season. One of the most famous beaches in Cyprus – Agia Napa's Nissi Beach – buzzes with activity from morning until night. Tourists remain in beach bars and nearby clubs until the small hours and, after a night of partying, head straight for the beach to enjoy a refreshing swim. Named after the nearby island (the word *nissi* means "island"), Nissi Beach has consequently been nick-named the "Cypriot Ibiza". The beach lures visitors with its clear water and sand, not seen in other parts of south Cyprus. According to legend, the sand was brought here from the Sahara.

Less famous but equally beautiful beaches can be found in the northern part of the island, in the region of Famagusta (Gazimağusa). Deckchairs, umbrellas and towels are available for hire, but watch out because in some places the owners charge exorbitant prices. Many beaches are set up with volleyball courts; you can also have a game of beach ball or frisbee. Numerous sport centres hire out diving or snorkelling equipment, as well as boats and canoes.

Since there is no shortage of daredevils, Cyprus's beaches also offer bungee jumping, water skiing, water scooters, paragliding and "banana" rides behind a motorboat.

The very popular water scooter

DIRECTORY

WATERSPORTS

Cyprus Federation of Underwater Activities
PO Box 21503,
1510 Nicosia.
Tel 22 754 647.
Fax 22 755 246.
www.cfua.org

DIVING

**Blue Dolphin
Scuba Diving**
Jasmine Court Hotel,
Kyrenia (Girne).
Tel 0533 861 5113.
Fax 0392 223 43 60.
www.bluedolphincyprus.com

Cydive Diving Centre
1 Poseidonos Ave,
MYRRA Complex, Pafos.
Tel 26 964 271.
Fax 26 935 307.
www.cydive.com

Scuba Cyprus
Santorio Village, PO Box 82,
Alsancak,
Kyrenia (Girne).
Tel 0533 865 2317.
www.scubacyprus.com

BOAT & YACHT CHARTER

Armata
Larnaka.
Tel 24 665 408.
Fax 24 627 489.

Interyachting Ltd.
Limassol.
Tel 25 811 900.
Fax 25 811 945.
www.interyachting.com.cy

Navimed Ltd.
Nicosia.
Tel 22 430 101.
Fax 22 430 313.

Sail Fascination Shipping Ltd.
Nikiforou Fokas 27,
Limassol.
Tel 25 364 200.
Fax 25 352 657.

SURVIVAL
GUIDE

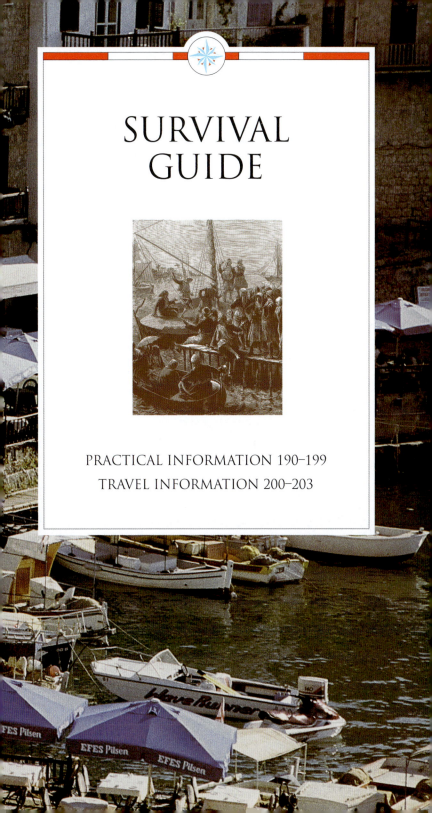

PRACTICAL INFORMATION

Cyprus is a popular year-round destination, due to its Mediterranean climate. It is easily accessible from mainland Europe and the Middle East, yet being an island is a true getaway. The Cypriots are extremely friendly and well inclined towards tourists.

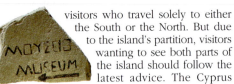

Stone road sign

The Greek South and Turkish North have very different characters. Entry requirements are straightforward for visitors who travel solely to either the South or the North. But due to the island's partition, visitors wanting to see both parts of the island should follow the latest advice. The Cyprus Tourism Organization (CTO), representing Southern Cyprus, has offices overseas and throughout the South. The Turkish Republic of Northern Cyprus Ministry of Economy and Tourism represents the North.

WHEN TO GO

Cyprus is a year-round destination, so any time of year is suitable for a visit. The main tourist season runs from April until October, and peaks during July and August, when the air and water temperatures are at their highest. At this time the late-night bars, taverns and restaurants fill up to capacity, and the beaches are packed with sun worshippers. The hotel swimming pools, pubs and discos are equally crowded. During peak season you can hear an international mix of languages in the streets, dominated by English, German and Russian.

Those who enjoy the mild, warm climate but prefer to avoid the crowds should visit Cyprus outside the peak season. In April, May and October it is warm enough to swim in the sea, but the beaches are not crowded. In winter (December–February), it is cool for swimming, but good for beach walks, while in the Troodos mountains you can even ski. In spring, Cyprus is an ideal place for hiking, cycling and horse riding.

The pretty harbour of Kyrenia, North Cyprus

PASSPORTS & VISAS (THE SOUTH)

Most visitors, including citizens of the EU, the USA, Canada, Australia and New Zealand do not require a visa to visit the Republic of Cyprus, and can stay there for up to three months. However, entry to the South will be refused if visitors' passports show they have previously entered North Cyprus.

Tourists may be asked to show that they have adequate means to support themselves for the duration of their stay. No vaccinations or health certificates are required.

PASSPORTS & VISAS (THE NORTH)

To visit North Cyprus, most visitors (including citizens of the EU, USA, Canada, Australia and New Zealand) require only a valid passport. But to avoid being refused entry on later visits to the South, passports should be stamped on a separate loose sheet of paper.

There are no currency restrictions in the North, which has no currency of its own and uses the Turkish lira.

CROSSING THE BORDER

Until 2003, the only entry route for travellers to North Cyprus was via plane or ferry from Turkey. Nowadays visitors can fly directly to the Republic of Cyprus and from there travel to the buffer zone. Most visitors do not require a visa to visit North Cyprus, but you will be issued a document free of charge when crossing the border between the two parts of the island.

A popular beach in a seaside resort

◁ The picturesque Kyrenia harbour in North Cyprus

There are seven border crossings (two for pedestrians and one for cars in Nicosia; a further four for cars outside the capital).

Apart from the largest cities, such as North Nicosia, Kyrenia and Famagusta, North Cyprus is less crowded than the South of the island. The climate is the same, so in spring it is pleasant to stroll among the orange groves, and in the summer to enjoy the beaches and the sea.

CUSTOMS

Customs regulations allow visitors to bring in, duty free, 200 cigarettes, one litre of spirits and two litres of wine. The import of perishable food items is strictly prohibited. Visitors may import any amount of banknotes, which should be declared to customs on arrival.

EMBASSIES & CONSULATES

Many countries have embassies or consulates in southern Nicosia, the capital of the Republic of Cyprus. There are no embassies or consulates north of the Green Line because North Cyprus is not recognized as an independent country.

WHAT TO TAKE

For the most part, Cyprus is a relaxed, casual holiday destination. Visitors should pack beachwear, sunglasses, hats and smart casual wear for the resorts. If you're staying in an upmarket hotel, or dining in a fancy restaurant, you will fit in better if you dress up more, as the Cypriots themselves do.

In summer you will seldom need a sweater, but in late autumn, winter and early spring temperatures are cooler and you will need to bring some warm clothing.

If you plan to visit the mountains, at any time of year, it is advisable to bring warm clothes and rain gear.

Visitors taking medication should travel with an adequate supply. It's also a good idea to bring high-factor sun lotion and insect repellent.

Some hotels don't supply bath or sink plugs, so you may consider bringing a universal plug.

ETIQUETTE

When visiting religious buildings, modest attire is expected. For churches, monasteries and mosques this means long trousers or skirts, and a shirt that covers your back and shoulders. Shoes must be removed before entering a mosque.

TOURIST ORGANIZATIONS

Tourist information bureaux can be found easily in all major tourist centres, such as Nicosia, Larnaka, Limassol, Pafos and Agia Napa. They distribute free information packs and maps, as well as providing useful advice on sightseeing. The **Cyprus Tourism Organization (CTO)**, with offices in many European cities, has a website with lots of information on the Republic of Cyprus. Visit their website at: www.visitcyprus.com.

The **Turkish Republic of Northern Cyprus Ministry of Economy & Tourism** has

Automatic tourist information kiosk

overseas offices, too. You can learn more about the North at www.go-north cyprus.com.

Nowadays travel agents, hotels, car hire companies, and organizations that offer special activities have their own websites. These websites are often in several languages, with pictures to illustrate the services offered. It's a good idea to browse through their websites to look for good offers before travelling; many arrangements can be made before you leave home, allowing you to start enjoying your visit from the moment you arrive in Cyprus. Just be sure to check when the website was last updated, as some of the information, particularly for the North, may be out of date and quote the last season's prices.

A range of brochures and illustrated booklets covering individual tourist sights is usually available for sale at the sights themselves.

LANGUAGES

Two languages – Greek and Turkish – have co-existed in Cyprus in the centuries between the Turkish conquest of 1571 and the partition of the island in 1974. Due to the current political situation, however, the South uses only Greek and the North uses only Turkish. In the holiday resorts of the South, English (as well as German and Russian) is commonly understood. Restaurant menus and shop signs are in several languages.

In the North it is more difficult to communicate in English and other European languages, although there is usually no problem in hotels. Road signs throughout the island carry the names of towns written in the Latin alphabet. In the North, however, only the Turkish names are given, so check your map to ensure that you know where you are going.

A tourist information centre

RELIGION

The Cypriot Orthodox Church, which is dominant in the south of the island, is independent from the Greek Orthodox Church. It is also the oldest national church in Christendom, its history tracing back to the times of St Paul.

In the towns you often encounter Orthodox priests dressed in long black robes. The main Orthodox services, lasting two to three hours, are held on Saturday evenings and Sunday mornings.

Monasteries have served as Cypriot pilgrimage sites for centuries. Today, they are visited by tourists in such vast numbers that access to some of them has been restricted.

In the North the dominant religion is Islam, though, like Turkey, the North is a secular state. All larger towns and cities have mosques, from which the muezzin's voice calls the faithful to prayer five times a day. Services are held on Friday afternoons.

Men at prayer in a mosque in North Cyprus

TRAVELLING WITH CHILDREN

Major brands of baby food, medicines and toiletries, including nappies (diapers) are sold in all supermarkets and pharmacies. Both parts of the island are family-friendly, with children welcomed everywhere and plenty of kids' facilities. However, risks for smaller children include sunburn, occasional rough waters and pests such as jellyfish, sea urchins and stinging insects.

Worshipper inside an Orthodox church in southern Cyprus

YOUNG VISITORS

Cyprus is an ideal holiday destination for young people. Its sunny beaches, clean waters, watersports facilities, and rich and varied nightlife attract young people in their thousands. Hundreds of nightclubs, discos, pubs and bars await the revellers.

Holders of ISIC or Euro<26 cards qualify for discounts on public transport and reduced admission to museums and some other tourist sights.

WOMEN TRAVELLERS

Women travelling alone or together should exercise normal caution. Cyprus is generally safe, but there have been reports of sexual assaults against women travellers so avoid walking alone at night.

DISABLED VISITORS

Facilities for the disabled have improved somewhat, but even so, few public buildings, shops or visitor attractions have wheelchair ramps so access can be very difficult for wheelchair users. Many museums are in older buildings without lifts. Access to archaeological sites is also difficult. Pavements in towns and villages (if there are any) are often uneven.

Sign prohibiting photography

A leaflet with information on facilities for wheelchair users is available from the CTO.

Only a few museums and archaeological sites in the south (and none in the North) offer Braille or audio guides for visually impaired people or induction loop devices for those with hearing difficulties. The British charity RADAR (for people with hearing and visual impairment) can supply information on facilities in Cyprus (www.radar.org.uk).

GAY & LESBIAN VISITORS

Homosexuality is no longer illegal in southern Cyprus, and gay visitors are generally welcomed; there are gay clubs and bars in Agia Napa, Larnaka, Limassol and Pafos.

In North Cyprus, homosexuality is still illegal.

SINGLE TRAVELLERS

Most visitors to Cyprus come as couples, families or groups of singles, and most hotels offer only double or twin rooms and charge a "single supplement" for those travelling alone. Individuals travelling independently may be able to negotiate a better deal out of season. Several companies specialize in tours for singles: lists are available from the CTO or the Association of Independent Tour Operators in the UK.

SENIOR CITIZENS

Both Cypriot communities are notably respectful to older people, but hazards include urban traffic (Cypriot drivers sometimes ignore pedestrian crossings) and noise – Agia Napa, especially, is geared to younger visitors.

PHOTOGRAPHY

Be aware that taking photographs of military bases or facilities, and the border between southern Cyprus and the North is strictly prohibited. United Nations soldiers guarding the Green Line are used to groups of tourists, but taking photographs at any point is strictly forbidden.

Archaeological sites can be photographed and filmed free of charge; however, the state museums generally charge a fee for taking photographs.

In places of worship, ask in advance whether photography is permitted. Most churches will not allow you to use flash photography.

ELECTRICAL EQUIPMENT

The mains supply on the island is 220/240V, with standard British triple rectangular-pin plugs. Most hotel reception desks will provide you with a suitable adaptor. Some hotel rooms are equipped with hairdryers, and irons are usually available to borrow. Most hotels have adapted their supply sockets to suit European plugs, so in theory there should be no problem using your own electrical equipment (but in practice this isn't always true).

TIME

Cyprus lies within the Eastern-European time zone, and local time is two hours ahead of GMT. Like the UK, Cyprus puts its clocks forward by one hour from late March to late September. "Morning" in South Cyprus is *proí*; "afternoon" – *mesiméri*; "evening" – *vrádhi*; and "night" – *níchta*.

WEDDINGS

Cyprus is one of the world's most popular wedding destinations and some hotels have their own wedding chapel. The bride and groom are required to have all the correct documentation.

DISCUSSING POLITICS

The events of 1974, when the island was divided between the Turkish and the Greek Cypriots, are still remembered with bitterness. In both the south and the North, local people vehemently argue the justice of their cause. Politics and recent history are subjects that are best avoided.

MILITARY ZONES

Britain's sovereign bases in the south, at Akrotiri (Episkopi) and Dhekelia, are also used by US forces and are likely to be on heightened alert in these security-conscious times. Do not intrude on military installations. The same applies to Turkish Army personnel, equipment and installations in the occupied North.

DIRECTORY

EMBASSIES & CONSULATES

Australia
Annis Komninis 4, Nicosia.
Tel *22 753 001.*
www.cyprus.embassy.gov.au

Germany
Nikitara 10, Nicosia.
Tel *22 451 145.*
www.nikosia.diplo.de

Ireland
Aianta 7, 1082 Nicosia.
Tel *22 818 183.*

Representation of the European Commission
Vyronos Avenue 30, 1096 Nicosia.
Tel *22 817 770.*
http://ec.europa.eu/cyprus/index_en.htm

Russia
Arch. Makarou III, 2406 Egkomi, Nicosia.
Tel *222 774 622.*
www.cyprus.mid.ru

UK
Alexandrou Palli 1, Nicosia.
Tel *22 861 100.*
http://ukincyprus.fco.gov.uk/en

USA
Ploutarchou, Nicosia.
Tel *22 393 939.*
www.american embassy.org.cy

TOURISM ORGANIZATIONS

Association of Cyprus Tourism Organization (CTO)
Leoforos Lemesou 19, Nicosia.
Tel *22 691 100.*
www.visitcyprus.com

Association of Independent Tour Operators
www.aito.co.uk

Cyprus Hotel Association
PO Box 24772, CY 1303, Nicosia.
Tel *22 452 820.*
www.cyprushotel association.org

Cyprus Tourist Guides Association
Tel *22 765 755.*
www.cytouristguides.com

Cyprus Travel Agents
Tel *22 666 435.*
www.acta.org.cy

Turkish Republic of Northern Cyprus Ministry of Economy & Tourism
Tel *0392 228 96 29.*
www.holidayin northcyprus.com

WEDDINGS

Union of Cyprus Municipalities
Nicosia.
Tel *22 445 170.*
Fax *22 677 230.*
www.ucm.org.cy

USEFUL WEBSITES IN THE REPUBLIC OF CYPRUS

www.cyprus-mail.com
www.visitcyprus.com
www.kypros.org
www.pio.gov.cy
www.windowoncyprus.com

USEFUL WEBSITES IN NORTH CYPRUS

www.cypnet.com
www.northcyprus.net
www.cyprustourist guide.com

Personal Security and Health

Policeman on a scooter

Cyprus has a low crime rate, but even here crimes do occur; these can be minimized by taking simple precautions. The risk of mugging and theft is greatest in crowded places. Take extra care on crowded promenades or streets and in markets to protect your belongings. Keep documents, money and credit cards hidden from view, and leave what you don't need in the hotel safe. Never leave anything visible in your car when you park it. When in need, you can always ask a policeman for help. Basic medical advice is available at pharmacies. All medical treatment must be paid for; insurance is strongly advised.

Entrance to a police station in the North

should be carried on a strap or inside the case. Your car should always be locked, with any valuables kept well out of sight.

Any case of theft should be reported immediately to the police. Passport theft should also be reported to your embassy in Nicosia.

PERSONAL BELONGINGS

Before travelling abroad, it is wise to ensure that you have adequate insurance to protect yourself financially from the loss or theft of your property. Even so, it is advisable to take precautions against loss or theft in the first place. Be vigilant when you are out and about but especially in crowded places, where the risk of theft or mugging is greatest.

Make photocopies of your important documents and keep these with you, leaving the originals behind in the hotel safe (where you can also deposit money and jewellery).

Make a note of your credit card numbers and the phone number of the issuing bank, in the event of loss or theft.

Cameras and camcorders

CYPRUS POLICE

The police in Cyprus are friendly towards tourists and ready to offer advice. The majority of them also speak English. But in the event that you are caught breaking the law, they can be stern and unwilling to accept excuses.

Heavy fines are levied for failing to wear a seat belt and for using a mobile telephone when driving a vehicle.

PERSONAL SECURITY IN THE NORTH

In terms of personal safety, North Cyprus is no different from the south. Special care should be taken when visiting the buffer zone and when

Typical southern Cyprus police car

passing by military facilities, of which there is no shortage. In particular, resist the temptation to photograph any military installations, vehicles or soldiers. The latter are visible in great numbers, but if you follow the rules of normal behaviour, they will not interfere with your visit.

Roads in North Cyprus are comfortable, wide and of very high quality, including the mountain roads.

Manned lifeguard post at one of the beaches

BEACHES

During the holiday season, most beaches employ lifeguards. The areas allocated for swimming are marked with coloured buoys. While swimming outside the marked areas is not prohibited, it is inadvisable, particularly for weaker swimmers. Some beaches have first-aid stations, with lifeguards trained to help casualties.

Beach facilities, such as showers, are standard almost everywhere. Hotels with direct access to the sea have stretches of beach allocated to them.

Smaller beaches have no lifeguards; they are generally found in coves sheltered from the open sea, so their waters are calm and safe. The most beautiful beaches are found in the regions of Agia Napa in the south, and Famagusta in North Cyprus. The south coast beaches are generally rocky and pebbly.

In summer, Cyprus has some of the highest temperatures in Europe, and it's easy to get sunburnt anytime from early

April to late October. Young children are especially vulnerable to the hot sun. Avoid being directly in the sun during the middle of the day, when the rays are strongest. Sunhats, sunglasses, a high factor sunscreen and sunblock are vital to protect your skin. During the day, carry bottled water with you, and drink lots of it, to avoid dehydration.

MEDICAL CARE

Cyprus is free from most dangerous infectious diseases (although AIDS is present), and no immunizations are required. Drinking tap water is safe. However, all medical treatment must be paid for, and comprehensive insurance to cover hospital and medical charges, as well as emergency repatriation, is advisable. Before travelling to the North, double check that your insurance policy will cover you there.

Some medical procedures (such as dental treatment) are not covered by insurance.

Emergency medical care in the Republic of Cyprus is free for all European Union citizens. The European Health Insurance Card (EHIC), available from the UK Department of Health or from a main post office, covers emergencies only. The card comes with a booklet that contains general health advice and information about how to claim free medical treatment when travelling abroad. You may find that you have to pay and reclaim the money later.

Hotels can usually recommend a local doctor or

Pharmacy sign with the easily recognisable green cross

dentist, many of whom speak English. All bills must be settled at the time of treatment, but these practitioners will provide a receipt for you to claim a refund from your insurance company.

Visitors on package holidays to Cyprus should check with their tour operator if medical insurance is included.

PHARMACIES

Most pharmacies keep normal shop opening hours *(see p178)*. They display the green cross sign and the word *farmakeio* or *eczane*. A list of pharmacies open at night and on holidays can be found in the English-language *Cyprus Mail*. In an emergency, an all-night pharmacy can offer medical help and advice. In tourist resorts and large cities most pharmacists speak English. They can usually advise and provide remedies for minor ailments and injuries, but if you need specialist prescription drugs it is best to bring an adequate supply with you.

A uniformed fireman

FIRE SERVICE

Winters are dry and mild, and summers are hot, creating prime conditions for fires,

which can spread with alarming speed and present a particular danger to forests. Mountain fires, especially, are difficult to put out.

Cyprus has two types of fire brigade; one that responds to general emergency calls, the other specifically dedicated to forest fires.

During excursions to the island's dry interior, or when camping, you must take particular care not to start a fire. Be especially careful to extinguish cigarettes thoroughly and dispose of them safely. When leaving a picnic area or campsite, ensure that bonfires are completely extinguished, and take all glass bottles with you to prevent accidental fires.

DIRECTORY

EMERGENCY SERVICES

Police
Tel 112 (South), 155 (North).

Fire Brigade
Tel 112 (South), 199 (North).

Forest Fire Teams
Tel 1407 (South), 177 (North).

Ambulance
Tel 112.

HOSPITALS

General Hospitals
Agia Napa/Paralimni.
Tel 23 821 211.
Larnaka. *Tel* 24 800 500.
Limassol. *Tel* 25 801 100.
Nicosia. *Tel* 22 801 400.
Pafos. *Tel* 26 803 100.

PHARMACIES

Information in English
Agia Napa. *Tel* 90 901 413.
Larnaka. *Tel* 90 901 414.
Limassol. *Tel* 90 901 415.
Nicosia. *Tel* 90 901 412.
Pafos. *Tel* 90 901 416.

Standard fire engine of the Cyprus Fire Brigade

Communications

Post office logo in South Cyprus

The quality of telecommunications services in Cyprus is very good, especially in the south. Public telephone booths are widespread. In larger towns and cities, you will have no trouble finding an Internet café, if your hotel doesn't have access. Postal services are decent. A good selection of newspapers is available, and there's no shortage of TV or radio stations.

most of the island, although reception may be patchy in the mountain region. Mobile phone usage is widespread in Cyprus, and visitors who bring their own phone are likely to experience few problems. Although individual calls cost more than at home, the convenience usually more than compensates.

Making and receiving calls requires an active roaming facility. While abroad, mobile telephone users are charged for both outgoing and incoming calls, as well as text messages. Information on the cost of calls can be obtained from individual mobile network operators.

Every hotel and many public buildings have Yellow Pages directories where, in addition to local phone numbers, you can find information on hotels, restaurants, and many outfits offering activities and entertainment.

A telephone card available in south Cyprus

USING THE TELEPHONE

Cyprus has a well-developed telephone network. Public phones accept coins, as well as phonecards, which can be purchased from newsagent kiosks, post offices and banks in various denominations. Instructions for using the phone are provided in both Greek and English. Calls to the police, fire brigade or ambulance service are free.

Hotel rooms are equipped with telephones, but calls made from them are usually very expensive; make sure you check the rates before using them.

The country code for Cyprus is 357 except for North Cyprus, where it is 90 (for Turkey) followed by (0)392. Local area codes in Cyprus include: Nicosia 22; Limassol 25; Larnaka 24; Pafos and Polis 26; Agia Napa and Protaras 23.

When making an international call from Cyprus, first dial 00, followed by the country code, and then the area code (omitting the zero that precedes some area codes). Useful country codes are: UK (44), USA and Canada (1), Ireland (353), Australia (61), New Zealand (64) and South Africa (27). All public telephones in the south can be used to make international calls. Calls are cheaper at night (after 6pm) and at weekends.

The mobile telephone (cellphone) network covers

Post office logo in North Cyprus

TELEPHONES IN NORTH CYPRUS

There are fewer public telephones in the North than in the South and the quality of connections can be poor. In the North, phones don't accept coins; instead you insert a pre-paid phone card (*telekart*). These are available from *Telekomünikasyon* offices, post offices and newsagents. There are also metred counter phones (*kontürlü telefon*) – where you speak first, and pay after completing the call. These calls are more

USING A CARDPHONE

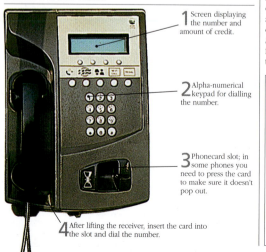

1 Screen displaying the number and amount of credit.

2 Alpha-numerical keypad for dialling the number.

3 Phonecard slot; in some phones you need to press the card to make sure it doesn't pop out.

4 After lifting the receiver, insert the card into the slot and dial the number.

USEFUL NUMBERS

- Directory enquiries 11892 (South), 192 (North)
- International directory enquiries 11894 (South), 192 (North)
- International calls via the operator 80000198
- Speaking clock 1895
- Infoline 132
- International access code 00

expensive than card-operated phones. Metered phones can be found in branches of the *Telekomunikasyon*.

Hotel room telephones are the most expensive. To avoid unpleasant surprises, check the rates first.

The area codes for Northern Cyprus are: 228 for Nicosia (Lefkoßa); 822 for Kyrenia (Girne); 366 for Famagusta (Gazimağuza); 723 for Morfou (Güzelyurt); and 660 for Lefke. The remaining area codes are the same as for southern Cyprus.

Postage stamp vending machine

POSTAL SERVICES

Most post offices in the south are open from 7:30am to 1:30pm and 3 to 6pm Monday to Friday (except in July and August, when they close daily at noon). They are closed from noon on Wednesdays. On Saturdays, main post offices are open only in the mornings. Letters and postcards sent to European countries arrive quite quickly, taking about four days to reach their destination.

In the North, post offices are open from 8am until 5pm on weekdays, with a lunch break from 1 to 2pm; and on Saturdays from 9am until noon.

Letterboxes throughout the island are painted yellow. The main post offices are in Plateia Eleftherias, Nicosia; 1 Gladstone Street, Limassol; and King Paul Square, Larnaka.

Post offices accept letters and parcels. Postage stamps

can be bought at post offices and almost any shop that sells postcards. You can also post your letter at the reception desk in most hotels.

Beware posting mail in the North – it will invariably take longer to reach its destination; due to the international non-recogition of North Cyprus, all mail sent from here has to travel via Turkey.

RADIO AND TELEVISION

Cyprus has an extraordinary number of TV channels for a country of its size. In the south there are five free-to-air islandwide channels plus several local stations in each town. Many Cypriots also subscribe to one or more Pay-TV channels. Greek national TV is relayed to the south and Turkish TV to the north. Most large hotels have satellite TV tuned to CNN, BBC World and other foreign-language channels.

The most popular English-language radio station in Cyprus is BFBS, aimed at the British Forces but listened to by English-speakers throughout the island. Its two channels resemble BBC Radio 1 and Radio 2, though the latter also transmits programmes from BBC Radio 4 and Radio Five Live. Cyprus's own national broadcaster, CyBC, provides a limited English-language service on Channel 2, and there are several independent English-language stations,

including Radio Napa (broadcast in Agia Napa) and Coast FM (in Limassol).

PRESS

The English-language newspapers published in southern Cyprus include the daily *Cyprus Mail* and the weekly *Cyprus Weekly*, as well as the *Cyprus Lion* – the British Forces newspaper. In the North, you can find the English-language *Cyprus Times*. Many popular British newspapers (*Daily Mail*, *Daily Express* and *Mirror*) are on sale on the day of publication.

These newspapers are sold at newsagent kiosks, airports and hotels. There are also a dozen or so local papers published in the island. The cultural bulletins, published in several languages, contain information on current events and activities, and may prove of interest to visitors.

Two popular newspapers from South Cyprus

INTERNET

The Internet provides a great way to research your trip before heading off. Many hotels have their own websites where you can view the facilities, and make reservations. The same is true of car hire companies and various organized activities. A particularly informative site is the CTO's own website **www.visitcyprus.com**.

Once you're in Cyprus, the Internet provides a great way to stay in touch with people back home, and to learn more about Cyprus. Internet cafés can be found in all the island's major towns, and most hotels provide Internet access for a fee. Fees for this service are usually reasonable.

Post office in Pafos, with the bright-yellow letterbox outside

Banking and Local Currency

Cyprus bank logo

Banks in Cyprus operate efficiently. There is a wide bank network on the island, and many foreign banks also have branches here. Cash machines can be found along the main streets and in hotel lobbies, making debit and credit cards a convenient way to withdraw cash. Most larger shops and boutiques, as well as hotels and restaurants, accept credit cards.

Tourists drawing money from a cash machine

BANKS AND CASH MACHINES

Bank opening hours are from 8:15am–1:30pm (Monday to Friday) in summer (8:30am–1:30pm, 3:15–4:45pm in winter) and closed Saturday and Sunday. Some banks in the tourist resorts are open every afternoon, from 3–5pm. The bank desks in Larnaka and Pafos International Airports remain open until the last plane of the day lands.

Cash machines operate around the clock. They are typically installed outside banks and some hotels, as well as in larger towns and holiday resorts. You can withdraw cash using all major credit cards. Follow the instructions (given in English) on the individual machine.

MONEY EXCHANGE

Bureaux de change are found in the centres of larger towns and at the airports. They are open 24 hours a day; currency exchange counters in the banks are open during normal banking hours. Money exchange transactions are always subject to a commission fee; look around to get the best deal – the rates are clearly posted for you to see.

Hotels also offer exchange facilities, but their rates of exchange tend to be less favourable than either banks or bureaux de change, and they usually charge a higher commission, too.

Both foreign currency and travellers' cheques are accepted, in exchange for euro or Turkish lira. Travellers' cheques are also honoured by many hotels, shops and restaurants.

Many shops in both the Republic of Cyprus and in North Cyprus accept common foreign currencies, including US dollars and British pound sterling.

ATM (cash machine) in one of Nicosia's streets

BANKS AND CURRENCY EXCHANGE IN NORTH CYPRUS

In North Cyprus, the bank networks are less extensive than in the south. Banks are open from 8am until noon. Travellers' cheques are widely accepted in shops, hotels and restaurants. They can also be exchanged for Turkish lira in banks and bureaux de change. When exchanging money, use only reputable dealers. In light of the high rate of inflation, it is worth changing smaller amounts of money more frequently, rather than a large amount.

Entrance to a Turkish bank in North Cyprus

TRAVELLERS' CHEQUES AND CREDIT CARDS

Banks, bureaux de change and other exchange facilities will cash your travellers' cheques into either euro or Turkish lira.

Credit cards are accepted by most larger shops, restaurants and hotels, although in markets and small shops only cash is accepted. Many debit cards are accepted, but check with your bank that your card is valid internationally. It may be difficult to find a cash machine in provincial towns and villages, so it is advisable to bring enough cash with you.

Money can be obtained from 24-hour cash machines and banks that accept credit cards. The most widely accepted cards are VISA, MasterCard and American Express.

CURRENCY

The Republic of Cyprus joined the Eurozone on 1 January 2008. Following a changeover period of one month, during which time both the Cyprus pound and the euro were in circulation, the Cyprus pound ceased to be legal tender.

The currency used in North Cyprus is the Turkish lira (TL or, more officially, TRY). This currency is not readily available abroad, so you need to change money on arrival in the island. North Cyprus also accepts payments in euro.

REPUBLIC OF CYPRUS

Banknotes

Euro banknotes have seven denominations. The €5 note (grey in colour) is the smallest, followed by the €10 note (pink), €20 note (blue), €50 note (orange), €100 note (green), €200 note (yellow) and €500 note (purple). All notes show the 12 stars of the European Union.

€5

€10

€20

€50

€100

€200

€500

Coins

The euro has eight coin denominations: €2 and €1; 50 cents, 20 cents, 10 cents, 5 cents, 2 cents and 1 cent. The €1 and €2 coins are both silver and gold in colour. The 50-, 20- and 10-cent coins are gold. The 5-, 2- and 1-cent coins are bronze.

€2 €1 50 cents 20 cents 10 cents 5 cents 2 cents 1 cent

NORTH CYPRUS

Banknotes

North Cyprus does not have its own currency; it uses the Turkish lira (abbreviated to TL). The banknotes, in six denominations from 1 to 100 TL, come in a range of colours, and bear Turkish national symbols and major historical figures. The euro is also accepted in the North.

1 lira

5 lira

10 lira

20 lira

50 lira

100 lira

1 lira

50 kuruş

Coins

There are six coins in circulation, ranging in value from 1 kuruş, 5 kuruş, 10 kuruş, 25 kuruş and 50 kuruş to 1 TL – Turkish Lira (100 kuruş).

TRAVEL INFORMATION

ost visitors travel to Cyprus on a package holiday which combines flights, accommodation, transport to and from the airport, and often car hire. This can be the most cost-effective option. International airports are located in Larnaka and Pafos; handling both scheduled flights and charters. Travel from mainland Europe to the island takes around 3–4 hours. Fares

Cyprus Airways flight attendant

and schedules can be obtained from travel agents, airline offices and on the Internet. You can also reach Cyprus by boat, although this takes much longer. Boats sail from Greece to Limassol, and from Turkey to Kyrenia and Famagusta. The road network is good, with clearly marked signs. Cars drive on the left side of the road. A decent bus service operates between main towns and big resorts.

AIR TRAVEL

The international airports in Pafos and Larnaka, both in the Republic of Cyprus, handle flights by the national carrier Cyprus Airways and other European airlines that serve many European capital cities and regional hubs. During summer, the airports become crowded due to the large number of charter flights. Scheduled flight tickets are generally more expensive than charters, but offer more flexibility and greater comfort.

Charter flights are at their busiest from April through October, with weekly departures. Most seats on charter flights are bought in blocks by tour operators, as part of their holiday packages, but "flight-only" charters are also available. These can be an affordable and convenient option for holidaymakers who prefer independent arrangements. Information concerning ticket availability can be obtained from travel agents and from airline

Terminal building at Larnaka airport

representatives. Airports have duty-free shops, cafés and restaurants, but the food and beverages on offer are over-priced.

Bus services from the airports to the main towns are frequent but it is worth checking the schedule to your destination in advance. The tourist information centres should be able to help you with this.

The best way of getting to town is by taxi or hired car. The taxi rank is situated immediately next to the exit from the arrivals hall. For short distances, taxis are a

comfortable and affordable mode of transport. Car hire companies have offices at the airports, as well as in towns.

Visitors travelling to Larnaka airport with a tour operator should turn left, towards the coach parking, after leaving the terminal building. Visitors hiring a car should turn towards the car park, situated some 400 m to the left, after leaving the terminal building.

At Larnaka as well as at Pafos airport, services, amenities and transport links are clearly signposted at the terminal.

FERRIES

Travel by ferry is often cheaper than flying, but currently there are few options to travel to Cyprus by sea. There are no passenger ferries to Cyprus at the present time.

Determined budget travellers can sail into Limassol from ports such as Piraeus (the port of Athens) and from some of the Greek islands, such as Patmos or Rhodes, but often this will be aboard a cargo ship. Journey times can be long: a direct sailing from Piraeus to Cyprus can take around 40 hours.

Those intending to travel by ferry are advised to contact a travel operator for the most up-to-date information concerning prices and sailing options.

Check-in hall at Larnaka international airport

Cruise ships provide regular links between Cyprus and Haifa (Israel), Beirut (Lebanon) and Port Said (Egypt).

Regular service begins in spring, at the start of the tourist season. Between May and October, the ferries sailing to the Middle East are used mainly by people on holiday in Cyprus. From the south there are a number of popular trips, including the journeys to Israel, Egypt, Lebanon and the Greek islands. Regular services operate between North Cyprus and Turkey.

Some travel operators offer organized three-day trips to Egypt and the Holy Land, which include visits to Jerusalem and Bethlehem. These excursion vessels depart from Limassol Port.

There are a number of luxury cruiseliners that travel the Mediterranean and Middle East, with Cyprus being a popular stopping-off point.

NORTH CYPRUS

The quickest way to reach North Cyprus is by plane. All flights to Ercan airport originate in Turkey – from Alanya, Dalaman, Istanbul and Izmir. It is not possible to fly direct to Northern Cyprus from any other country. Flights are operated by Turkish Airlines. In order to reach Ercan airport you have to travel to Turkey from one of the European airports and then change for the flight to North Cyprus.

Convenient package holidays offer the same combination of flights, accommodation, airport transfers and, generally, car hire as those to the south,

Ferry harbour in Kyrenia, North Cyprus

making this the easiest way to visit. You can also reach the North by ferry, which is a cheaper option, recommended for those who wish to bring their own car to the island. The ferry companies serving these routes include Turkish Maritime Lines and Fergun Lines. Ferry journeys take much longer than flying: the journey from Taşucu to Kyrenia lasts six hours; from Mersin to Famagusta 10 hours.

Travelling to North Cyprus can test your patience, as it usually involves long hours of waiting at Turkish airports for connecting flights – an important consideration when travelling with children or the elderly. These delays are due to the timetables not being very well coordinated.

Since the Republic of Cyprus joined the European Union in 2004, all citizens from the south are allowed to cross the border into North Cyprus without any hindrance, at least in theory, and stay as long as they wish. Visitors to the south who want to see North Cyprus can also cross the border to the North at the official checkpoints. Crossing anywhere other than an official checkpoint may result in arrest.

DIRECTORY

CYPRUS TOURISM ORGANIZATION (CTO)

www.visitcyprus.com

Larnaca
Tel 246 54322.

Limassol
Tel 253 62756.

Nicosia
Tel 226 74264.

Pafos
Tel 269 32841.

Troodos
Tel 254 21316.

INTERNATIONAL AIRPORTS

Ercan
Tel 0392 600 5000.

Larnaca
Tel 24 816 400.
Fax 24 643 633.
www.hermesairports.com

Pafos
Tel 24 816 400.
Fax 26 007 100.
www.hermesairports.com

CYPRUS AIRWAYS

www.cyprusairways.com

PORTS

Famagusta
Tel 0392 365 43 88.

Larnaca
Tel 24 815 225.

Limassol
Tel 25 207 182.

Pafos
Tel 26 946 840.

Airport terminal building at Ercan, North Cyprus

Travelling by Car

The logo of a Cypriot petrol station

Most visitors to Cyprus explore the island by bus or hire car. Buses provide good links between the towns, while for shorter distances taxis are a good option – both comfortable and affordable. In Cyprus, vehicles are right-hand drive. The roads throughout the island are in good condition, and signposting is clear.

North Cyprus sign indicating cars should drive in the left lane

CAR HIRE

It is expensive to hire a car on the island, especially in the main tourist season from April through October. You may find more attractive prices during low season. The price usually includes full insurance, a certain mileage allowance and VAT (value-added tax). Drivers under the age of 25 require additional insurance. Cypriot authorities honour international diving licences, as well as foreign licences. Both manual and automatic cars are available for hire, as are motorcycles and scooters.

You really only need a four-wheel-drive vehicle if you are planning to tour the mountain regions in winter using some of the rough tracks, or go off-road in the Akamas peninsula. Major international car hire companies – Hertz, Avis and Europcar – have offices at the airports and in large cities, including Nicosia, Larnaka, Limassol and Pafos. Driving a hire car across the border to North Cyprus is not prohibited, but you will have to take out extra insurance on the Turkish side.

RULES OF THE ROAD

Driving is the easiest way to get around Cyprus. Roads are good, with motorways connecting Nicosia with Larnaka, Limassol, Pafos and Agia Napa. Distances are short – it is less than 160 km (100 miles) from Pafos to Nicosia.

Cypriots drive on the left side of the road, and drivers should give way to vehicles approaching from the right. Road signs are provided in both Greek and English in the south.

Distances and speed limits are in kilometres – 100 kmph (60 mph) on motorways,

Road sign in the south: sharp bend

80 kmph (50 mph) on most other roads, and 50 kmph (30 mph) in built-up areas. There are on-the-spot fines for speeding and for failing to wear a seat belt. Driving under the influence of alcohol is a criminal offence with serious consequences, as is using a mobile phone while driving.

ROADS

The condition of the roads in Cyprus is very good. Since the 1980s many stretches of road have been built, and others modernized. Roundabouts (traffic islands) have also appeared at intersections; the right of way goes to drivers approaching from the right.

Finding your way to the major historic sites is not difficult, as brown road signs show the way. Difficulties may arise, however, in the narrow streets of small towns, where signs are usually absent.

Pedestrians, especially those who may not be used to left-hand traffic, should exercise caution when crossing the road, and warn children to be particularly careful when stepping into the road.

MAPS

When hiring a car, you will usually be given a very basic road map of the island. It is certainly worth purchasing a more detailed map of Cyprus or the part of the island you'll be exploring; these are available in many bookstores and petrol stations. It may be easier to purchase a map from home and bring it with you, so that you'll be prepared from the outset. Bear in mind that many mountain roads are accessible only by four-wheel drive vehicle or motorcycle (or scooter).

Remember, too, that place names in the North may be different from those on a map purchased in the South, so you may have to cross-reference maps.

A well-maintained road in the Troodos mountains

DRIVING IN NICOSIA

The capital of Cyprus is the biggest and most congested city on the island. Traffic jams occur during rush hour and tourists may have difficulty negotiating the traffic here, and the narrow streets of parts of the city. The worst congestion can be expected on the trunk roads leading into and out of the city and – particularly in high season – on roads to the main historical sites. Outside the rush hour, driving in Nicosia is relatively easy and comfortable.

Street names throughout the city are clearly visible, and major tourist attractions are well signposted.

BUSES

Bus service between the large towns is efficient and comfortable, and tickets are inexpensive. There are at least six services daily between the four main southern towns. Transport links to major seaside resorts are also good.

Local buses also connect outlying communities with the nearest main town, but they are geared to the needs of schoolchildren and villagers, so departures are only early morning and mid-afternoon. Travellers will find it harder to get to and from the smaller towns and villages.

Before travelling, check the timetable to see when the last return bus departs, to ensure that you will be able to get back. At weekends, there are reduced services.

Traffic moving along one of Kyrenia's busy streets

TAXIS

Metered taxis operate in all the main towns in Cyprus. Unmetered rural taxis serve most larger villages, charging 31–49 cents per kilometre. There are also shared "service taxis" or minibuses, which take passengers door to door so you can choose the most convenient point for getting on or off. Service taxis operate between all the major towns half-hourly between 6am and 6pm (to 7pm in summer) Monday to Friday, and 7am to 5pm at weekends.

A taxi sign in North Cyprus

Taxi fares are reasonable – particularly when you take a larger car and share the cost between several people – and provide a very convenient way of getting around.

HITCHHIKING

Hitchhiking is not illegal in Cyprus, nor is it recommended. It is better avoided altogether in the larger towns, where a decent public transport system and affordable taxis provide safer alternatives. In remote areas, the locals readily give lifts to people standing by the road.

It can be difficult to hitch a lift during the peak holiday season, and temperatures soar, making the wait uncomfortable. Be sure to carry a bottle of water with you and wear a sunhat. Women who hitchhike should take special care.

DIRECTORY

BUS TIMETABLES

Intercity
Intercity Buses
Tel 24 643 492.
www.intercity-buses.com

Larnaka
Zinonas Buses
Tel 24 665 531.
www.zinonasbuses.com

Nicosia
Nicosia City Bus Lines
Tel 77 777 755.
www.osel.com.cy

Pafos
Osypa/Alepa Limited
Tel 26 934 252.
www.pafosbuses.com

TAXIS

Acropolis Vassos Taxi
Akamia Centre, Larnaka.
Tel 24 655 555.

Euro Taxi
Ifigenias 24, Nicosia.
Tel 22 513 000.

Golden Taxi
Lysis Fasis 33, Limassol.
Tel 25 311 711.

Mayfair Taxi
Agapinoros 46, Pafos.
Tel 26 954 202..

CAR HIRE

Avis
Tel 22 713 333.
www.avis.com.cy

Europcar
Tel 25 880 222.
www.europcar-cyprus.com

Hertz
Tel 22 208 888.
www.hertz.com.cy

A traditional village bus – today they are a lot more modern

Index

Acknowledgments

Dorling Kindersley and Wiedza i Życie would like to thank the following people and institutions, whose contributions and assistance have made the preparation of this guide possible.

Publishing Manager
Kate Poole

Managing Editors
Vivien Antwi, Vicki Ingle

Publisher
Douglas Amrine

Senior Cartographic Editor
Casper Morris

Senior DTP Designer
Jason Little

Additional Picture Research
Rachel Barber, Rhiannon Furbear, Ellen Root

Revisions Editor
Anna Freiberger

Revisions Designer
Maite Lantaron

Design and Editorial Assistance
Beverley Ager, Uma Bhattacharya, Emer FitzGerald, Carole French, Vinod Harish, Mohammad Hassan, Jasneet Kaur, Juliet Kenny, Vincent Kurien, Laura Jones, Jude Ledger, Alison McGill, Sonal Modha, Catherine Palmi, Andrea Pinnington, Rada Radojicic, Sands Publishing Solutions, Azeem, Siddiqui, Roseen Teare, Dora Whitaker

Production Co-ordinator
Wendy Penn

Jacket Design
Tessa Bindloss

Consultant
Robin Gauldie

Factchecker
John Vickers

Proofreader
Stewart Wild

Index
Hilary Bird

Additional Photography
Wojciech Franus, Carole French, Konrad Kalbarczyk, Grzegorz Micuła, Bernard Musyck, Ian O'Leary, Ronald Sayegh, Andrzej Zygmuntowicz

Special Assistance
Dr. Fotos Fotiou, Aleksander Nikolaou, Irfan Kiliç, Suleyman Yalin, Latif Ince, Artur Mościcki, Joanna Egert-Romanowska, Maria Betlejewska, Małgorzata Merkel-Massé.
The publishers would also like to thank all the people and institutions who allowed us to use photographs from their archives:

Bernard Musyck, Ronald Sayegh
(www.CyprusDestinations.com, skiing and agrotourism site)

Picture Credits
a = above; b = below/bottom; c = centre; f = far; l = left; r = right; t = top.

4Corners Images SIME Johanna Huber 8cl; SIME/Schmid Reinhard 9br, 142-143. **Alamy** Peter Horree 169tl; imagebroker/Maria Breuer 190cr; imagebroker/Siepmann 169c; Werner Otto 8br; Robert Harding Picture Library Ltd/ John Miller 96-97; Rodger Tamblyn 9tr; Rawdon Wyatt 203t. **The Trustees of the British Museum** 93bc. **Coral Beach Hotel and Resort** 156cl, 167br. **Corbis** 10t; Nathan Benn 40; Bettmann 26, 34bl, 71br; Jonathan Blair 11t, 24c, 25c, 34t; Tom Brakefield 151cr; James Davis/Eye Ubiquitous 16clb, 91crb, 148cla; John Heseltine 168cl; Dave G. Houser 1; Jo Lillini 22b, 185bl; Chris Lisle 24b; Hans Georg Roth 6–7. **Cyprus Police** 194bc. **Cyprus Tourism Organisation** 8tc. **Loel Winery** 181tl. **Grzegorz Micuła** 12; 16t; 17ca, bl; 18t; 19br; 36–37; 52b; 57cb; 67cr; 92t; 186b; 187t; 190t; 196cla. **PunchStock** Digital Vision 9cl. **TAGO** Konrad Kalbarczyk 13b, 182t; Wojciech Franus 15b. **Andrzej Zygmuntowicz** 168–169 (except for the box).

Jacket
Front – **4Corners** AWC Images/SIME. Back – **AWL Images** Katja Kreder clb; **Dorling Kindersley** Robin Gauldie bl; Jon Spaull tl; **Getty Images** Gallo Images/Travel Ink cla. Spine – **4Corners** AWC Images/SIME t.

All other images © Dorling Kindersley
For further information see www.dkimages.com

English-Greek Phrase Book

There are no clear-cut rules for transliterating modern Greek into the Latin alphabet.

The system employed in this guide follows the rules generally applied in Greece, adjusted to fit in with English pronunciation. On the following pages, the English is given in the left-hand column, the right-hand column provides a literal system of pronunciation and indicates the stressed syllable in bold.

It is also worth remembering that both the Cypriot Greek and Cypriot Turkish alphabets differ slightly from those used on the mainland, and their accents are distinctive, too.

In Emergency

Help!	Voítheia	vo-ee-theea
Stop!	Stamatíste	sta-ma-tee-steh
Call a doctor!	Fonáxte éna yatro	fo-nak-steh e-na ya-tro
Call an ambulance!	Kaléste to asthenofóro	ka-le-steh to as-the-no-fo-ro
Call the police!	Kaléste tin astynomía	ka-le-steh teen a-sti-no mia
Call the fire brigade!	Kaléste tin pyrosvestikí	ka-le-steh teen pee-ro-zve-stee-kee
Where is the nearest telephone?	Poú eínai to plisiéstero tiléfono?	poo ee-ne to plee-see-e-ste-ro tee-le-pho-no?
Where is the nearest hospital?	Poú eínai to plisiéstero nosokomeío?	poo ee-ne to plee-see-e-ste-ro no-so-ko-mee-o?
Where is the nearest pharmacy?	Poú eínai to plisiéstero farmakeío?	poo ee-ne to plee-see-e-ste-ro far-ma-kee-o?

Communication Essentials

Yes	Nai	neh
No	Ochi	o-chee
Please	Parakaló	pa-ra-ka-lo
Thank you	Efcharistó	ef-cha-ree-sto
Excuse me	Me synchoreíte	me seen cho-ree-teh
Goodbye	Antío	an-dee-o
Good morning	Kaliméra	ka-lee-me-ra
Good evening	Kalinychta	ka-lee-neech-ta
Morning	Proí	pro-ee
Afternoon	Apógevma	a-po-yev-ma
Evening	Vrádi	vrath-i
Yesterday	Chthés	chthes
Today	Símera	see-me-ra
Tomorrow	Avrio	av-ree-o
Here	Edó	ed-o
There	Ekeí	e-kee
What?	Tí?	tee?
Why?	Giatí?	ya-tee?
Where?	Poú?	poo?
How?	Pós?	pos?

Useful Phrases

How are you?	Tí káneis?	tee ka-nees
Very well, thank you	Poly kalá, efcharistó	po-lee ka-la, ef-cha-ree-sto
Pleased to meet you	Cháiro polę	che-ro po-lee
What is your name?	Pós légeste?	pos le-ye-ste?
Where is/where are…?	Poú eínai?	poo ee-ne?
How far is it to…?	Póso apéchei…?	po-so a-pe-chee?
I understand	Katalavaíno	ka-ta-la-ve-no
I don't understand	Den katalavaíno	then ka-ta-la-ve-no
Can you speak more slowly?	Miláte lígo pio argá parakaló?	mee-la-te lee-go pyo ar-ga pa-ra-ka-lo?
I'm sorry	Me synchoreíte	me-seen-cho-ree teh

Useful Words

big	Megálo	me-ga-lo
small	Mikró	mi-kro
hot	Zestó	zes-to
cold	Kreyo	kree-o
good	Kaló	ka-lo
bad	Kakó	ka-ko
open	Anoichtá	a-neech-ta
closed	Kleistá	klee-sta
left	Aristerá	a-ree-ste-ra
right	Dexiá	dek-see-a
straight	Eftheía	ef-thee-a
between	Anámesa/ Metaxey	a-na-me-sa/ Metaxý
on the corner….	Sti gonía tou…	stee go-nee-a too
near	Kontá	kon-da
far	Makriá	ma-kree-a
up	Epáno	e-pa-no
down	Káto	ka-to
early	Norís	no-rees
late	Argá	ar-ga
entrance	I eísodos	ee ee-so-thos
exit	I éxodos	eee-kso-dos
toilets	Oi toualétes	eee-kso-dos

Shopping

How much is it?	Póso kánei?	po-so ka-nee?
Do you have…?	Echete…?	e-che-teh
Do you accept credit cards?	Décheste pistotikés kártes	the-ches-teh pee-sto-tee-kes kar-tes
Do you accept ' travellers cheques?	Décheste pistotikés travellers' cheques?	the-ches-teh pee-sto-tee-kes … travellers cheques
What time do you open?	Póte anoígete?	po-teh a-nee-ye-teh?
What time do you close?	Póte kleínete?	po-teh klee-ne-teh?
this one	Aftó edó	af-to e-do
that	Ekeíno	e-kee-no
expensive	Akrivó	e-kree-vo
cheap	Fthinó	fthee-no
size	To mégethos	to me-ge-thos
white	Lefkó	lef-ko
black	Mávro	mav-ro
red	Kókkino	ko-kee-no
yellow	Kítrino	kee-tree-no
green	Prásino	pra-see-no
blue	Mple	bleh
antique shop	Magazí me antíkes	ma-ga-zee me an-dee-kes
bakery	O foúrnos	o foor-nos
bank	I trápeza	I trápeza
bazaar	To pazári	to pa-za-ree
bookshop	To vivliopoleío	o vee-vlee-o-po-lee-o
pharmacy	To farmakeío	o far-ma-kee-o
post office	To tachydromeío	to ta-chee -thro-mee-o
supermarket	Supermarket	"Supermarket"

Sightseeing

tourist information	CTO	CTO
beach	I paralía	ee pa-ra-lee-a
Byzantine	vyzantinós	vee-zan-dee-nos
castle	To kástro	to ka-stro
church	I ekklisía	ee e-klee-see-a
monastery	moní	mo-ni
museum	To mouseío	to moo-see-o
national	ethnikós	eth-nee-kos
river	To potámi	to po-ta-mee
road	O drómos	o thro-mos
saint	ágios	a-yee-os
theatre	To théatro	to the-a-tro

Travelling

When does the … leave?	**Póte févgei to…?**	po-teh fev-yee to..
Where is the bus stop?	**Poú eínai i stási tou leoforeíou?**	poo ee-neh ee sta-see too le-o-fo-ree-oo?
Is this bus going to…?	**Ypárche I leoforeío gia…?**	ee-par-chee le-o-fo-ree-o yia…?
bus ticket	**Eisitírio leoforeíou**	ee-see-tee-ree-o le-o-fo-ree-oo?
harbour	**To limáni**	to lee-ma-nee
bicycle	**To podílato**	to po-thee-la-to
taxi	**To taxí**	to tak-see
airport	**To aero-drómio**	to a-e-ro-thro-mee-o
ferry	**To „ferry-boat"**	to fe-ree-bot

In a Hotel

Do you have a vacant room?	**Echete domátia?**	e-che-teh tho-ma-tee-a?
double room	**Díklino me dipló kreváti**	thee-klee-no meh thee-plo kre-va-tee
single room	**Monóklino**	mo-no-klee-no
room with bathroom	**Domátio me mpánio**	tho-ma-tee-o meh ban-yo
shower	**To douz**	To dooz
key	**To kleidí**	to klee-dee
I have a reservation	**Echo kánei krátisi**	e-cho ka-nee kra-tee-see
room with sea view	**Domátio me théasti thálassa**	tho-ma-tee-o meh the-a stee tha-la-sa
room with a balcony	**Domátio me théasti mpalkóni**	tho-ma-tee-o meh the-a stee bal- ko-nee
Does the price include breakfast	**To proïnó symperi-lamvánetai stin timí?**	to pro-ee-no seem-be-ree-lam-va-ne-tehsteen tee-mee?

eating out

Have you got a free table?	**Echete trapézi?**	e-che-te tra-pe-zee?
I'd like to reserve a table	**Thélo na kratíso éna trapézi**	the-lo na kra-tee-so e-na tra-pe-zee
The bill, please	**Ton logariazmó parakaló**	tonlo-gar-yas-mo pa-ra-ka-lo
I'm a vegetarian	**Eímai chortofágos**	ee-meh chor-to-fa-gos
menu	**O katálogos**	o ka-ta-lo-gos
wine list	**O katálogos me ta oin-opnevmatódi**	o ka-ta-lo-gos meh ta ee-no-pnev-ma-to-thee
glass	**To potíri**	to po-tee-ree
bottle	**To mpoukáli**	to bou-ka-lee
knife	**To machaíri**	to ma-che-ree
fork	**To piroúni**	to pee-roo-nee
spoon	**To koutáli**	to koo-ta-lee
breakfast	**To proïnó**	to pro-ee-no
lunch	**To mesimerianó**	to me-see-mer-ya-no
dinner	**To deípno**	to theep-no
main course	**To kyrios gévma**	to kee-ree-os yev-ma
starter	**Ta orektiká**	ta o-rek-tee-ka
dessert	**To glykó**	to ylee-ko
dish of the day	**To piáto tis iméras**	to pya-to tees ee-me-ras
bar	**To „bar"**	To bar
tavern	**I tavérna**	ee ta-ver-na
café	**To kafeneío**	to ka-fe-nee-o
wine shop	**To oinopoleío**	to ee-no-po-lee-o
restaurant	**To estiatório**	o e-stee-a-to-ree-o
ouzeria	**To ouzerí**	To ouzerí
kebab take-away	**To souvlatzídiko**	To soo-vlat-zee dee-ko

Menu Decoder

coffee	**O Kafés**	o ka-fes
with milk	**me gála**	me ga-la
black coffee	**skétos**	ske-tos
without sugar	**chorís záchari**	cho-rees za-cha-ree
tea	**tsái**	tsa-ee
wine	**krasí**	kra-see
red	**kókkino**	ko-kee-no
white	**lefkó**	lef-ko
rosé	**rozé**	ro-ze
raki	**To rakí**	to ra-kee
ouzo	**To oúzo**	to oo-zo
retsina	**I retsína**	ee ret-see-na
water	**To neró**	to ne-ro
fish	**To psári**	to psa-ree
cheese	**To tyrí**	to tee-ree
halloumi cheese	**To chaloúmi**	
feta	**I féta**	ee fe-ta
bread	**To psomí**	to pso-mee
hummus	**To houmous**	to choo-moos
halva	**O chalvás**	o chal-vas
Turkish Delight	**To loukoúmi**	to loo-koo-mee loo-koo-mee
baklava	**O mpaklavás**	o bak-la-vas
kléftiko (lamb dish)	**To kléftiko**	to klef-tee-ko

Numbers

1	**éna**	e-na
2	**dyo**	thee-o
3	**tría**	tree-a
4	**téssera**	te-se-ra
5	**pénte**	pen-deh
6	**éxi**	ek-si
7	**eptá**	ep-ta
8	**ochtó**	och-to
9	**ennéa**	e-ne-a
10	**déka**	the-ka
100	**ekató**	e-ka-to
200	**diakósia**	thya-kos-ya
1,000	**chília**	cheel-ya
2,000	**dychiliádes**	thee-o cheel-ya-thes
1,000,000	**éna ekat--ommyrio**	e-na e-ka-to-mee-ree-o

Days of the Week, Months, Time

one minute	**éna leptó**	e-na lep-to
one hour	**mía óra**	mee-a o-ra
half an hour	**misí óra**	mee-see o-ra
a day	**mía méra**	mee-a me-ra
week	**mía evdomáda**	mee-a ev-tho-ma-tha
month	**énas mínas**	e-nas mee-nas
year	**énas chrónos**	e-nas chro-nos
Monday	**Deftéra**	thef-te-ra
Tuesday	**Tríti**	tree-tee
Wednesday	**Tetárti**	te-tar-tee
Thursday	**Pémpti**	pemp-tee
Friday	**Paraskeví**	pa-ras-ke-vee
Saturday	**Sávvato**	sa-va-to
Sunday	**Kyriakí**	keer-ee-a-kee
January	**Ianouários**	ee-a-noo-a-ree-os
February	**Fevrouários**	fev-roo-a-ree-os
March	**Mártios**	mar-tee-os
April	**Aprílios**	a-pree-lee-os
May	**Máios**	ma-ee-os
June	**Ioúnios**	ee-oo-nee-os
July	**Ioúlios**	ee-oo-lee-os
August	**Avgoustos**	av-goo-stos
September	**Septémvrios**	sep-tem-vree-os
October	**Októvrios**	ok-to-vree-os
November	**Noémvrios**	no-em-vree-os
December	**Dekémvrios**	the-kem-vree-os

English-Turkish Phrase Book

Pronunciation

Turkish uses a Roman alphabet. It has 29 letters: 8 vowels and 21 consonants. Letters that differ from the English alphabet are: **c**, pronounced "j" as in "jolly"; **ç**, pronounced "ch" as in "church"; **ğ**, which lengthens the preceding vowel and is not pronounced; **ı**, pronounced "uh"; **ö**, pronounced "ur" (like the sound in "further"); **ş**, pronounced "sh" as in "ship"; **ü**, pronounced "ew" as in "few".

In an Emergency

Help!	İmdat!	eem-dat
Stop!	Dur!	door
Call a doctor!	Bir doktor çağrın!	beer dok-tor chah-ruhn
Call an ambulance!	Bir ambulans çağrın!	beer am-boo-lans chah-ruhn
Call the police!	Polis çağrın!	po-lees chah-ruhn
Fire!	Yangın!	yan-guhn
Where is the nearest telephone?	En yakın telefon nerede?	en ya-kuhn teh-leh-fon neh-reh-deh
Where is the nearest hospital?	En yakın hastane nerede?	en ya-kuhn has-ta-neh neh-reh-deh

Communication Essentials

Yes	Evet	eh-vet
No	Hayır	h-'eye'-uhr
Thank you	Teşekkür ederim	teh-shek-kewr eh-deh-reem
Please	Lütfen	lewt-fen
Excuse me	Affedersiniz	af-feh-der-see-neez
Hello	Merhaba	mer-ba-ba
Goodbye	Hoşça kalın	bosh-cha ka-luhn
Good morning	Günaydın	gewn-'eye'-duhn
Good evening	İyi akşamlar	ee-yee ak-sham-lar
Morning	Sabah	sa-bah
Afternoon	Öğleden sonra	ur-leh-den son-ra
Evening	Akşam	ak-sham
Yesterday	Dün	dewn
Today	Bugün	boo-gewn
Tomorrow	Yarın	ya-ruhn
Here	Burada	boo-ra-da
There	Şurada	shoo-ra-da
Over there	Orada	o-ra-da
What?	Ne?	neh
When?	Ne zaman?	neh za-man
Why?	Neden	neh-den
Where?	Nerede	neh-reh-deh

Useful Phrases

How are you?	Nasılsınız?	na-suhl-suh-nuhz
I'm fine	İyiyim	ee-yee-yeem
Pleased to meet you	Memnun oldum	mem-noon ol-doom
That's fine	Tamam	ta-mam
Where is/are ...?	... nerede?	...neh-reh-deh
How far is it to ...?	... ne kadar uzakta?	...neh ka-dar oo-zak-ta
I want to go to ...	... a/e gitmek istiyorum	... a/eh geet-mek ees-tee-yo-room
Do you speak English?	İngilizce biliyor musunuz?	een-gee-leez-jeh bee-lee-yor moo-soo-nooz?
I don't understand	Anlamıyorum	an-la-muh-yo-room
Can you help me?	Bana yardım edebilir misiniz?	ba-na yar-duhm eh-deh-bee-leer mee-see-neez?

Useful Words

big	büyük	bew-yewk
small	küçük	kew-chewk
hot	sıcak	suh-jak
cold	soğuk	sob-ook
good/well	iyi	ee-yee
bad	kötü	kur-tew
open	acık	a-chuhk
closed	kapalı	ka-pa-luh
left	sol	sol

right	sağ	saa
straight on	doğru	dob-roo
near	yakın	ya-kuhn
far	uzak	oo-zak
early	erken	er-ken
late	geç	gech
entrance	giriş	gee-reesh
exit	çıkış	chuh-kuhsh
toilets	tuvaletler	too-va-let-ler

Shopping

How much is this?	Bu kaç lira?	boo kach lee-ra
I would like ...	... istiyorum	... ees-tee-yo-room
Do you have ...?	... var mı?	...var muh?
Do you take credit cards?	Kredi kartı kabul ediyor musunuz?	kreh-dee kar-tuh ka-bool eb-dee-yor moo-soo-nooz?
What time do you open/close?	Saat kaçta açılıyor/ kapanıyor?	Sa-at kach-ta a-chuh-luh-yor/ ka-pa-nuh-yor
this one	bunu	boo-noo
that one	şunu	shoo-noo
expensive	pahalı	pa-ba-luh
cheap	ucuz	oo-jooz
size (clothes)	beden	beh-den
size (shoes)	numara	noo-ma-ra
white	beyaz	bay-yaz
black	siyah	see-yah
red	kırmızı	kubr-muh-zuh
yellow	sarı	sa-ruh
green	yeşil	yeh-sheel
blue	mavi	ma-vee
bakery	fırın	fub-ruhn
bank	banka	ban-ka
cake shop	pastane	pas-ta-neh
chemist's/pharmacy	eczane	ej-za-neh
hairdresser	kuaför	kwaf-fur
barber	berber	ber-ber
market/bazaar	çarşı/pazar	char-shuh/pa-zar
post office	postane	pos-ta-neh
travel agency	seyahat acentesi	say-ya-hat a-jen-teh-see

Sightseeing

castle	hisar	bee-sar
church	kilise	kee-lee-seh
mosque	cami	ja-mee
museum	müze	mew-zeh
square	meydan	may-dan
theological college	medrese	med-reh-seh
tomb	türbe	tewr-beh
tourist information office	turizm danışma bürosu	too-reezm da-nuhsh-mah bew-ro-soo
town hall	belediye sarayı	beh-leh-dee-yeh sar-'eye'-ub
Turkish bath	hamam	ba-mam

Travelling

airport	havalimanı	ba-va-lee-ma-nub
bus/coach	otobüs	o-to-bewss
bus stop	otobüs durağı	o-to-bewss doo-ra-ub
ferry	vapur	va-poor
taxi	taksi	tak-see
ticket	bilet	bee-let
ticket office	bilet gişesi	bee-let gee-sheh-see
timetable	tarife	ta-ree-feh

Staying in a Hotel

Do you have a vacant room?	Boş odanız var mı?	bosh o-da-nuhz var muh?
double room	iki kişilik bir oda	ee-kee kee-shee-leek beer o-da
twin room	çift yataklı bir oda	cheeft ya-tak-luh beer o-da
single room room with a bathroom	tek kişilik banyolu bir oda	tek kee-shee-leek ban-yo-loo beer o-da

key	anahtar	*a-nah-tar*
room service	oda servisi	*o-da ser-vee-see*
I have a reservation	Rezervasyonum var	*reh-zer-vas-yo-noom var*
Does the price include breakfast?	Fiyata kahvaltı dahil mi?	*fee-ya-ta kah-val-tuh da-heel mee?*

Eating Out

Do you have a table for ...people	... kişilik bir masa	*... kee-shee-leek*
The bill please	Hesap lütfen	*beb-sap lewt-fen*
I am a vegetarian	Et yemiyorum	*et yeh-mee-yo-room*
restaurant	lokanta	*lo-kan-ta*
waiter	garson	*gar-son*
menu	yemek listesi	*ye-mek lees-teb-see*
wine list	şarap listesi	*sba-rap lees-teb-see*
breakfast	kahvaltı	*kab-val-tuh*
lunch	öğle yemeği	*ur-leh yeh-meb-ee*
dinner	akşam yemeği	*ak-sham yeh-meb-ee*
starter	meze	*meh-zeh*
main course	ana yemek	*a-na yeh-mek*
dish of the day	günün yemeği	*gewn-ewn yeb-meb-ee*
dessert	tatlı	*tat-luh*
glass	bardak	*bar-dak*
bottle	şişe	*shee-sheh*
knife	bıçak	*buh-chak*
fork	çatal	*cha-tal*
spoon	kaşık	*ka-shuhk*

Menu Decoder

bal	*bal*	honey
balık	*ba-luhk*	fish
bira	*bee-ra*	beer
bonfile	*bon-fee-leb*	fillet steak
buz	*booz*	ice
çay	*cb-'eye'*	tea
çilek	*cbee-lek*	strawberry
çorba	*cbor-ba*	soup
dondurma	*don-door-ma*	ice cream
ekmek	*ek-mek*	bread
elma	*el-ma*	apple
et	*et*	meat
fasulye	*fa-sool-yeb*	beans
fırında	*fub-rubn-da*	roast
gazoz	*ga-zoz*	fizzy drink
kkahve	*kab-veh*	coffee
karpuz	*kar-pooz*	water melon
kavun	*ka-voon*	melon
kayısı	*k-'eye'-ub-suh*	apricots
kıyma	*kuby-ma*	minced meat
kızartma	*kub-zart-ma*	fried
köfte	*kurf-teh*	meatballs
kuzu eti	*koo-zoo eb-tee*	lamb
lokum	*lo-koom*	Turkish delight
maden suyu	*ma-den soo-yoo*	mineral water

meyve suyu	*may-veh soo-yoo*	fruit juice
muz	*mooz*	banana
patlıcan	*pat-lub-jan*	aubergine (eggplant)
peynir	*pay-neer*	cheese
pilav	*pee-lav*	rice
piliç	*pee-leech*	roast chicken
şarap	*sba-rap*	wine
sebze	*seb-zeh*	vegetables
şeftali	*shef-ta-lee*	peach
şeker	*sheb-ker*	sugar
su	*soo*	water
süt	*sewt*	milk
sütlü	*sewt-lew*	with milk
tavuk	*ta-vook*	chicken
tereyağı	*teb-reh-yab-ub*	butter
tuz	*tooz*	salt
üzüm	*ew-zewm*	grapes
yoğurt	*yoh-urt*	yoghurt
yumurta	*yoo-moor-ta*	egg
zeytin	*zay-teen*	olives
zeytinyağı	*zay-teen-yab-ub*	olive oil

Numbers

0	sıfır	*suh-fubr*
1	bir	*beer*
2	iki	*ee-kee*
3	üç	*ewcb*
4	dört	*durt*
5	beş	*besb*
6	altı	*al-tuh*
7	yedi	*yeb-dee*
8	sekiz	*seb-keez*
9	dokuz	*dob-kooz*
10	on	*on*
100	yüz	*yewz*
200	iki yüz	*ee-kee yewz*
1,000	bin	*been*
100,000	yüz bin	*yewz been*
1,000,000	bir milyon	*beer meel-yon*

Time

one minute	bir dakika	*beer da-kee-ka*
one hour	bir saat	*beer sa-at*
half an hour	yarım saat	*ya-ruhm sa-at*
day	gün	*gewn*
week	hafta	*baf-ta*
month	ay	*'eye'*
year	yıl	*yubl*
Sunday	pazar	*pa-zar*
Monday	pazartesi	*pa-zar-teb-see*
Tuesday	salı	*sa-luh*
Wednesday	çarşamba	*cbar-sham-ba*
Thursday	perşembe	*per-sbem-beh*
Friday	cuma	*joo-ma*
Saturday	cumartesi	*joo-mar-teb-see*200

Road Map

Mediterranean Sea

Antalya

Cape Kormakitis
(Koruçam Burnu)

Lambousa
(Lambusa)

Kormakitis
(Koruçam)(Lapta)Lapithos

Karavas
(Alsancak)

Saint Hilarion Castle

Bellap

Larnakatis
Lapithou (Kozan)

Güzelyurt (Morfou Bay)

Serrachis

N   O   R   T

NICOSI
(LEFKOS

Chrysochou Bay

Morfou
(Güzelyurt)

Cape Arnaouitis

Vouni (Vuni Sarayi)

Peristerona

B9

B9

A9

Soloi
(Soloi Harabeleri)

Elaia

Tilliria

Archa
Mich

Akaki

Baths of
Aphrodite

Lefka
(Lefke)

Panagia
Chrysospiliotissa

Akamas
Peninsula

Marion

E704

Limniti

Asinou
(Panagia
Forviotissa)

Peristerona

Tamassos

E906

Agios
Irakleidios

Alyk

Polis

Makounta

Xiros

Panagia
tis Podithou

E907

Stavros Tou
Agiasmati

R

E903

Lara

E713

E709

Kalopanagiotis

Kakopetria

Panagia tou Arakia

Machairas

Profitis Ilias
Monastery

E902

Agios
Georgios

Cedar
Valley

Kykkos

Pedoulas

Agios Nikolaos
tis Stegis

Lagoudera

Agros

E903

Palaichori

Pegeia

E703

Panagia
Chrysorrogiatissa

Mount
Olympus

Troodos

Trooditissa
E802

E907

Germasogeia

Lefkara

Coral Bay

Agios
Neophytos

E702

E606

Omodos

Platres

Timios
Stavros

Agios Minas

Lempa

E701

Koilani

Lofou

Louvarás

Choirokoitia

Pafos

A6

Potamiou

Vouni

Monagri

E110

Kalavasos

Xeros valley

Diarizos Valley

B8

Geroskipou

Ezousa

Palaipafos

Kouklia

Asprokremnos Dam

A6

E601

Amathous

A1

Agios Georgios
Alamanos

Sanctury of
Apollo Ylatis

A1

Limassol (Lemesos)

Petra Tou
Romiou

B6

Episkopi

Kolossi

Akrotiri Bay

Kourion

Cape Akrotiri

Cape Aspro

Agios Nikolaos
ton Gaton

Rodos

Episkopi Bay

Cape Gata

KEY

Border	
Airport	
Motorway	
Main road	
Secondary road	
Ferry route	
Ferry port	

0 km   20

0 miles   20